YORKSHIRE SIEGES OF THE CIVIL WARS

YORKSHIRE SIEGES OF THE CIVIL WARS

DAVID COOKE

Pen & Sword
FAMILY HISTORY

First published in Great Britain in 2011 by
PEN AND SWORD FAMILY HISTORY
an imprint of
Pen & Sword Books Ltd
47 Church Street
Barnsley
South Yorkshire
S70 2AS

Copyright © David Cooke 2011

ISBN 978 1 84415 917 8

Typeset in 10pt Palatino by Mac Style, Beverley, East Yorkshire
Printed and bound in the UK by CPI

Pen & Sword Books Ltd incorporates the Imprints of Pen & Sword
Aviation, Pen & Sword Family History, Pen & Sword Maritime,
Pen & Sword Military, Pen & Sword Discovery, Wharncliffe Local
History, Wharncliffe True Crime, Wharncliffe Transport, Pen & Sword
Select, Pen & Sword Military Classics, Leo Cooper, The Praetorian Press,
Remember When, Seaforth Publishing and Frontline Publishing

For a complete list of Pen & Sword titles please contact
PEN & SWORD BOOKS LIMITED
47 Church Street, Barnsley, South Yorkshire, S70 2AS, England
E-mail: enquiries@pen-and-sword.co.uk
Website: www.pen-and-sword.co.uk

CONTENTS

Introduction   1

Chapter 1   Hull's Managing   8

Chapter 2   The Great and Close Siege of York   25

Chapter 3   The Siege of Helmsley Castle   63

Chapter 4   The Siege of Knaresborough Castle   70

Chapter 5   'O Thou Bloody Prison': Pontefract Castle   81

Chapter 6   The Siege of Scarborough Castle   163

Chapter 7   The Siege of Sandal Castle   182

Chapter 8   The Siege of Bolton Castle   195

Chapter 9   The Siege of Skipton Castle   203

Bibliography   216

Index   217

INTRODUCTION

Massive artillery pieces pound the walls of a castle. The defenders respond in kind but the besieging guns are well protected. Eventually, their target, one of the castle's towers, collapses into the dry moat. The besieging commander summons the castle's governor: 'Surrender now and avoid the effusion of Christian blood.' His troops are ready to storm the breach in the castle's wall should the garrison commander refuse.

The peace of a church service is disturbed by a massive explosion. Besiegers and besieged watch intently as a tower and a section of its adjoining wall lift into the air and then collapse back into the crater formed by the explosion. As quiet once again descends on the scene, storming parties rush into the jagged wound in the town's walls, meeting little resistance. The defenders rally quickly and put up a gallant defence. Unsupported, the attackers are slowly but surely driven back until the wall is once again secure. Now the silence is broken only by the moans of the wounded.

The defenders have been driven back into the tower of the church which forms part of the castle's outer defences. The enemy cannot make any progress up the tower due to the tight, steep, spiral staircases but the brave defenders are cut off from any succour. Night falls. Their commander decides that their desperate situation requires a desperate remedy. Cutting the ropes from the bells they climb out onto the church roof and make their way to the end closest to their comrades. Using the ropes to climb down, they then run a gauntlet of musket fire until they reach the shelter of their own lines, several of their number receiving wounds as they go.

Forty thousand men form line of battle on a moor. On one side is a force intent on relieving a besieged city and on the other an enemy force just as intent on preventing them from doing so. The battle is bloody and the relieving force is defeated. The besiegers return to their siege lines and await the fall of the city, now bereft of any hope of relief.

Another day: another field. A large body of mounted men approach the enemy's siege lines. The enemy respond and deploy troops to block their route into the castle. Soon battle is joined. Charge follows charge and the besiegers are driven from their lines. The route to the castle is open. The victorious horsemen make haste for the castle, bringing with them supplies and a herd of cattle, gathered on their march. The relieving force cannot tarry for long and must soon march away. The defenders, with full stomachs for the first time in days, know that the enemy will soon return and once again lay siege.

It is a bright summer's morning. Towering above the scene is a massive gatehouse. Lining the road leading away from the city a victorious army awaits the opening of the gates. At the prescribed time the wooden gates creak open and the forlorn defenders begin their march away. They have put up a brave fight and have been allowed the honours of war. They march away with their flags flying and carrying their weapons. The musketeers carry lit matches in their hands and a musket ball in their mouths. Their march will take them to the nearest friendly garrison. After that, who knows?

All this sounds very dramatic but each of the scenes described actually took place during one of the numerous sieges of the English Civil Wars in Yorkshire.

Siege warfare often plays the poor relation to the cut and thrust of mobile campaigns with their constituent battles and skirmishes. Who, after all, really wants to read a book about a few hundred men inside a castle being starved into submission over a period of weeks or months? I have to confess to that being my attitude towards siege warfare. How could it compare to massed ranks of horse and foot, with banners flying and drums beating, charging back and forth across an open heath? To be quite blunt, it cannot compare to the grandeur of an open field battle, at least in our imagination, but probably not in the eyes of the participants, but nonetheless is full of interest.

As I researched my previous books on the Civil Wars and Yorkshire military history (see bibliography) I began to acquire a lot of contemporary information covering a number of the major sieges in the county and was very surprised by the amount of action that took place during them. The defenders of Hull, York and Pontefract, to name but three, did not sit still behind their walls and wait for the enemy to grind them down. The garrisons carried out active defences, sallying forth and attacking the enemy siege lines on an almost daily basis, seriously affecting their ability to bring the siege to a successful conclusion. Although some of these actions were on a large scale, many involved no more than an officer and a few dozen men. The fascination is with the detail provided by the participants in these events in diaries and letters.

A further source of interest is that, with the exception of Hull, all of the sites covered in this book still exist and most, if not all of them, show the marks of the sieges or their aftermaths – the last of Hull's defences were demolished centuries ago, although their course can still be traced on a modern-day street plan. Not only do the defences still exist but in many cases the modern towns still follow their medieval street plans and the course of many of the skirmishes can be followed on the ground.

Another aspect of siege warfare is the attempted relief of a beleaguered garrison. Just such an attempt led to the largest battle of the Civil Wars, Marston Moor – it may be the largest battle on British soil, depending on whose numbers for the Battle of Towton you believe. Relief attempts could be on a grand scale, as at Marston Moor, or just a few dozen horsemen. Not only relief attempts but also sieges varied greatly in scale. At York upwards of 24,000 Parliamentary and Scots troops laid siege to the city, while the Marquess of Newcastle held the town with around 5,000 men. Sandal Castle goes to the other end of the scale with around 100 Royalist defenders holding the castle against several hundred Parliamentary troops.

My previous book – *The Civil War in Yorkshire – Fairfax versus Newcastle*, Pen and Sword, 2004 – covered the field operations in the county during the First Civil War. Many of the sieges covered in this work were mentioned in passing. Pontefract and Scarborough were also besieged during the Second Civil War. The intention of the current work is to provide the reader with as detailed an account of these sieges as possible, in line with the coverage of battles in my previous book. It is hoped that the two together will give a comprehensive account of the military operations in the county during the Civil Wars.

Siege Warfare

A siege was an attempt to capture a defended location by a superior attacking force. In the context of the English Civil Wars, a defended location could be a number of different things. Most of the sieges covered in this book were of castles, for example, Pontefract, Sandal, Helmsley and Skipton, or walled towns like Hull and York. Such locations were essential to military operations.

First, they provided secure bases for the vying armies. Throughout his campaign against Lord Fairfax, the Earl, later Marquess, of Newcastle used

York as his main supply base. Fairfax initially used several West Riding towns as his main base of operations but after his defeat by Newcastle at Adwalton Moor in June 1643 this was no longer possible and he withdrew to Hull which became his base for the Marston Moor campaign in 1644.

Castles and towns also provided control of their surrounding area. This facilitated the gathering of 'contributions' from the area and the raising of troops. The loss of an area could gravely affect a side's ability to recruit and if the area was later recaptured a large influx of new troops could take place. A good example of this was in Lancashire in the summer of 1644. The local Royalists had been defeated at Sabden Brook during the summer of 1643 and control of the county, with the exception of Lathom House, had been lost, denying a fruitful source of recruits. When Prince Rupert advanced through the county on his way to relieve York, storming Bolton and capturing Liverpool on his way, he received a major influx of recruits from the local populace, many of whom supported the King's cause.

A fortified town or castle could also provide a rallying point for a defeated army. This could be a two-edged sword as the victorious army could follow up and lay siege to the location, thus trapping the defeated army inside. This happened at the Second Siege of Hull and the Siege of York, as will be seen in due course. In 1645 the Royalist Northern Horse was able to rally at Skipton Castle following a defeat at Sherburn-in-Elmet, before they moved on into Cumbria to meet their final defeat.

It can be seen from the preceding paragraphs that fortified locations were of vital importance to the conduct of warfare during the Civil Wars period and many major battles were fought in an attempt to deny or take such locations.

How did an attacking force go about taking a fortified location? The first objective was to isolate the location and prevent the influx of supplies and reinforcements. This was not always practical. At York, for example, when Lord Fairfax's army combined with the Scots, commanded by the Earl of Leven, they were too few to completely surround the city and the northern sector was covered only by cavalry patrols. To remedy this problem Fairfax and Leven invited the Earl of Manchester to bring his army from East Anglia, which he duly did. Sometimes the inability to isolate a fortified location was not due to a lack of troops but for reasons of geography. At Hull the Humber provided a ready-made access point for both supplies and reinforcements. Although the Royalists raised gun batteries on the north shore, they were unable to close the river to shipping.

Once a fortified location had been isolated, or as near isolated as it could be, the besieging commander would summon the garrison to surrender. If this was refused, as it invariably was, the attacker had a number of options. The first was to simply starve the defenders into submission. This was often the chosen option if the attacker had been able to isolate the location and there was no imminent threat of a relief force arriving. To counter this, the defenders could evacuate as many superfluous personnel, military and civilian, as could be spared. At York the Marquess of Newcastle sent his horse from the city before the Scots and Parliamentary armies had completely surrounded it. This achieved two ends: it removed a large number of men and horses that would have had very limited use during the siege and who would have consumed a lot of provisions and it also provided the nucleus of a relief force.

If the attacker was in a hurry to reduce the garrison he could carry out an assault with little if any preparation. This could be a very bloody undertaking for both sides. More often an assault would not be carried out until the defences had been breached by bombardment or mining. All of the locations covered in this book were defended by medieval walls which, being vertical, were highly vulnerable to bombardment. The attacker would attempt to place his heavy siege guns as close as possible to the chosen area of the walls, the nearer the more effect the guns would have and the quicker the walls would be breached. Conversely, the defender tried to keep the attacker as far away as possible by building outer defensive earthworks which could be some distance from the main fortification. At Hull the defenders used this tactic to keep Newcastle's cannon at arm's length but also used another ploy which was even more effective. The banks of the Humber and River Hull had sluice gates which would inundate the surrounding land if opened at high tide. Lord Fairfax was able to keep the Royalist artillery at very long range by doing exactly this.

As well as attempting to breach the walls the besiegers' guns could be used to try and set fire to the buildings within the walls. Contemporary accounts speak of forges being set up by the Royalists during the siege of Hull, where cannon balls were heated until red hot and then fired into the town. Lord Fairfax set up efficient fire-fighting arrangements in the town and little damage was done. Another weapon which could be used for this tactic was the mortar. These were very short barrelled weapons which fired at a high trajectory, lobbing their explosive shells over the defences and into the heart of a town or garrison. Evidence for the use of mortars has been found at

Sandal Castle and one of the Civil War burials at the castle may have been killed by a piece of a mortar shell as a fragment was found in the grave along with the skeletal remains.

Another method of breaching a wall was by mining. This is exactly what its name suggests. A mine was dug with a chamber under the wall. In pre-gunpowder days the mine was collapsed by lighting a large fire in the chamber which burnt away the props supporting the roof of the chamber, thus collapsing the earth above and bringing down a section of wall along with it. By the time of the Civil Wars mine chambers were packed with gunpowder and the mine exploded. Mines were used at the sieges of York and Pontefract Castle. At York two mines were dug although only one was exploded, the second was flooded during heavy unseasonable rain. If defenders suspected that a mine was being built they could counter-mine by digging a shaft and tunnel and breaking into the enemy mine. There is archaeological evidence of several counter-mines being dug at Pontefract Castle.

Once a practicable breach had been made in a wall the attacker had two options: he could assault immediately or he could summon the garrison to surrender once again. If a garrison refused to surrender at this point, and the attacker was forced to make an assault, little mercy could be expected. If terms were agreed then often the garrison would be granted the honours of war and allowed to march to another garrison with their arms and possessions.

Having looked at the theory of siege warfare, it is now time to look in detail at the sieges that took place in Yorkshire during the First Civil War. The story of the First Civil War begins with the First Siege of Hull in July 1643, more than a month before the King raised his standard at Nottingham, an act which many historians mark as the start of the war. In the autumn of 1643 Hull stood its second siege and remained the only Parliamentary bastion in the whole of Yorkshire. After a major reverse in fortune the Parliamentary forces, ably assisted by a Scots army, gained the upper hand and laid siege to our county town. The Siege of York led to the largest battle of the Civil Wars when a large Royalist force marched to relieve the city. With the fall of York on 16 July 1643, and the destruction of the Royalist field army in Yorkshire, all that was left for the Parliamentary commander, Lord Ferdinando Fairfax, to do was to reduce the few remaining Royalist fortresses: Pontefract Castle, Sandal Castle, Knaresborough Castle, Bolton Castle, Scarborough Castle,

The keep of Helmsley Castle after it had its east wall demolished to prevent the castle being defended.

Helmsley Castle and Skipton Castle. By the end of 1645 he had achieved his objective.

Many of the castles mentioned above were slighted – rendered indefensible. One often used tactic, and not only in Yorkshire, was to demolish gatehouses and remove one wall of the keep, for example, at Helmsley. Usually this was done on the orders of Parliament. One exception to this was Pontefract Castle. Rather than Parliament ordering the castle's demolition, the citizens of the town petitioned Parliament to allow them to demolish it – the three sieges of the castle had cost them much.

Chapter 1

HULL'S MANAGING

The village of Wike nestled at the confluence of the Rivers Humber and Hull. Its inhabitants made their living mainly through fishing. Edward I realized the strategic importance of the location, and from that time on it became known as Kingston-upon-Hull. The town's fortunes fluctuated over the next 400 years but by the mid-seventeenth century it was the main port on the Humber and the main arms magazine for the North of England. Successive kings added to the town's defences and by Henry VIII's reign the town was walled, with the exception of its eastern side which was adjacent to the River Hull. During medieval times this had not been a major concern but with the advent of reliable artillery in the fifteenth and sixteenth centuries, it laid the

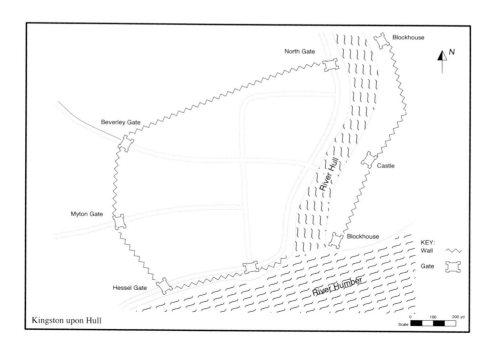

Kingston upon Hull

1610 map of Hull by John Speede.

town open to bombardment from the east bank of the River Hull. Henry VIII remedied this oversight by building a wall with two blockhouses and a 'castle' on the eastern side of the river, thus providing the town with all round defences.

By the reign of Charles I, Hull was very much a mercantile town and many of its inhabitants had Calvinist leanings and were against Archbishop Laud's religious reforms. The King's Scots subjects were of a similar mind and in 1639 they raised an army to defend their religious rights against the King's and Laud's religious reforms, particularly the introduction of bishops. The ensuing conflict became known as the First Bishops War. Charles began to raise troops in the North to bring his rebellious Scots subjects to heel. Hull would be his main magazine and a conduit for arms and supplies arriving from the Tower of London. He despatched Captain William Legge to govern the town and this seems to have rankled a number of local gentry, Sir John Hotham in particular. In April 1639 Charles visited the town and Hotham's name is noticeably absent from a list of local worthies who attended the King. Sir John's perceived snubbing by the King, in regards to the governorship of

Hull, led to major repercussions for the King's cause in the North, as will be seen in due course.

The First Bishop's War ended in an agreement between the King and the Scots, with little military action having taken place. In 1640 the continuing antagonism between Charles and the Scots led to the outbreak of the Second Bishops War. For the first time in eleven years the King called a parliament, which lasted for only three weeks, when Charles dissolved it because it disagreed with his policies – the Short Parliament. In the North military matters took a decided turn for the worse, when the King's army was defeated by the Scots at the Battle of Newburn on 28 August 1640. Following this the Scots occupied Newcastle and forced the King to pay reparations. This meant Charles had to call another parliament on 3 November. With the calling of the Long Parliament, as it became known, the road to the English Civil Wars had been laid.

In the North, the King had despatched Sir Thomas Glemham, with a force of 1,000 men, to garrison Hull, as he feared the loss of his northern arms magazine. The mayor and town council of Hull protested at this but Charles threatened a royal visit, with the massive expenses entailed, if the garrison was not admitted. The mayor demurred and Sir Thomas and his men were admitted to the town. To add to Hull's problems a body of cavalry was quartered in the surrounding villages which, obviously, added to the expense borne by the area. In July 1641 the crisis in the North came to an end and the garrison was disbanded, with Sir Thomas Glemham departing for London. Hull would see less than twelve months of peace.

On 4 January 1642 the King took a major step towards war with his intransigent Parliament, when he unsuccessfully attempted to arrest five members of the House of Commons and one member of the Lords. In the aftermath of the King's attempted coup, Parliament appointed Sir John Hotham as governor of the town and magazine of Hull. Hotham despatched his son, Captain John Hotham, to Hull immediately, while he remained in London until early March. At about the same time as Parliament appointed Hotham as governor of Hull, the King had appointed the Earl of Newcastle. When Newcastle arrived at Hull, with no military force to back him up, the mayor wrote to the King and Parliament asking whose representative he should accept. Parliament summoned Newcastle to take his seat in the House of Lords. Newcastle sought the King's advice and Charles, not wanting to force a final breach with Parliament, ordered the earl to London.

Sir John Hotham.

By mid-April Sir John Hotham was ensconced in the town with a sizeable garrison, made up from the local trained bands – the militia force raised by each county. The King was at York and had gathered a good number of supporters to him, along with trained band troops. Hull was high on both the King's and Parliament's agenda, as the magazine in the town held enough arms and armour to equip a substantial force. Parliament petitioned the King to be allowed to move the magazine to the Tower of London, something he had little intention of allowing them to do. The local gentry counter-petitioned the King not to allow the magazine's removal as it would leave the North bare of military stores in case of a foreign invasion. The Scots had invaded the North only two years earlier. More worrying was that the Queen had sailed to the Continent in February with a large part of the crown jewels, to raise money for weapons and powder and possibly raise a foreign or mercenary army.

On 22 April the King made his first move to gain control of Hull. James, Duke of York, with a small retinue arrived unannounced at the town and entered with the locals going to attend the town market. The prince was quickly recognized and feasted in a manner befitting his rank. On the morning of the 23rd the royal party was being given a tour of the town's defences when a letter arrived announcing that the King intended to dine with the governor, Sir John Hotham, on that very day. The King, with 300 'attendants', was well on his way from Beverley to Hull. It was rumoured that a force of 400 more of his supporters were following at a discreet distance. Hotham met with Sir Peregrine Pelham, one of the town's MPs and a staunch anti-royalist, and it was decided that allowing the King and his party entrance to the town would breach Parliament's orders and the faith they had put in Sir John. The King would not be allowed to enter Hull.

Hotham despatched a messenger to the King, who was by this time only three miles away from the town, asking him 'to forbear his coming to the town at this time' as the governor could not allow his entrance without breaking faith with Parliament. The messenger quickly returned and told Hotham that the King had received his message with great displeasure and would not be denied entrance. Hotham ordered the town gates to be closed and the drawbridges raised. The town's inhabitants were ordered to remain in their homes and the garrison manned the walls.

At eleven o'clock the King and his retinue arrived before the Beverley Gate. Hotham had climbed onto the wall at the side of the gatehouse. A heated discussion followed, with the King threatening Sir John with being declared a traitor. Hotham stuck to his guns. Both sides broke for lunch and Sir John had provisions lowered from the walls for the waiting Royalists. After the break the King again demanded entry and this time Sir John said he could enter the town with a small party of attendants. The King countered this by saying he would enter with a party of twenty to thirty supporters. Once again Hotham refused. The King then ordered two heralds to declare Sir John a traitor. By this time the Duke of York and his party had been allowed to leave the town and join his father. The Royalists then withdrew to Beverley for the night.

On the 24th, prior to departing for York, the King gave Hotham a final chance, when he sent two heralds to ask if he had changed his mind. When the governor replied in the negative, he was once again declared a traitor.

For the next two months a 'paper' war ensued, with the propaganda sheets of both sides detailing the righteousness of their causes and the iniquities of their opponents. Both sides continued to raise troops and it must have become obvious that open warfare between the King and his Parliament was inevitable.

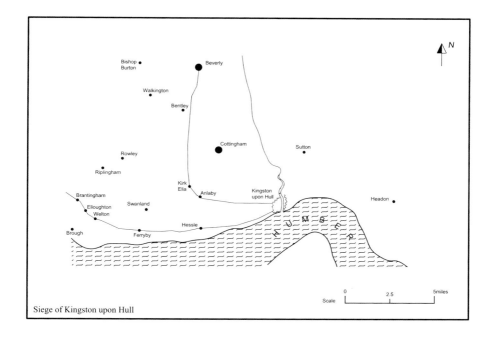

Siege of Kingston upon Hull

The First Siege of Hull

Many historians have dated the start of the First Civil War as 22 August 1642, when the King raised his standard at Nottingham – an inauspicious start as the standard blew down! By this date shots had been fired in a number of places and Hull had stood its first siege.

After a fruitless exchange of communications with Parliament, the King decided to make a show of force against the town, which he hoped would cow them into surrender. By 3 July the King, with 3,000 foot and 1,000 horse, arrived at Beverley. This force was much less effective than it sounds. The foot were badly equipped, with only 800 muskets. The ratio of musket to pike at the time should have been 2:1, which means that there should have 2,000 muskets in a force of 3,000 foot. The whole force was under the command of the Earl of Lindsey.

Lindsey began his preparations for the siege by sending mounted troops to reconnoitre the land around the town. Hotham had few cavalry with which to prevent this. The town was well fortified and the defenders were much better equipped than their Royalist opponents. A suggestion was made to cut the town's water supply but this was deemed impossible as the River Hull ran with fresh water when the tide was going out. The town's water table was so high that it only took a couple of feet of digging for the hole to start filling with water, indeed it was said that when a burial took place in the town the corpse would drowned before the grave was filled in! It was decided that the most promising route for the siege to take would be to cut off the town then starve the inhabitants and garrison into surrender.

Several windmills lay between Hull and Beverley, and Lindsey, on or about 5 July, despatched a force of one troop of horse, about fifty men, and 100 foot to burn them down. This raiding force carried out their attack at close to midnight. It is not clear whether Sir John Hotham received prior information of the raid or whether it was the windmills going up in flames that alerted the garrison. Several cannon shots were fired by the defenders and the Royalist foot abandoned their weapons and fled back towards Beverley, followed closely by their horse.

Both sides continued their preparations. Hotham ordered earthworks to be raised before the North, Beverley and Myton Gates and guns mounted in them and on the walls. Only the North and Beverley Gates were left open, with the Myton and Wressle Gates being blocked up with earth. Hotham also ordered a rampart to be built between each of the earthworks at the gates.

The Royalists continued with their plan to isolate and starve the town. The King made a proclamation that anyone providing supplies to the town would be declared a traitor. The Earl of Lindsey ordered two forts to be built at Paull and Anlaby, one each side of the town. It was planned that the guns in these forts would close the Humber and prevent supplies coming to the town along the river – in reality this was not the case. He also despatched Lord Willoughby and Sir Thomas Glemham into Lincolnshire to patrol the southern bank of the Humber and prevent supplies and reinforcements from reaching the town from that direction. A small ship was despatched across the Humber with cannon and supplies to build a fort on the south bank but it was intercepted and sunk by a Parliamentary warship.

A council of war was held in the town and a decision made to cut the banks of the Rivers Hull and Humber and inundate the low-lying land around the town. The flood waters stretched up to two miles from Hull and could only be crossed easily along the main roads into the town, which were on raised embankments, and along the riverside dykes. The main effect this flooding had was to prevent the Royalists raising gun batteries close to the town. Parliament promised to compensate the landowners for the damage caused but, as most of the landowners around the town were of Royalist sympathies, little money was paid out.

On 10 July, the garrison received a welcome reinforcement. Parliament had despatched Sir John Meldrum and 500 soldiers to the town. Sir John Meldrum, a Scot, was an experienced campaigner who had served King Charles faithfully for many years but refused to join him in his impending fight against Parliament. There is some evidence for Meldrum having been in the town prior to the siege commencing, so it may only have been the 500 reinforcements who arrived on the 10th. A further 1,500 men were to arrive before the siege was over. Parliament had one warship, *The Hercules*, already stationed at Hull and two further warships were ordered to the town: *The Rainbow* and *The Unicorn*. The Royalists now had little chance of isolating the town.

The King continued to demand the town's surrender and exchanged a number of communications with Parliament. After despatching one of these messages, the King, and his court, left Beverley for Nottingham and Leicester. In his absence Lindsey continued to besiege the town.

The garrison was much more active. One sally reached as far west as Anlaby, where the Royalist troops were driven from their quarters and a powder store blown up. The Parliamentarian troops returned to Hull triumphant with a dozen prisoners. On another occasion Sir John Meldrum led 500 foot from the Beverley Gate to attack the Royalist positions in that direction. A large body of horse formed up to oppose him, supported by foot. The Royalist foot quickly turned on their heels and Meldrum was able to drive their horse back towards Beverley, causing numerous casualties and bringing back 30 prisoners.

When the King returned to Beverley he realized that his ill-equipped force would not be able to take the town. The successful Parliamentary raids on his army's quarters had sapped their morale. The King made a decision to withdraw the whole army to York. Several weeks later King Charles had decided that the breach between himself and his Parliament had grown so wide that only open warfare would decide the issue. As armies have done for many centuries, the Royalist army marched believing that it would take one successful battle to bring Parliament to heel. It would all be over by Christmas!

The Fight for Yorkshire

With the departure of the King's army, the Royalists in Yorkshire were in an unenviable position. A large proportion of the troops raised in the North had marched south with the King. The Earl of Cumberland, the King's commander in Yorkshire, gave orders to recruit new forces to hold the county against the Parliamentary forces being raised in several areas around. The Royalist army was mainly gathered in and around York. Parliament had three separate forces being raised in the county. In the West Riding, Lord Ferdinando Fairfax raised his troops from the mill towns around Halifax and Bradford and these troops began to put pressure on the Royalists from the west. From the southeast the Hothams marched their forces from Hull towards Selby and from the coast Sir Hugh Cholmley marched towards Malton and Stamford Bridge.

The Earl of Cumberland knew his limitations and realized that he was not a soldier. Further north, the Earl of Newcastle was raising another Royalist army in Northumberland and County Durham. On 26 September Cumberland and his officers wrote to Newcastle, requesting that he marched into Yorkshire with his army and assumed command of all the forces in the county. After some negotiation, Newcastle's army marched south on 1 December, arriving at York on the 3rd.

Lord Fairfax had stationed his troops at Tadcaster, just to the west of York. On the 7th Newcastle marched his army of 4,500 men against the gathered Parliamentarian forces. Lord Fairfax had decided to withdraw towards Leeds but the Royalists arrived before this happened. In a hard-fought action, Fairfax's 1,000 men held their ground against several Royalist attacks. The Parliamentarians were very low on gunpowder and had to withdraw to Selby during the night – powder was more readily available in Hull than in the West Riding. In the aftermath of the battle, Newcastle garrisoned Pontefract Castle and Ferrybridge, almost cutting off Fairfax from his main area of support.

The Royalists attempted to push into the West Riding. On 18 December a substantial Royalist force attacked Bradford. The town's garrison was made up of locally raised, ill-equipped troops but they stood their ground and halted the enemy attack. Reinforcements arrived from Halifax later in the day and the Parliamentarians were able to drive the Royalists from Bradford, causing them to withdraw to Leeds.

Ferdinando, Lord Fairfax.   *Sir Thomas Fairfax.*

A few days after the fight at Bradford, Sir Thomas Fairfax arrived with reinforcements from his father's army. On 23 January 1643 he led an attack against a large Royalist force garrisoning Leeds. Breaking into the town at the bottom of Briggate and along the Headrow, the Parliamentarians drove the Royalists from the town. The Royalists also abandoned Wakefield, which was quickly occupied by Parliamentary forces from Huddersfield.

The Earl of Newcastle's army heavily outnumbered their fragmented Parliamentary opponents but Newcastle was unable to move over to the offensive. His army was short of arms and gunpowder and a large convoy was due to arrive at York in early February. Newcastle had despatched James King, his lieutenant-general, with a large force, to escort the convoy safely to York. Sir Hugh Cholmley, the Parliamentarian commander of the Scarborough garrison, led a force to intercept King at Yarm Bridge on 1 February. Cholmley was quickly defeated and the convoy continued on to York.

Newcastle now had his military supplies but was still unable to commence his campaign. Queen Henrietta-Maria had left for the Continent twelve months earlier, to raise money for weapons and armour. Her arrival on the East Coast was imminent and Newcastle had been ordered to ensure her safety and despatch her arms convoy to Oxford, where the King awaited her arrival. On 22 February the Queen arrived at Bridlington. During the night the town, and the Queen's quarters, were bombarded by several Parliamentarian warships. The Queen and her entourage had to take shelter in a ditch but were saved by the timely arrival of Admiral van Tromp, with a small Dutch squadron. Van Tromp threatened to open fire on the Parliamentarian ships if they did not cease fire. The threat and the falling tide persuaded the English captains that a withdrawal would be a good idea. Newcastle had marched most of his army to Pocklington, where he heard of the Queen's arrival at Bridlington. He turned his army towards the coast, rendezvoused with the Queen and safely escorted her to York, where they arrived on 7 March.

In Scarborough, Sir Hugh Cholmley, a lukewarm Parliamentarian, was having doubts as to whether he was supporting the right side. Following the arrival of the Queen in York, and an exchange of letters – it is possible that Cholmley actually visited the Queen in York – Sir Hugh declared his support for the King on 25 March, and much of the Scarborough garrison supported him.

With Cholmley's defection, Lord Fairfax's situation in Selby had completely changed. He now had Royalist forces to his north, northwest and northeast. The Hothams in Hull were also becoming less cooperative. Fairfax's main support was in the West Riding and he decided that a withdrawal to Leeds on 30 March would be a strategically sound move. While Fairfax's main army marched directly to Leeds from Selby, he despatched his son, Sir Thomas, on a diversionary raid to Tadcaster. Sir Thomas lingered in Tadcaster for too long before departing for Leeds. He was intercepted by Colonel George Goring, and 1,000 Royalist horse, at Seacroft Moor, where Fairfax's force was virtually destroyed. In the meantime Lord Fairfax had safely arrived at Leeds with his main army.

In early May, Newcastle began his offensive into the south of the county, clearing a route for the Queen to march south. Wakefield was reoccupied and Rotherham and Sheffield captured on 4 and 6 May respectively. Newcastle ordered the ironworks at Sheffield to begin casting cannon for his army, which he had moved to Pontefract in preparation for the Queen's departure. On 21 May he received disturbing news: Wakefield had fallen.

Newcastle had left a garrison of over 3,000 men in Wakefield, commanded by George Goring. Poor military intelligence had led the Fairfaxes to believe that the garrison was only 800 men and a decision was taken to attack the town. During the night of 20/21 May, Sir Thomas Fairfax led an army of 1,500 men to attack the town, believing that he outnumbered the garrison by almost two to one. The Parliamentarians successfully stormed the town, capturing the bulk of the garrison in the process. When the prisoners were counted it was realized that Fairfax had actually been outnumbered by two to one rather than the opposite. His father said it was more a miracle than a victory, in a letter to Parliament.

Rather than turn and confront the enemy immediately, Newcastle carried on with his plan to send the Queen's convoy south. By 16 June the Queen, and her escort, had arrived safely in Newark. From there they carried on to Oxford. Newcastle was now free to take the war to his enemies in the West Riding.

On the 22nd Newcastle's army stormed Howley Hall, near Batley, held for Parliament by Sir John Saville. For the next week the rains poured and the roads were unfit to move an army along. By the 30th the roads had dried enough for Newcastle to continue his march to Bradford, where Lord Fairfax's army was quartered. Lord Fairfax realized that Bradford could not stand a siege. The town sits in a bowl, surrounded by high ground on all sides. With the success of the attack on Wakefield fresh in his mind, Fairfax decided to attack the Royalists in their encampment at Howley Hall. The attack was planned for early on the 30th but his army was late in departing from Bradford. Both armies were marching along the same road towards each other.

The two armies clashed at Adwalton Moor, close to Morley. Initially, the Parliamentarians got the better of the fighting, although they were heavily outnumbered, having 4,000 regular soldiers and an unspecified number of clubmen (local levies), while Newcastle had between 10,000 and 12,000, including a substantial body of cavalry. The Parliamentarian attack was so successful that Newcastle was on the verge of ordering his army to withdraw. One of his officers, Sir Posthumous Kirton, requested permission to lead a counter-attack, which quickly turned the tide of the battle. With the success of Kirton's attack, Newcastle threw more men into the fray and the Parliamentarian centre and left were quickly broken. On their right flank, Sir Thomas Fairfax held his ground for some time after the rest of the army had broken and may have been unaware of the Royalist success. While the remainder of his father's army had routed towards Bradford, Sir Thomas had to take a more circuitous route, initially falling back to Halifax and then riding through the night to Bradford.

Newcastle's army continued its advance to Bradford and prepared to assault it on 1 July, with orders to give no quarter. The Earl spent the night at Bolling Hall and local tradition has it that he was visited by a spirit which implored him to 'Pity poor Bradford'. Whether caused by a supernatural visitor or not, Newcastle had changed his mind by the next morning and began negotiations with Sir Thomas Fairfax. Lord Fairfax and the bulk of his surviving troops had marched to Leeds during the night. During the negotiations, Newcastle's guns opened fire on the town. Sir Thomas realized that Newcastle did not really want to come to an agreement but was simply playing for time while his artillery was positioned. Fairfax decided to break out with his remaining mounted men during the early hours of the 2nd. After an eventful ride, during which his wife was captured by pursuing Royalist horse, he arrived at Leeds.

After Sir Hugh Cholmley had defected to the King's side, the Hothams had become uncooperative. It was likely that they too would change sides. On 29 June things came to a head when the citizens of Hull attempted to arrest the pair. Captain John was arrested but his father escaped from the town and rode to Beverley, where his pursuers caught him. The pair were now considered traitors by both sides and would meet their ends with the executioner's axe on Tower Hill in January 1644. A letter was despatched from Hull to Lord Fairfax, which reached him at Leeds as a council of war was deciding what to do after the defeat at Adwalton Moor. A decision was made to withdraw the pitiful remnants of the army to Hull.

After Adwalton Moor the situation in Yorkshire had changed completely. The Earl of Newcastle, soon to be elevated to Marquess, had complete control of the county, with the exception of Hull. Many historians have written of a possible three-pronged attack on London at this point by Newcastle's northern army, Sir Ralph Hopton's western army and the King's own army, based in Oxford. Newcastle may well have wanted to march south but the Yorkshire gentry would have none of it, not while Hull stood firm for Parliament. Newcastle decided to lay siege to the town while pushing some of his mounted troops into Lincolnshire. On 2 September the Royalist army arrived before the walls of Hull and the town's second siege had begun. Just over three weeks later another event took place, which was a direct reaction to the Parliamentary defeat at Adwalton Moor. Both King and Parliament had been courting the Scots for some time but their defeat caused Parliament to come to an agreement with the Scots. On 25 September the Solemn League and Covenant was signed. Parliament had agreed that England would become a Presbyterian nation and the Scots had agreed to supply a 20,000 strong army in January 1644.

The Second Siege of Hull

On 22 July Parliament appointed Lord Fairfax as the governor of Hull. Although Newcastle had pushed part of his army into Lincolnshire, and captured Lincoln and Gainsborough, the Royalists exerted little pressure on Hull and gave the defeated Parliamentarians time to recover. The Royalists did not advance on the town until late in August. Sir Thomas Fairfax had been quartered in Beverley to relieve the supply situation in Hull. As the Royalist army advanced towards Beverley Sir Thomas awaited orders from his father to withdraw. By the time the order arrived it was almost too late. Sir Thomas sent the bulk of his troops back towards Hull and covered their retreat with a mounted rearguard. The initial clash between Fairfax and the Royalist advance guard took place just north of Beverley. Fairfax then withdrew into the town, closely followed by the enemy, and a bloody skirmish took place. Fairfax had some difficulty in extricating his men from the town and then continued to fight a gallant rearguard action most of the way back to Hull.

The Royalist army, 12,000 strong, continued to move into position and on 2 September the siege began. The Royalists first move was to cut the town's water supply by diverting the stream which provided most of the town's water. As has already been mentioned, this would have had little effect on the defenders. The Royalists began to build a battery, the Fort Royal, to the north of the Charterhouse Hospital, which stood a few hundreds yards north of the Northgate. Lord Fairfax evacuated the hospital and demolished most of it to build a battery to oppose the Royalist work. The besiegers raised another at Sculcoates, close to the Beverley road. Fairfax added more guns to the Charterhouse fort to oppose this new battery. The Royalist forces were divided in two by the River Hull and a pontoon bridge was built to join the troops on both banks of the river.

On 9 September the Parliamentarians made their first large sally. The plan was for a large force to attack the Royalists quartered around Anlaby, to the west of Hull. The Royalists were not taken by surprise and the attacking force was quickly driven back to the town's defences, having suffered a number of casualties.

William Cavendish, Earl of Newcastle.

Colonel Oliver Cromwell.

The Royalist batteries could now effectively bombard the town and they began to fire red-hot shot into the town in the hopes of setting fire to the town's buildings. This seems to have had a limited effect but worried Lord Fairfax enough for him to take measures against it. On 14 September the banks of the Rivers Humber and Hull were cut and the land around Hull inundated for the second time in fourteen months. Many of the Royalist siege works were flooded. The north and northwest sides of the town could not be approached except through the flooded fields or along the raised roadways. Because of this most of the fighting during the rest of the siege took place in the area around the Derringham Dyke and opposite the Hessle Gate, close to the banks of the Humber. Both sides erected new earthworks and batteries in the area.

The east bank of the River Hull was protected by modern fortifications built in the time of Henry VIII: the North and South Blockhouses and the

Castle. Towards the middle of September the Northern Blockhouse suffered a serious explosion, when an over-eager gunner ran into the powder store with a lighted match. Although the interior of the blockhouse was damaged, its exterior remained intact and defensible. The Royalists also had a similar incident. Late in September, about twelve days after the explosion in the North Blockhouse, a powder store in a barn in Cottingham exploded.

On 26 September, Lord Willoughby of Parham and Colonel Oliver Cromwell visited Hull to discuss the situation with Lord Fairfax. It was decided that Sir Thomas Fairfax and Lord Fairfax's mounted men would be ferried across the Humber into Lincolnshire and join with the Earl of Manchester's Eastern Association Horse to oppose Newcastle's forces in the north of the county. As will be seen shortly, this decision paid real dividends.

The Royalists had attempted to isolate Hull by building a fort at Paull and another opposite on the Lincolnshire shore. In early October two Parliamentary ships, *The Lion* and *The Unicorn*, attacked and destroyed both forts. The Humber remained open to shipping and supplies and reinforcements could arrive at Hull uninterrupted. One of these reinforcements was the redoubtable Scots soldier, Sir John Meldrum, who arrived at Hull on 5 October. Meldrum's arrival seems to have revitalized the defenders and within a few days sallies had been made along the Derringham Bank and to Sculcoates. On the 9th the Royalists carried out two attacks in retaliation. The first took the Charterhouse fort, the fort's commander being killed. The garrison quickly organized a counter-attack and drove the Royalists from the fort. The second attack went in against the fortifications by the Hessle Gate. Captain Strickland led the attack, which was initially successful, but as his men attempted to occupy the fort they came under heavy fire from the half-moon work in front of the Myton Gate. Strickland was struck down and his men driven back by a counter-attack from the town.

By the 11th the defenders' confidence had grown to such an extent that a major sally was planned. Sir John Meldrum, ably assisted by Colonels Lambert and Rainsborough, would lead 1,500 foot, including sailors, and four troops of horse against the Royalist works between Derringham and the Humber. In a letter to Parliament, Lord Fairfax gave details of the attack:

> Yesterday, being the eleventh of this instant, I thought fit to draw forth what strength I could well make, in a salley, to drive the Enemy from a new worke that in the night hee had encroacht very near us, on the West side of the Towne, and it pleased God to give a blessing to the attempt.

My men I divided into two bodies, under the command of Colonell Lambart [Lambert] and Colonell Rainborrow [Rainsborough], Captaine of the Lyon, who brought some sea men for our assistants, and all under the command in chiefe for that service of Sir John Meldrum; whose valour and discretion with the other two Colonels throughout the whole action, I cannot mention without high commendation. About nine of the clocke by an assault two severall waies, the service begun; for, the truth is, we could not take that early advantage that I desired for such an enterprise: in a short time we gained one of their workes, and assaulted them in another; and it was not long ere we were unhappily forc't to retreat, and the enemy recovered all againe. But through the goodnesse of God my men soone rallied, their spirits recovered, and they suddenly repossess't of the last worke, beate them out of all the rest in that part, and got possession of one of their great Brasse demy Cannon. The Enemy thus fled, and the ground ours, we drew that great Gunne out of danger of their reprisal: About two houres after our possession of those workes, the enemy had drawne down a full body of reserves of Horse and Foot, from their Quarters, their numbers we know not, but about 36 Colours some of our men could tell; with these they opposed our tired men, and that in truth with excellent resolution, but it pleased God after two houres sharpe encounter, or thereabouts, they left the Field.

As night fell, the townsfolk sent food and drink to their men occupying the enemy positions and the captured Royalist cannons were dragged back to the town.

The successful Parliamentary sally on the 11th must have seriously damaged Newcastle's resolve. It was not the only bad news he received on that day. While his besieging forces had fought against the Parliamentary sally from Hull, his forces in Lincolnshire had been confronted and defeated by Lord Willoughby, Oliver Cromwell and Sir Thomas Fairfax. During the night of 11/12 October Newcastle began to withdraw his forces from before Hull. Newcastle had also received news of the death of his wife. Hull had successfully stood its second siege. It would be the last time the town was threatened. Prior to the siege the Royalist campaign in the North had reached its high point. After the siege their cause would steadily slip into decline and defeat.

Chapter 2

THE GREAT AND CLOSE
SIEGE OF YORK

The Scots Invasion

After his withdrawal from Hull on 12 October 1643 the Marquess of Newcastle quickly settled his army into winter quarters near his house at Welbeck. This was very early in the campaign season but the death of his wife seems to have knocked the wind from his sails. Lord Fairfax remained at Hull while his son Sir Thomas continued to support the Earl of Manchester's Eastern Association army in Lincolnshire.

Several weeks prior to the Battle of Winceby and Newcastle's withdrawal from before the walls of Hull, an event which would change the course of the war had taken place. On 25 September 1643 Parliament came to an agreement with the Scots: the Solemn League and Covenant. Both sides had made approaches to the Scots but Fairfax's defeat at the Battle of Adwalton Moor had forced Parliament's hand. Parliamentary defeats in the North and in the West Country had turned the course of the war in the King's favour. He now had three armies available to march towards London; his own based around Oxford, Sir Ralph Hopton's in the South and Newcastle's in the North. Parliament saw this as a real threat and a treaty with the Scots as the best way out of a bad situation.

The treaty of the Solemn League and Covenant had two main clauses. The first stated that England would adopt the Presbyterian faith as its national church. Parliament would later renege on this part of the agreement and this would subsequently be a cause of conflict between the Scots and Parliament. The second clause, and the one much more relevant to our story, was that a Scots army of some 20,000 men would invade the North of England early in the following year.

On 19 January 1644 a Scots army of 18,000 men crossed the Tweed and marched into Northumberland, heading south towards Newcastle-upon-Tyne. News quickly reached Newcastle, elevated from Earl to Marquess after his victory at Adwalton Moor. By 29 January he had gathered a substantial force and headed north, leaving a small force to defend Yorkshire under the command of Colonel John Belasyse, a cousin of the Fairfaxes. Newcastle arrived at Newcastle-upon-Tyne hours before the Scots army summoned the town to surrender. Alexander Leslie, Earl of Leven, the Scots commander, must have been surprised that his summons was answered by the Marquess of Newcastle, who Leven thought was still in Yorkshire.

The Scots were in an unenviable position. They had hoped that an unsupported Newcastle-upon-Tyne would surrender quickly and provide them with a secure base of operations. The harbours along the Northumberland coast were too small to use as supply bases and most of the Scots supplies would have to come by sea as the road back to Berwick was in no fit state to transport the large logistic tail the Scots army would need. With Newcastle's arrival it seemed unlikely that the town would fall in the foreseeable future. A second consideration was that, while the south shore of the Tyne remained in Royalist hands, the town could be supplied and receive reinforcements, a similar situation to that at Hull several months earlier. With this in mind Leven decided that his army would cross the Tyne and head for Sunderland.

For almost a month the Scots army sidestepped west along the north shore of the river with the Royalist army keeping pace with them, blocking any attempt they made to cross. It was not until 28 February that the Scots managed to cross the river. The weather had worsened and Newcastle had withdrawn his army into Durham to rest and recuperate. The Scots continued their march over several days and occupied Sunderland on 4 March. Several contemporary Scots accounts express surprise that Newcastle did not do more to impede their march.

Newcastle moved his army towards Sunderland. For the next month he tried to draw the Scots army into the open where his substantial body of horse would give him a distinct advantage and would counteract Scots numbers. Leven was a canny, experienced commander and would not commit his troops beyond the enclosures surrounding Sunderland and its nearby villages. Although the Royalists seem to have got the better of the actions they were unable to inflict a major defeat on the Scots.

In early April Newcastle once again pulled his worn-out forces back to Durham. This time Leven felt confident enough to follow him and made camp close to the city. On 12 April Newcastle received shocking news from the south: his forces in Yorkshire had been defeated and their commander captured. The Fairfaxes were on the march and York was seriously threatened.

The Fight for Yorkshire

While Newcastle had been confronting the Scots in the North, what had been happening in Yorkshire? Colonel John Belasyse was threatened from three directions. Lord Fairfax's troops in Hull were resurgent. Fairfax despatched cavalry forces up the East Coast which raided as far north as Whitby and as far west as Stamford Bridge, only a short distance from York. In Nottinghamshire the town of Newark was besieged by a substantial Parliamentary force and it was only a short march from there into the southern part of Yorkshire. The third threat came from across the Pennines, where Sir Thomas Fairfax awaited an opportunity to advance into the West Riding.

Over the autumn and winter of 1643/4 Parliament seems to have used Sir Thomas to deal with any dangerous situations in the northern part of the Midlands. As has been mentioned, Sir Thomas and the bulk of his father's horse were ferried across the Humber to join Oliver Cromwell's Eastern Association horse. The pair were victorious at the Battle of Winceby on 11 October 1643 and this was the start of a partnership which would win the war. In Cheshire the Royalists, under Sir John Byron, had laid siege to the important town of Nantwich, Parliament's main base in the area. Sir Thomas was despatched to relieve the town, which he did successfully on 25 January 1644, after a hard-fought action.

After the relief of Nantwich, Fairfax marched into Lancashire where he remained for several weeks, recruiting troops ready for a return to his home county. This he began in early March. The exact date is not known, but what is clear is that John Lambert, who led Fairfax's advance guard, was at Bradford by 6 March. While Lambert occupied Bradford, Belasyse gathered his small army at Selby and awaited developments. On 21 March Belasyse's situation improved when Prince Rupert, the King's German nephew, surprised and defeated the Parliamentary besiegers at Newark. This allowed Colonel George Porter, one of Newark's defenders, to march with reinforcements of horse from Newark to Selby, which gave Belasyse an opportunity to strike at the enemy force in Bradford.

The date of the action at Bradford is not known, although it is very likely that it was in late March. Porter took part in the action so it could not have been earlier than the 27th and Sir Thomas Fairfax had reinforced Lambert by the end of the month. The action at Bradford was very confused. First Lambert, who was heavily outnumbered, withdrew from the town and then the victorious Royalists in turn withdrew. By nightfall Lambert had reoccupied the town. There seems to have been some disagreement among the Royalist commanders about the day's events. Belasyse blamed Porter for Lambert's force escaping from the town and Porter took such offence at this that he immediately marched his troops back to Newark. Within a couple of weeks they would be sadly missed.

By 9 April the Fairfaxes, father and son, had combined their forces at Ferrybridge and on the following day they advanced towards Belasyse's defensive position at Selby. On the 11th they attacked. The course of the ensuing action can still be traced through the streets of the town. The street ends were barricaded and defended by the Royalist foot. After hard fighting Sir Thomas Fairfax's column broke into the town on Ousegate, a street which runs along the side of the river, as its name suggests. Once his foot had cleared the barricade, Sir Thomas led his horse in an attack along the street. Belasyse led a mounted counter-attack and Sir Thomas became unhorsed and separated from his men. In turn the Parliamentary horse counter-attacked and relieved Sir Thomas. During this fighting Colonel Belasyse was wounded and captured. Lord Fairfax sent his own physician to tend his relative's wounds. Many of the Royalist horse escaped from the town, crossing the Ouse on a pontoon bridge, which must have stood close to where the present road bridge stands. The remainder of the Royalist force was captured. Belasyse's army had been all but destroyed and its commander captured. Other than a small garrison and the survivors from Selby, York was open to the enemy.

News reached Newcastle at Durham on the day after the battle. During the night of 12/13 April he began a forced march south. The Scots quickly realized what was happening and began a pursuit and they seem to have got the better of the Royalists in a number of skirmishes during the pursuit. By 19 April Newcastle had arrived at York. The Scots had broken off their pursuit and marched to join with Lord Fairfax's army at Tadcaster on the 20th. On the 22nd the combined force began its short march towards York. During

1617 map of York by Braun and Hogenberg.

the night Newcastle sent his horse south from the city. They would be much more useful outside the siege lines, forming part of a relief force. On 23 April the siege of York began.

York's Defences

York had been founded as a fortress in AD 71 when the Roman army had marched into Brigantian lands. The XI Legion (Hispana) had built a fortress close to the confluence of two rivers, an ideal defensive spot. Remnants of the

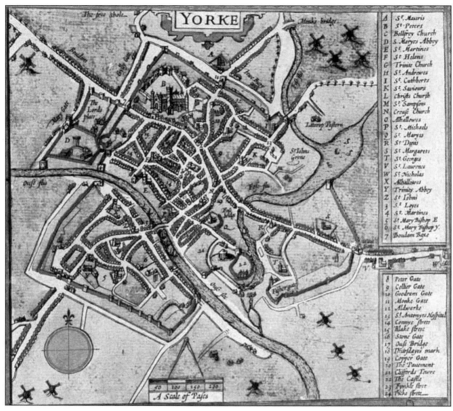

1610 map of York by John Speede.

Roman walls still exist and parts of the existing medieval walls follow the line of the original walls, which are buried under earth banks. By the seventeenth century it was these medieval walls which formed the bulk of York's defences.

The main gate into York from the south was Micklegate Bar. At the end of 1460 and into early 1461 it was adorned by the heads of Richard, Duke of York, the Earl of Rutland and the Earl of Salisbury, along with a number of their senior followers, slain at the Battle of Wakefield (30 December 1460). It is said that York's head was adorned with a paper crown in mockery of his royal pretensions. Micklegate Bar was the only one of the main gates not to be blocked up during the siege. The area south of the Ouse also included a small gate known as Skeldergate Postern.

After crossing the Ouse into the main part of the city, and continuing in a clockwise direction, the next gate is Bootham Bar, which stands on the site of one of the original Roman gateways. The Bar was the main route into the town from the north. For many years it had a sign stating that no vagabonds or Scots would be allowed inside the city after dark. Beyond Bootham Bar lies the King's Manor. During his time in York in the lead-up to war King Charles had used the manor house as his headquarters. Along with the ruins of St Mary's Abbey it stands in a large walled enclosure which included St Mary's Tower. The defences of the King's Manor were completely outside those of the city.

The walls between Bootham Bar and Monk Bar closely follow the line of the Roman fortress walls. Just to the east of Monk Bar the Roman walls turned south but by the time of the Civil Wars the wall continued in an easterly direction towards the River Foss where there was another small

The King's Manor was King Charles's headquarters in York in the lead-up to the Civil Wars.

postern gate, Layerthorpe Postern. For some distance to the south the city was protected by the Foss.

Beyond the Foss lay another salient in the city's defences. Walmgate, the main road from the city towards the east, led to Walmgate Bar which is the only gate that still retains its barbican. The gate is said to still show the signs of the Civil War fighting but I have to say I found it difficult to see where. The city's walls were completed by the Castle, Clifford's Tower and a short section of wall, which together covered the area between the Foss and the Ouse.

Earthworks had been dug in several places outside the city walls. Contemporary documents write of the Scots attacking several fieldworks in the Acomb area and a large fort has recently been excavated on the Mount, south of Micklegate Bar. These fieldworks played a dual role. First, they impeded the enemy's approach to the town and forced their artillery to be emplaced further away than would have been desirable for an effective bombardment. Secondly, they also provided an area of land between the city wall and the outer defences on which cattle and horses could be grazed.

The Siege

When the siege commenced on 23 April 1644 the Scots moved into positions on the south side of the Ouse, facing the defences around Micklegate Bar, while Lord Fairfax's troops were positioned on the east bank of the Foss facing Walmgate Bar. The main quarters for the Scots were at Bishopthorpe and Middlethorpe while Fairfax's were at Fulford and Heslington. These dispositions left the area between the Ouse and the Foss covered by only a few cavalry patrols. Sir Henry Slingsby, commanding a regiment of foot in the garrison, reports:

> Thus we were blockt up upon two sides of ye town, & the rest we had open 3 weeks, until, such time as my Ld Manchester came with his Norfolk men.

In actual fact it would be five weeks before Manchester's army arrived. Obviously this caused a major problem to the Allied, Scots and Parliamentary, army. Both reinforcements and supplies would be able to arrive at the city from the North. Another problem faced by the Allied commanders was that of a sally from the city. They took two measures to alleviate this problem. Their main siege lines were set some distance back from the walls so that they would have some warning of an attack by the Royalists. *Hull's Managing,* a Parliamentary tract, tells us that:

> Our guards being at such a distance from the City, they cannot well sally forth in any parties to our prejudice, for first our men have more time to make ready and then while they assault one quarter, the two next can more easily strike in betwixt them and home, to intercept their retreat.

The Allied commanders also had a pontoon bridge built over the Foss to allow the two forces to reinforce one another quickly should the need arise. This was necessitated by Newcastle's ability to move his men along interior lines within the city to attack at any point he chose. As will be seen in due course these measures seem to have had the desired effect and the subsequent Royalist sallies were quite ineffective.

The supply situation within the city was good, Slingsby writes 'of provisions we had in good store in ye town', while *Hull's Managing* reports that the Royalists were 'much straitned for flesh, meat, & salt, but of corne they have no lack'. This would certainly have not been the case had Newcastle retained his horse within the city and was a major contributory factor for him sending them south.

There still remained the problem of the Allies not having enough troops to completely blockade the city. Where could additional troops be found? Fortunately for the Allied commanders another Parliamentary army lay to the south in Lincolnshire. If the Earl of Manchester could be persuaded to bring his army north then the city could be completely surrounded. A deputation was sent to Lincoln to consult Manchester, the two main members of which were the Scots Earl of Crawford-Lindsey and Sir Thomas Fairfax. They seem to have been very persuasive and Manchester agreed to march north. On 24 May Manchester's Eastern Association troops began their march to York. The journey does not appear to have been problem-free and Simeon Ashe, who was Manchester's chaplain and wrote a series of letters during the campaign, tells us that 'we were compelled to leave our greatest Ordinance behind us, the wayes being deep, by reason of the great rain which hath been in these parts'.

On 31 May, as Manchester's army continued its march, the three Allied commanders, Leven, Fairfax and Manchester, held a council of war in Lord Howard's house at Escrick, where they discussed the siege and Manchester's role in it. It was decided that the Eastern Association troops would cover the arc between the Ouse and the Foss. On 1 June Manchester wrote a letter to the Committee of Both Kingdoms to tell them that Sir John Meldrum had been despatched from York with two regiments of foot to reinforce the garrison of Manchester and oppose Prince Rupert's march through Lancashire. Manchester also stressed the importance of the siege:

> I believe we shall use all means to give some speedy issue to this siege of York that so all our forces may be ready to oppose any enemy wheresoever they are, for the engagement is such now, and the consequences of carrying this place so great, as they cannot undertake any other action until this be finished.

While Manchester moved north Leven and Fairfax despatched a large body of horse into the West Riding to shield the passes through the Pennines and to cover the movements of Newcastle's cavalry, the Northern Horse. They had also captured Cawood Castle, an important position on the Ouse between Selby and York. The Royalists attempted to recapture it by sending a body of horse from Pontefract Castle but were unsuccessful.

On 3 June Manchester's army completed its march and moved into its quarters between the Ouse and Foss. While this was going on the Royalists attempted to break out with a body of horse towards Scarborough. *Hull's Managing* reports the ensuing fight:

> In particular upon Munday the third of June instant, a partee of horse sallyed out towards our quarters at Clifton, intending to break through and advance towards Scarborough, being discovered our horse divided themselves into three Squadrons, the middle charged them, the other two wheeled about upon their right and left, and charged them in the reare, and so having encompassed them, cut most of them off; took 67 horse, very few escaped to carry the news to Yorke.

The Parliamentary horse were able to catch the Royalists in a classic pincer movement and capture the bulk of them.

After their long march it should be expected that many of Manchester's men would have wanted to rest on the 4th but this does not seem to have been the case. Simeon Ashe reports some of them, without orders, advanced beyond the siege lines to capture cattle and horses grazing close to the city walls. On the same day the Allied commanders held a council of war to decide on the course of action to be taken and the results of these decisions soon became apparent. A number of small skirmishes took place on the 4th and the Duchess of Newcastle reports an attempt by Allied troops to clear one of the gates while the Royalists tried to block it!

On 5 June the Allies made their first move. Initially the Scots and Eastern Association troops deployed in line of battle and looked as though they intended to attack the city, drawing the defenders' attention. Under cover of this distraction Lord Fairfax made a move towards Walmgate Bar. Fairfax raised a five-gun battery on Windmill Hill close to the Bar. Simeon Ashe mentions that the battery was within a musket shot of the gate. Fairfax pushed on to capture the suburbs outside the gate and placed two more guns in the street opposite and a third one close to 'ye Dovecoat' which must have

York: Bootham Bar looking from Bootham.

been a local landmark. This incident highlights an error in the defenders' planning for the defence of the city. At Newcastle-upon-Tyne, the Marquess of Newcastle had ordered the suburbs close to the town's walls to be burnt, thus denying cover to the enemy. This had not happened at York and Fairfax used the cover of the buildings to approach Walmgate Bar and set up his guns close enough to the walls and gate to do damage. A similar problem also existed at Bootham Bar.

Also on the 5th the Allied commanders wrote to the Committee of Both Kingdoms to give them a situation report. They were under pressure from the Committee to respond to Prince Rupert's advance into Lancashire. The Committee had despatched Sir Henry Vane to York to be their man on the spot. The Committee suggested that troops be despatched across the Pennines to deal with Prince Rupert. The commanders at York were less than impressed by this suggestion and put forth their objections:

> For by this accession of forces Prince Rupert's army is so increased as we think it not safe to divide our men, and send a part to encounter him in Lancashire. If we should raise our siege before York and march with all our forces against him, it is in his discretion to avoid us, and either pass by another way than we take, and so come into Yorkshire, or else retire into Cheshire, whither if we should pursue him, it would be in the Marquis of Newcastle's power, in our absence, to recover all Yorkshire again and increase his army to as great a strength as ever it was.

At this time of the Civil War Prince Rupert was a thorn in Parliament's side and had gained an aura of invincibility. The Committee of Both Kingdoms' suggestions to march against him, and the Allied commanders' refusal, is a recurring theme when examining the correspondence between the two. Their refusal made sound strategic sense, as later events were to prove.

On the 6th the next phase of the siege was put into operation when Manchester's men attacked into the suburbs along Bootham. For the loss of five men Manchester had begun his approach to Bootham Bar and the King's Manor.

The 7th passed quietly but on the 8th it was the Scots' turn to attack, in the first major action of the siege. To the west of the city, close to Acomb, lay three small Royalist forts which prevented the Scots from approaching within effective range of the city walls. In the early hours of 8 June the Scots attacked, as Simeon Ashe reports:

About midnight, a commanded Company of the courageous Scots, assaulted fiercely and bravely the three Forts on the west side of the City, and after a very hot service, for the space of two houres (whereof many of us, with deepe affections were eye witnesses at a distance) they became possessors of two of them. The one of the Forts (which was nearest to the Towne) was strengthened with a double ditch, wherein were 120 souldiers, above 60 were slaine, and all the rest taken prisoners. The other Fort taken, had only 50 men to maintaine it, who were all either killed, or taken prisoners desiring quarter. And the 3d Fort had been possessed by the Scots also, if that a strong party both of Horse and Foot, had not come out of the Towne for the reliefe thereof. In this brave and bold service, the Scots lost 3 Captaines and some others (whether 6, 7, or some few more as yet is not manifested) were killed, one Lieftenant-Colonell and 2 Captaines deadly wounded, with many others wounded, but (as is hoped) not in danger of death.

Sir Henry Slingsby also writes of the attack:

Some redoubts they took by storm, as one in Bishopfeilds, & another on a windmill hill towards Bishopthorp. But this was no great loss more yn ye killing of ye men; for but one they kept, ye other they slight'd, & we still send [to] ye fields to keep our cows and horses.

While the Scots attacked the fieldworks to the west of the city, Newcastle had sent men out into the suburbs around Bootham to set light to the buildings and deny them to Manchester's men. This was unsuccessful as Simeon Ashe tells us:

Upon Saturday the 8 day in the morning, a souldier of the Marquess of Newcastle was taken in the Earl of Manchesters leager: he was in a red suit, he had pitch, flax, and other materials upon him for fiering of the suburbs there, as yet free from the wasting flames. Some more of the

Marquesse his souldiers were taken prisoner also; they had white coats (made of plundred cloath taken from Clothiers in these parts) with crosses on the sleeves, wrought with red and blew silk, an ensigne as wee conceive of some Popish Regiment.

Ashe goes on to describe an attempt by Manchester's men to burn the wooden gate at Bootham Bar. The defenders prevented this by throwing grenades – ceramic spheres filled with gunpowder – from the walls and gate.

By nightfall on 8 June all three Allied armies had made progress in their respective areas of operations. Manchester and Fairfax had advanced into the suburbs at Bootham and Walmgate Bars respectively, while the Scots had cleared the way to advance their batteries closer to the walls on the south side of the Ouse. Newcastle's army was now firmly shut within the city and Sir Henry Slingsby complains that he was even unable to get a letter to his wife at Red House to the west of York. Unbeknown to Newcastle the Allies had almost completed two mines, one under St Mary's Tower, part of the defences of the King's Manor, and the other at Walmgate Bar.

The Marquess of Newcastle knew that he had to play for time to allow Prince Rupert to arrive and relieve the city. He was aware of Rupert's advance as signals were regularly received by beacon from the top of the keep of Pontefract Castle which could be seen from the tower of York Minster. With this in mind Newcastle opened communications with the Allied commanders. On the evening of the 8th he sent two identical letters to Leven and Fairfax:

I cannot but admire that your Lordship hath so neere beleagured the Citie on all sides, made batteries against it, and so neere approached to it, without signifying what your intentions are, and what you desire or expect, which is contrary to the rules of all military discipline and customes; therefore I have thought fit to remonstrate thus much to your Lordship, to the end that your Lordship may signifie your intentions and resolutions therein, and receive ours, and so I remain my Lord.

This letter began a series of communications and meetings that gained Newcastle seven days. Leven's reply was to the point:

At this distance I will not dispute in points of militarie discipline, nor the practice of Captains in such cases, yet to give your Lordsh. satisfaction in that your letter desires from me, your Lordship may take notice, I have drawn my forces before this citie with intention to reduce it to the obedience due to the King and Parliament, whereunto if your Lordship shall speedily confer me, it may save the effusion of much innocent blood, whereof I wish your Lordship to bee no lesse sparing than I am, who rest …

Throughout the First Civil War the Scots and Parliament both professed to be fighting not against the King but against his evil advisers and were, indeed, his loyal subjects. In a meeting held by the Allied commanders it became apparent that Manchester had not received a letter from Newcastle. When Newcastle was informed of this on the 9th he quickly despatched a copy of his original letter and the replies from Leven and Fairfax. In a covering letter Newcastle stated that he would have 'done the like to your Lordship then, if I had had any assurance of your Lordship being in these parts in your own person'. It does seem a little surprising that Newcastle remained unaware of Manchester's presence in the siege lines six days after the latter's arrival.

The Allied commanders held another meeting to discuss Newcastle's communications. They agreed to send a letter to Newcastle to open discussions about the surrender of the city. Newcastle said that he would consider their offer and reply to them on Tuesday the 11th. He had gained two more days.

While they waited for a reply from Newcastle, the Allied commanders held a meeting with the representative of the Committee of Both Kingdoms, Sir Henry Vane, to discuss the situation in the North. After the meeting Sir Henry wrote to the Committee supporting the commanders' decision to continue the siege and not to dance to Prince Rupert's tune. As these discussions were taking place the Royalists attempted to break two bodies of horse out of the city. To the north 200 horsemen sallied out but were quickly driven back. Another body of eighty rode from Micklegate Bar towards Acomb but had as little success as the first body.

Promptly on the 11th Newcastle replied to the Allied commanders:

I have received your Lordshipps Letter with the names of the Commissioners appointed by your Lordshipps, But since your Lordshipps have declared in your Letter to allow a Cessation of Armes only on that side of the Towne during the time of the Treaty, I finde it not fit for me to incline to it upon those conditions, and had returned your Lordshipps this answer long before this tyme if some weighty affaires had not retarded my desires in that particular, I am …

Newcastle was refusing to parley unless there was a general ceasefire for the duration of the talk. This seems to have riled the Allied commanders and their reply, sent on the 12th, was straight to the point:

We the Generalls of the Armies raised for the King and Parliament, and now imployed in this expedition about Yorke, That no further effusion of blood be done, and that the City of Yorks and Inhabitants may be preserved from ruine; We hereby require your Lordship to surrender the said City to us in name and for the use of King and Parliament within the space of 24. houres after the receipt hereof, which if you refuse to doe, the inconvenience ensuing upon your refuseall must bee required at your Lordships hands, seeing our intentions are not for blood or destruction of Townes, Cities, and Counties, unlesse all other meanes being used, we be necessitated hereunto, which shall be contrary to the mindes and harts of …

If Newcastle did not surrender the city then the loss of blood would be on his head! Newcastle replied on the following morning:

I have received a Letter from your Lordships dated yesterday about four of the clock in the afternoon, wherein I am required to surrender the City to your Lordships within 24. hours after the receipt; but I know your Lordships are too full of honour, to expect the rendring the City upon a demand, and upon so short an advertisement to me, who have the Kings Commission to keep it, and where there is so many generall persons, and men of honour, quality and fortune concerned in it. But truly I conceive this sad demand high enough to have been exacted upon the meanest Governor of any of his Majesties Garrisons: And your Lordships may be pleased to know, that I expect Propositions to proceed from your Lordships, as becomes Persons of honour to give and receive one from another; and if your Lordships therefore think fit to propound honourable and reasonable terms, and agree upon a generall cessation from all acts of hostility during the time of a Treaty, then your Lordships may receive such satisfaction therein, as may be expected from persons of honour, and such as desire as much to avoid the effusion of Christian blood, or destruction of Cities, Towns, and Counties as any whatsoever, yet will not spare their own lives, rather then to live in the least stain of dishonour, and so desiring your Lordships resolution.

Even though Newcastle seems to have assumed the moral high ground, Fairfax, Leven and Manchester were quick to reply, agreeing to a general ceasefire and parley on the following day.

At 1500 hours on the 14th the parley began and was scheduled to continue until 2000 hours. The ceasefire would last from three hours before the parley until three hours after its completion and would cover the whole of the city. The commissioners would meet in a tent between the lines and each side would be allowed 100 musketeers as an honour guard. The seven Royalist commissioners were:

Lord Widdrington
Sit Thomas Glemham
Sir Richard Hutton
Sir William Wentworth
Sir Robert Strickland
Sir Thomas Metham
Master Robert Rockley

The Allies sent commissioners from all three armies. They were:

The Earl of Crawford-Lindsey
Lord Humbey
Lieutenant General Baillie
Sir William Fairfax
Colonel Hammond
Colonel Russell
Colonel White

The Royalist commissioners began by stating the conditions under which Newcastle would consider surrendering the city. Simeon Ashe reported them in full:

Propositions made to the three Generalls by the Earl of Newcastle, concerning the rendering of the City of York, entitled, Propositions to be tendered to the Enemy.

I. That the town shall be rendered within twenty dayes, in case no relief come to it by that time from the King or Prince Rupert, upon these conditions:

    That the Marquess Newcastle with all officers and souldiers therein have free liberty, to depart with colours flying and match light, and to take with them all Arms, Ammunition, Artillery, Money, Plate, and other goods belonging to them; for which end, that carriages be provided them, and victualls and other provision for their march.

    That they be conveyed with our Troops to the King, Prince Rupert, or any other garrisons of the Kings where they please; And that they be not forced to march above 8. miles a day.

    That they shall have liberty to stay or appoint others to stay 40. dayes in the town for sale of such goods, or for conveying of them to other places which they shall not be able to carry away with them.

    That no Oath, Covenant, or Protestation be administred to any of them, further then is warranted by the known lawes of the land.

II. That the Gentry herein have liberty to go to their houses, and there be protected from violence, and not questioned for what they have done to the other partie: that no Oath or Covenant be tendered them as above said.

III. That the townes-men injoy all their priviledges and libertie of trade and merchandice, as before, and not to be questioned for any things they have done against the Parliament; and that no Oath be tendered to any of them, &c.

    That the Garrison to be sent into York be only Yorkshiremen.

    That all the Churches therein be kept from prophanation, and no violation offered to the Cathedral Church.

    That the service be allowed to be performed therin as formerly had bin.

    That the Revenues of the Church remain to the Officers thereof as hath done, and that the Prebends continue their Prebendaries and other Revenues as formerly according to the Lawes.

IV. That all Ministers and other Ecclesiasticall persons therein, of what countrey soever, have liberty to depart with the army, or to their own livings, there to serve God and to enjoy their estate without disturbance.

That no oath or covenant be proffered them as aforesaid, nor they questioned hereafter, for what they have done to the Kings party.

That good Hostages be given, and to remain in their custodie: And that Cliffords Tower (the chiefe Fort in York) be still kept garrisoned by them, untill the Articles abovesaid, and some others then offered with them, be punctually performed. And then the said Garrison, and all Armes, Ammunition and Cannon therein, be safely conveyed to what Garrison of the Kings they pleased.

The Allied commissioners could not agree to these conditions without referring to their commanders. Three of the commissioners left the parley, returning one and a half hours later with their commanders' reply, a set of counter-proposals, once again reported by Simeon Ashe:

That the City of York and all the Forts, together with all Arms, Ammunition, and other warlike provisions whatsoever in and about the same be tendered and delivered up to us for and to the use of King and Parliament, upon the conditions following, viz.

That the common souldiers shall have free liberty and licence to depart and go to their own homes, and to carry with them their clothes and their own money (not exceeding 14. days pay) And shall have safe conduct and protection of their persons from violence, they promising that they will not hereafter take up Arms against the Parliament or Protestant Religion.

That the Citizens and ordinary inhabitants of the said City shall have their persons and house protected from violence; and shall have the same free trade and commerce as others under obedience of King and Parliament, And that no Regiment or Companies shall be admitted or quartered in the Town of York, except for those that are appointed for the Garrison thereof.

That the Officers of all qualities shall have liberty to go to their own homes with swords and horses, and shall have licence to carry their apparell and money along with them (the money not exceeding one months means for every severall officer).

Any officer who shall be recommended by the Marquess of Newcastle shall have a pass from one of the Generalls to go beyond the seas, they promising not to serve against the Parliament and Protestant Religion.

That the Gentry and other inhabitants of the County of York, now residing in the City of York, shall have liberty to go to their own homes, and shall be protected from violence.

That a positive Answer be returned to these Propositions by 3. of the clock tomorrow afternoon, being the 15. instant; And in case they shall not have been accepted, we shall not hold our selves bound to them, and in the mean time we declare there is no cessation after the 3. hours already granted.

The two sets of propositions had a number of differences but the major one was the existence of Newcastle's army. In the Royalists' propositions his army would march out with the full honours of war, carrying their arms and armour, while in the Allied propositions his army would cease to exist, although its members would be allowed to return home. The Parliamentary counter-propositions make perfect sense. The last thing the Scots and Parliament needed was Newcastle to combine with Prince Rupert and then march back into Yorkshire. If this was allowed to happen then the work of the previous months could come to nothing. The Royalist commissioners were so angered by the Allied proposals that they refused to even take a copy to the Marquess.

On the morning of the 15th the Allied commanders sent a drummer into the city with a copy of their demands, and Newcastle's reply could not have come as a great surprise to them, as Simeon Ashe tells us:

I have perused the Conditions and demands your Lordship sent, but when I considered the many professions made to avoide the effusion of Christian blood, I did admire to see such propositions from your Lordshipps, conceiving this not the way to it, for I cannot suppose that your Lordshipps doe imagine that persons of honour can possibly condescend to any of these propositions, and so I remaine …

Once the Allied commanders had received Newcastle's reply they declared the ceasefire at an end. During the following night the Royalists lit a beacon on top of the Minster tower which was answered by one from the roof of

Pontefract Castle's keep. Both sides seem to have taken this as an indication that Prince Rupert was about to march from Lancashire to York and this may have prompted the Allied commanders to make their next move.

On 16 June Sir Henry Vane was in his quarters writing to the Committee of Both Kingdoms. He reports the completion of the two mines, one under St Mary's Tower and the other at Walmgate Bar, and the repair of the largest siege gun the Allies had which was capable of firing a 64lb ball. He was then disturbed by an explosion. Returning to his letter some time later he writes:

> Since my writing thus much Manchester played his mine with very good success, made a fair breach, and entered with his men and possessed the manor house, but Leven and Fairfax not being acquainted therewith, that they might have diverted the enemy at other places, the enemy drew all their strength against our men, and beat them off again, but with no great loss, as I hear.

Here Sir Henry gives a bare-bones account of the only Allied assault during the siege. There are a number of accounts of the attack on the King's Manor by both Royalist and Allied correspondents. The manor stood outside the city walls but its grounds were walled and defended. As the mine exploded St Mary's Tower and part of the adjacent wall collapsed, leaving a breach through which Manchester's men could attack. At the time of the siege the area behind the breach was a bowling green, as it still is today. The wall next to the tower had already suffered from the attentions of a battery of cannon raised by Lawrence Crawford, Manchester's Major General, and the Royalist defenders had barricaded the breach with a wall of earth and sods. At noon on the 16th Crawford ordered the mine to be blown but does not seem to have given the other commanders any notice of what he was about to do. Why did Crawford do this?

One of the reasons given by contemporary correspondents is that the mine was in danger of flooding due to the heavy rain that had recently fallen. Simeon Ashe reports exactly this reason and is backed up by Sir Henry Slingsby who wrote of the other mine at Walmgate Bar having to be abandoned because it had flooded. Sir Thomas Fairfax, on the other hand, gives a rather different reason for Crawford blowing the mine, and states that

The bowling green close to where Parliamentarian troops stormed the breach made by a mine at St Mary's Tower, which can be seen behind the building in the foreground.

Crawford was 'Ambitious to have the honour, alone, of springing the mine'. Even if the reason given by Ashe was correct it seems highly unlikely that the mine was flooding so quickly that Crawford did not have time to inform Leven and Fairfax. Their troops could have provided a diversion while Crawford's men attacked but his failure to coordinate his attack with such a diversion brought the full weight of the Royalist defenders down on his men's heads.

As the smoke cleared Crawford ordered his assault force of 600 men to attack. Some attacked the tower while others attacked the breach and a third group assaulted the walls with ladders. The stunned Royalist defenders quickly fell back and the Parliamentary troops were soon in possession of the bowling green. Sir Phillip Byron, the local Royalist commander, led a counter-attack into the bowling green but was killed as he opened the gate. With their leader dead his men fell back and the Parliamentary troops advanced further into the manor's grounds. It seems that the attackers' initial success was not supported by other troops and Newcastle was able to gather a force of up to 2,000 men to oppose the assault force. Newcastle even led some of his own foot, the Whitecoats, in this counter-attack. Some of the Royalist troops retook the area of the breach and many of Crawford's men were trapped. Crawford seems to have been so confident of his men's initial success that he did nothing to support them. Trapped by a much larger force of defenders the attackers fought gallantly until their ammunition was expended and they were forced to yield.

Most of the accounts give a similar number for Crawford's losses, with 35 dead, 100 wounded and 200 taken prisoner out of his original force of 600. Royalist losses were much lighter. They had had 100 men captured during the initial assault but these would have been recovered when the attackers surrendered. On the following day some of Manchester's troops heard the groans of the wounded lying among the ruins of the tower and went to their assistance. The defenders opened fire possibly thinking it was another attack, and drove them off. It was not until the 19th that the Royalists gave permission for Manchester's men to recover their dead and wounded.

After the attack on the King's Manor the siege seems to have quietened, almost as though both sides were holding their breath and waiting for Prince

High Petergate seen from Bootham Bar.

Rupert's next move. At Walmgate Bar Lord Fairfax's guns had reduced the height of the gate to that of the city walls and the Royalist had filled the gate with earth and barricaded the houses behind it as an assault seemed imminent. The attack never came as Lord Fairfax was desperately short of powder and ammunition, as he reported to the Committee of Both Kingdoms in a letter written on the 18th:

> I must solicit you for a speedy supply of gunpowder, match, and bullet for my own and the Scotch armies in very large proportions, otherwise the service of these armies will be much retarded, contrary to our desires and your expectations. For my own particular I must intreat a supply of muskets, pistols, and carbines, concerning which I have often written. I am necessitated still to move you to acquaint the Parliament with my want of money, for my men are like to mutiny and many run away, whom I cannot in justice punish having nothing to pay them withall, while Manchester's men are very well paid, and a considerable supply furnished to the Scott's army. I beseech you to consider what it is to have an army and nothing to give them, while joined with other armies that are well paid. The pay of my army comes to 15,000l. a month, and I have received only 10,000l. for these four months past at least.

Fairfax's supply and financial situations were a recurring theme in his letters to the Committee and to Parliament. His frustration is understandable.

On 24 June Newcastle tried another sally from the city. This time a large body of musketeers left Monk Bar to attack Manchester's quarters but with little success. They were quickly driven back into the town with the loss of 20 dead and 20 prisoners, while Manchester lost only three.

Once again the siege settled into a round of skirmishing and cannon fire with both sides waiting for news of Prince Rupert. On 30 June news reached the Allied commanders that Rupert had reached Knaresborough, a day's march from York. A council of war decided that the army's main task would be to prevent Rupert relieving York and with this in mind the Allied army left its siege lines in the early hours of the morning of 1 July and marched west to Hessay and Long Marston where the Allied horse awaited them. Throughout the day the Allied army waited for the arrival of Rupert's army. Late in the day a body of Royalist horse appeared from the direction of Wetherby but very quickly withdrew along the road they had arrived on. Shortly after this Leven, Fairfax and Manchester received news that Rupert had marched around their northern flank and relieved the city.

The Relief of York

It is now time to digress briefly and examine how Prince Rupert achieved the relief of York. After relieving Newark in late March he returned to the Midlands where he received orders from his uncle, the King, to march north to York. His march began on 16 May. After combining with Sir John Byron's Cheshire forces the army began to move north. By the 25th they had reached the Mersey. At the time there were three crossing points between Manchester and the sea: one at Warrington which had been garrisoned by troops from Manchester, one at Hale Ford which was covered by the garrison of Liverpool and one at Stockport. Rupert chose the latter and quickly routed the local militia and crossed into Lancashire.

By the 28th Rupert had reached Bolton, a staunchly Parliamentary town. Its garrison had been reinforced by the besiegers of Lathom House, near Preston, the last Royalist stronghold in the county, who had withdrawn to the town on Rupert's approach. Bolton rebuffed Rupert's call to surrender. The first assault was driven off and the defenders then hanged a Royalist officer, said to be Irish, in full view of the Royalist forces. Inflamed, the Royalists attacked again and quickly stormed the town. If Parliamentary accounts are to be believed, there then followed one of the bloodiest episodes of the Civil Wars when Rupert's men rampaged through the streets killing anyone who crossed their path, regardless of age or sex. The Parliamentary accounts were almost certainly exaggerated for use as propaganda and study of local burial records does not back up the story they tell.

Prince Rupert of the Rhine.

From Bolton Rupert moved on to Bury where he was joined by the Northern Horse. Newcastle's decision to send them out of

York to form part of a relief force had proven correct. Next Rupert turned his attention on Liverpool. If things should go awry in Yorkshire he would need a secure base to fall back on. Many of Sir John Byron's foot regiments were 'Irish', not native Irish regiments but English regiments which had been stationed there prior to the start of hostilities. Liverpool also gave the Royalists a secure port for the arrival of more of these reinforcements. The siege of Liverpool lasted from 7 to 11 June. During the final night of the siege, as the Royalist forces prepared for an assault in the morning, the garrison slipped away to the ships anchored in the harbour basin. With morning the Royalist army was able to occupy the town unopposed.

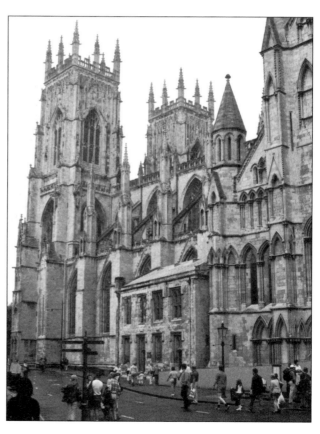

York Minster.

During the siege Rupert received a letter from his uncle which has become one of the most debated pieces of correspondence from the Civil Wars. Historians have long debated whether the letter was a firm command from the King to fight the Scots army wherever and whenever he found it and the debate still goes on. It is irrelevant how modern historians interpret the letter, Rupert took it as a command to fight. After his subsequent defeat at Marston Moor he would carry the letter until his death, as an excuse for his decision to fight.

For almost two weeks Rupert rested his army and used the time to prepare for his march across the Pennines and raise local troops. Much of Lancashire

St Olave's Church stands within the walls of the King's Manor in York and was used as an observation post by the Royalists.

had strong Royalist leanings and now the county was free of Parliamentary forces, other than the garrisons of Manchester and Warrington, recruits flocked to his standard.

By 23 June Rupert had moved his army to Preston and it was from this town that his rapid march across the hills began. On the 26th Rupert arrived at Skipton, where his army rested for a couple of days. By evening on the 30th the Royalist army had arrived at Knaresborough, within striking distance of York. The obvious route from Knaresborough to York was via Wetherby and it was this route that the Allied army had moved to block. Rupert chose not to use this route but marched to Boroughbridge and then along the north bank of the River Ure to Poppleton. From his camp at Poppleton he sent Colonel George Goring into York with orders for Newcastle to march to join him to fight the Allied army the next day.

In the Allied camp a council of war was called to decide on a course of action. The Scots were for a march to the south to cover the arrival of a substantial force of Cheshire and Lancashire troops and prevent Rupert's march south. The English commanders wanted to fight Rupert. The Scots had their way and early on the morning of 2 July 1644 the Allied army began its march to the south, covered by the combined horse. Rupert was firmly set on fighting and began to deploy his troops onto Marston Moor. Sir Thomas Fairfax, Oliver Cromwell and David Leslie, the Allied cavalry leaders, sent warnings to their commanders that the Royalists were deploying for battle and they in turn ordered the Allied foot to retrace its steps. Some of the Scots had reached as far south as Tadcaster so it took some time for the Allied army to deploy onto the ridge above Marston Moor. Rupert was also biding his time on the moor waiting for Newcastle's infantry to arrive. By the time both armies had deployed it was late in the day. Not expecting fighting to break out until the following morning, Rupert and Newcastle had retired from the field to refresh themselves. They were wrong. At approximately 7.30 in the evening of 2 July 1644 the Allied army began its advance. The Battle of Marston Moor had begun.

Standing at the monument today, or walking down one of the battlefield's lanes surrounded by birdsong, it is difficult to imagine over 40,000 men fighting for their lives in the fields around you. That is exactly what happened. The Allied army outnumbered the Royalist one, 24,000 to 17,000. The battle started with a general advance by the Allies which was initially successful but things then began to go wrong. Sir Thomas Fairfax's horse, supported by three regiments of Scots horse, forming the right (eastern) flank of the Allied army, were quickly routed by George Goring's Royalist horse. At about the same time, part of Lord Fairfax's and several regiments of Scots foot were broken and prospects looked bad for the Allies. Goring's second line of horse were in a position to attack the flank of the Allied army which they did. Two regiments of Scots foot, Maitland and Crawford-Lindsey's, held their ground against successive attacks by horse and foot and gave time for other regiments to come to their aid and stabilize the Allied line. The Allied left flank was commanded by Oliver Cromwell and quickly defeated their Royalist counterparts, commanded by Sir John Byron, which allowed them to turn into the flank of the Royalist army.

By this stage of the battle all five army commanders had left the field. Leven, Fairfax and Manchester had followed their routing foot south. Leven is reported to have reached either Leeds or Bradford by the time news reached him that his army had won the battle, while Fairfax got as far as Hull! One Parliamentary account of the battle sent from Hull to London by ship even

A side view of the King's Manor, York.

reports the battle as being a Parliamentary defeat. Manchester had also fled from the field but did return and was the only army commander on the field at the close of the day. On the Royalist side, Newcastle had attached himself to a troop of gentlemen who had offered their service as his bodyguard and ended the day chasing routing Allied troops to the south of the battlefield, playing the part of a troop leader rather than an army commander. Rupert returned to the field but after briefly rallying some of the horse defeated by Cromwell and David Leslie and leading them in an unsuccessful counter-charge, he left the field along with his routing troopers. One Parliamentary account has him hiding in a bean field from Cromwell's pursuing troopers.

With the defeat of Byron's horse and Cromwell's flank attack, the Royalist army began to collapse. A body of Newcastle's white-coated foot made a gallant stand but after a hard fight were overrun. By nightfall the Royalist army was streaming back towards York, hotly pursued by the Allied horse. The city gates were closed to prevent enemy troops penetrating into the city along with the routers. Marston Moor was the biggest battle of the Civil Wars and had the largest butcher's bill. Locals reported gathering and burying over 4,000 bodies on the field, by far the bulk of them were Royalists. How many men died subsequently of their wounds is not known but contemporary accounts report thousands of Royalist wounded in York in the days after the battle.

The Fall of York
During the night of 2/3 July 1644 the defeated Royalist commanders had hard decisions to make. Their army had been shattered, with a large proportion of its foot killed, wounded or prisoner. The army's horse was reasonably intact but was no use for defending a town. A number of contemporary accounts cover the ensuing discussions. Newcastle was one of the richest men in the country prior to the Civil Wars but his fortune had been spent on raising and maintaining an army for the King. With its defeat at Marston Moor he resolved himself to going into voluntary exile on the Continent rather than face the scorn of the King's courtiers. Rupert was determined to march north with the horse and try and raise another army. It was inevitable that the victorious Allied army would return to their siege lines around the city so a relief force would almost certainly become necessary. Sir Hugh Cholmley tells us that Rupert managed to dissuade

Newcastle from going into exile but the Marquess changed his mind again during the night. It is a strong possibility that James King, Lord Eythin, who had no love for Rupert, was instrumental in Newcastle's change of heart.

On the 3rd both Rupert and Newcastle departed from York. Escorted by a troop of horse and another of dragoon, Newcastle rode to Scarborough from where he departed for Hamburg on either 5 or 6 July. Rupert marched north with between 1,500 and 4,000 horse, depending which account is believed, and less than 1,000 foot. At Thirsk Rupert was met by Sir Robert Clavering and a force of between 1,300 and 2,000 men, which he had raised in the North East. The combined force then moved on to Richmond. On 7 July Rupert marched to Bolton Castle from where he wrote a letter to Sir Philip Musgrave, who commanded the King's forces in Westmorland and Cumberland, requesting that Sir Philip send any reinforcement he could. To speed the arrival of these reinforcements Rupert crossed the Pennines into Lancashire.

Between 10 and 18 July he marched to and fro across northern Lancashire, still with the intention of marching back into Yorkshire and relieving York. On the 18th a communication reached Rupert telling him of the city's surrender two days earlier. There was no point remaining in the North and his uncle, the King, had need of him in the South. Rupert's force crossed the Mersey at Hale Ford, near Liverpool, on 23 July and had reached Chester by the 25th. Newcastle's surviving cavalry, the Northern Horse, did not follow Rupert straight away. On 20 August a force commanded by Sir John Byron, including the Northern Horse, were defeated at Ormskirk, and by the 21st the whole force had withdrawn into Cheshire.

The Allied army spent the night of 2 July on the battlefield. Simeon Ashe describes the sight that met the Allied soldiers' eyes when they awoke on the 3rd: 'In the morning, there was a mortifying object to behold, when the naked bodies of thousands lay upon the ground, and many not altogether dead.' The Earl of Manchester was the only one of the three Allied commanders on the field when dawn broke on the 3rd. Fairfax and Leven returned during the course of the day and the Allied army received a welcome reinforcement of Cheshire and Lancashire troops on the 4th, commanded by Sir John Meldrum and Sir William Brereton. With the arrival of these reinforcements the Allied army returned to the siege lines. The city was summoned but its commander, Sir Thomas Glemham, refused to surrender and wrote to Prince Rupert to tell him that he would defend the city to the last man.

The wall of the King's Manor close to Bootham Bar, showing where houses had been built against the wall. The Marquis of Newcastle sent men out to try and burn these dwellings down and prevent the Parliamentarians using them for cover.

Once the Allied army had settled into its siege lines once more, plans were set in motion to deal with Prince Rupert. Many of Meldrum and Brereton's reinforcements returned to Lancashire to try to prevent Rupert from withdrawing south and a large body of horse was sent into North Yorkshire to pursue him. Neither force was able to impede Rupert's movements. By the time York surrendered on 16 July Manchester's horse was camped close to York, so their pursuit could not have lasted very long.

Sir Thomas Glemham's small garrison was in no state to stand a protracted siege of the city. Sir Henry Slingsby, commanding one of the foot regiments in the garrison, writes:

Thus were we left at York, out of all hope of releif, ye town much distract'd, & every one ready to abandon her: & to encourage ym yt were left in ye town, & to get ym to stay, they were fain to give out false reports, yt ye prince had fallen upon ye enemy suddenly & rout'd ym, & yt he was coming back again to ye Town; yet many left us, not liking to abide another seige; wch after began.

The Allies' first move was to raise several new batteries, one between Walmgate and Layerthorpe Postern and another on a hill in Bishopfield. The Foss was bridged with a pontoon bridge to allow rapid communication between the various areas of the siege and the Royalist could see the Allies building numerous ladders. It looked like an assault was imminent and Sir Henry Slingsby was certain that it would take place around Layerthorpe Postern; due to the dry weather the ditch that protected the gate was almost dry and left it vulnerable.

On Thursday 11 July the Royalist commanders requested a parley and Simeon Ashe reports the ensuing negotiations:

Hereupon a treaty being desired by the enemy, Sir William Constable and Colonell Lambert, were sent by the Lord Fairfax into the Citie, upon Hostages sent out for their securite and safe return. They went in on Saturday morning, and having spent that day in parley, they returned with this request to the three Generals, That there might be Commissioners authorized, to treat and conclude upon Articles for the peaceable surrender of the Citie. Our three Generalls having demanded the judgement of some Ministers, whether the work of the Treaty, might be approved on the Lords day, and receiving incouragement, they appointed the Lord Humby, Sir William Constable, and Colonell Mountague, to go the next day into the Town, three Hostages being sent out of the Town for their securitie: They continued their debate till Munday, about noon they returned, with Articles to be subscribed by the Generals.

After a long discussion the following articles were agreed:

Articles agreed upon betweene Alexander Earle of Leven, Generall of the Scottish Forces, Ferdinando Lord Fairfax, and the Earle of Manchester, Generalls of the English Forces about Yorke on the one part, and Sir

Thomas Glenham Knight, Governour of the City of Yorke, and Colonell Generall of the Northerne Army, of the other part Anent the surrender and delivery of the said City, with the Forts, Townes, Cannon, Ammunition, and furniture of Warre belonging thereto, in manner after specified to the said Generalls, for the use of King and Parliament, the 15 day of July, 1644.

1. The said Sir Thomas, as Governour of the said Citie, shall surrender and deliver up the same, with the Forts, Tower, Cannon, Ammunition, and furniture of Warre, belonging thereunto, betweene this and the sixteenth of Iuly instant, at or about the 11 houre thereof in the forenoone, to the said Generals or any in their names for the use aforesaid, in manner, and upon the condition after written.

2. That the Governour, and all Officers and Souldiers, both Horse and Foot, the Governours, Officers, and Souldiers of Cliffords-Tower, the Officers and Souldiers of the Sconce, the Officers and Souldiers belonging to the traine and outworkes, shall march out of the City on Horse-back & with their Armes, flying Colours, Drums, beating Matches lighted on both ends, Bullets in their mouths, and withall their bag and baggage, that every souldier shall have 12 charges of Powder.

3. That Officers and souldiers shall not march above ten miles a day, that they have accommodation of Quarter and convenience of carriages, that a Troope of Horse out of every of the three Armies, shall attend upon them for their convoy in their march, that no injurie or affront be offered them to Skipton, or the next Garrison Towne within sixteene miles of the Princes Army.

4. That such Officers and souldiers as are sicke and hurt, and cannot march out of the Towne, shall have liberty to stay within untill they be recovered, and then shall have passage given them to goe into the Princes Army, where ever it shall be, or to their owne houses and estates, where they may rest quiet, or whither else they shall please, That it may be recommended to my Lord Fairfax for their subsistence during their cure or being ill.

5. All Officers and souldiers wives, children and servants, now in Towne, may have libertie to goe along with their husbands, or to

them, or if they please to returne to their owne houses and estates, to enjoy them under such contributions as the rest of the Country payes, that they may have liberty to carrie with them their goods, and have a convenient time and carriages allowed to carrie them away.

6. That no Officer or souldier shall be stopt or plundered upon his march.

7. That no man shall intice any Officer or souldier as he marches out of the Towne with any promises of preferment or reward, or any other grounds whatsoever.

8. That the Citizens and Inhabitants may enjoy all their priviledges which formerly they did at the beginning of these troubles, and may have freedome of trade both by Land and Sea, paying such duties and customes as all other Cities and Towns under the obedience of King and Parliament.

9. That the Garrison that shall be placed here, shall be two parts of three at the least of Yorkshire men, and no free quarter shall be put upon any without his owne consent, and that the Armies shall not enter the City.

10. That in all charges, the Citizens resident and inhabitants shall bear such part with the County at large as was formerly used in all other Assessments.

11. That all Citizens, Gentlemen, and Residents, Sojourners, and every other person within the City, shall at any time when they please have free liberty to move themselves, their families, and goods, and to dispose thereof and of their Estate at their pleasure, according to the Law of the Land, either to live at their owne houses or elsewhere, and to enjoy their Goods and Estates without molestation, and to have protection and safeguard for that purpose, so that they may rest quietly at their aboad, and to travell freely and safely about their occasions, and for their better removall they shall be furnished with carriages, paying for their carriages reasonable rates.

12. That all those Gentlemen and others whatsoever that have Goods within the Citie, and are absent themselves, may have free liberty to take, carry away, and dispose of those Goods, as in the last Article.

13. That no building be defaced, nor any plundering, nor taking of any mans person, or of any part of his Estate, and that Iustice, according to Law, within the Citie shall be administred in all cases by the Magistrates, and be assisted there if need be by the Garrison.

14. That all persons whose dwellings are in the City, though now absent, may have the benefit of these Articles, as if they were present in the City.

By the Articles of Agreement touching the Rendition of the City of York.

The Generals of the Armies have treated as Generals in reference onely to themselves and their Souldiers, and it was not intended to intrench upon any Ordinances of Parliament, but all such persons and estates as were subject to Sequestrations, might still be liable and subject thereto, notwithstanding any generall words in the Articles.

And thus these Generals doe declare under their hands, and the Commissioners of the Treaty doe declare, That they did severall times during the Treaty expresse to the other Commissioners, that they had no order to meddle with any Ordinance of Parliament, or to goe further then the bounds of the Army. Subscribed by

The Lord Fairfax.
Sir Adam Hepborne.
The Earle of Manchester.
Lord Humby.
Sir William Constable.

It is interesting to compare these articles with those proposed by Newcastle a month earlier which the Allied commanders refused to accept. They are very similar and differ only in the detail. Simeon Ashe goes on to explain the leniency of these terms:

If any upon the perusall of those Articles do imagine too much favour was granted to the enemy, we desire that this may be considered for their satisfaction. That the benefit which could be expected for our Armies, or the Kingdom, by taking the Town by storm, could not possibly in any measure counterveil the miserable consequences thereof, to many thousands. Who knows how much precious blood might have been spilt upon so hot a service. How few in the Town could have preserved their houses and shops from spoyl, if more than 20 thousand Souldiers had broken in upon them, with heat and violence? How much would this County have suffered in the ruines of this Citie? And how many of our good friends in other places who drive Trades with Citizens, here, would have been pintched in their estates, by the impoverishing of their Debtors.

Although Ashe's sentiments are laudable a quick resolution of the siege was of paramount importance to the Allied commanders. They still had the spectre of Prince Rupert lurking across the Pennines and must have expected his return at any time – Rupert did not start heading south until he heard of the city's surrender. If the city could be taken quickly by granting the garrison the honours of war and promising to protect the citizens, then so be it.

At eleven o'clock on the morning of 16 July the Royalist garrison marched out of Micklegate Bar. Simeon Ashe describes the garrison as it marched from the city:

York: the remains of St Mary's Abbey stands within the walls of the King's Manor. Royalist troops counter-attacked and beat off a Parliamentarian assault in this area.

The fourth part of them, at least, who marched out of the Town were women, many very poor in their apparell, and others in better fashion. Most of the men had filled, and distempered themselves with drink; the number of the Souldiers, as we conjectured, was not above a thousand, besides the sick and wounded persons.

Once the garrison had departed the Allied generals and many of their officers attended a service in the Minster. The city was in a bad state with many of its suburbs burnt. Simeon Ashe stated that it would take more than £100,000, an enormous sum, to repair the damage caused during the siege. The town was packed with Royalist wounded who had been unable to leave with the garrison and many more inhabitants were suffering from the 'spotted fever'. Lord Fairfax and his army took over the care of the city, an event which is commemorated by a plaque in the Minster's Chapter House.

York had fallen and now the Allied armies could go their separate ways. Only Fairfax's army still remained around and in York by 22 July. Initially, the Scots army moved into the West Riding around Leeds and Wakefield. It was then decided to march north to join with the Earl of Callendar's besieging force at Newcastle-upon-Tyne. Manchester's Eastern Association troops headed south and on 26 July received the surrender of Tickhill Castle, near Doncaster. Other garrisons in South Yorkshire, Nottinghamshire and Derbyshire surrendered in turn as their march progressed. Lord Fairfax was left to mop up in Yorkshire. After the defeat at Marston Moor, and Rupert's subsequent withdrawal, no Royalist field army remained in the county but a number of garrisons still held out. It would take almost eighteen months to subdue them and it is now to the ensuing sieges we must turn.

Chapter 3

THE SIEGE OF HELMSLEY CASTLE

The Early History of the Castle

Following his campaign in the North, William I, the Conqueror, granted the manor of Helmsley to Robert de Mortain, the King's half-brother. It is possible that de Mortain built a wooden castle on the site but the manor was confiscated in 1088 following de Mortain's attempt to overthrow the King.

In 1120 the manor was granted to Walter Espec who was one of England's most powerful nobles and held the position of Justiciar of the Northern Counties. In 1138 he commanded King Stephen's northern army, leading them to victory over the Scots at the Battle of Northallerton, also known as the Battle of the Standard. Soon after the manor was awarded to Espec he began work on the stone castle. It remained Espec's main residence until his death in 1154.

On Espec's death his estates passed into the hands of his sister's husband, Peter de Roos. De Roos's son, Robert is recorded as being in possession of the castle by 1157. After 1186 Robert's grandson, another Robert but also known as Fursan, began a major rebuild of the castle. Fursan was a very wealthy man, married to the illegitimate daughter of King William of Scotland. As well as rebuilding Helmsley Castle he carried out major building work on Wark Castle in Northumberland and endowed a number of religious houses. Fursan was chosen as one of the twenty-five barons who would be responsible for enforcing the Magna Carta. He also joined the Knights Templar. He died in 1227 and was buried in the Temple Church in London.

The castle continued to be owned by the de Roos family until the time of the Wars of the Roses. Thomas de Roos, the third lord of that name, fought for the house of Lancaster and was captured and executed in the aftermath of the Battle of Hexham in 1464. King Edward IV awarded the castle to his younger brother George, Duke of Clarence. On Clarence's death the castle passed to his brother, the much maligned Richard, Duke of Gloucester. In 1483 Richard was crowned as Richard III. On 22 August 1485 he met his end

Model of Helmsley Castle.

at the Battle of Bosworth and the castle passed back to the de Roos family, to Edmund the eleventh Lord Roos.

In 1508 Edmund de Roos died without issue and was succeeded by his nephew, Sir George Manners. Possession of the castle continued in the Manners family until the death of Francis Manners, the sixth Earl of Rutland. The estate passed to his daughter, Katherine, who was the Duchess of Buckingham and then on to her eldest son, George Villiers, second Duke of Buckingham.

The castle was built on an outcrop of rock overlooking the River Rye and the town of Helmsley. The main entrance to the castle was through its outer bailey and massive southern barbican. If an attacker managed to penetrate both of these he would still be faced by the main southern gate. At the northern end of the castle stood a smaller barbican and gateway. Surrounding

Helmsley Castle: entrance to the South Barbican.

the castle were two deep, steep-sided ditches, separated by a bank which had at times a defensive wall, although this may have gone by the time of the Civil Wars. The two barbicans stood on an enlarged area of this bank.

The main ward of the castle was surrounded by high curtain walls which extended across the ditch to join the end towers of the South Barbican. The curtain walls were interspersed with towers. The castle's keep, the East Tower, stood about halfway down its eastern wall. Opposite the East Tower on the western wall stood a range of buildings which had been converted into a comfortable Tudor dwelling between 1563 and 1587, although by the time of the Civil Wars there is little evidence of the castle being occupied.

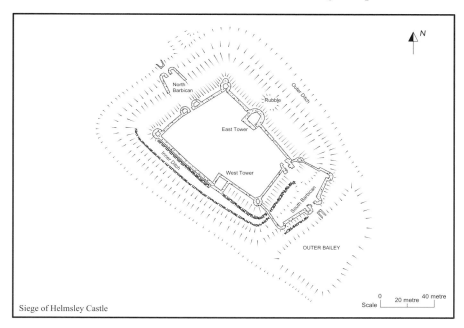

Siege of Helmsley Castle

The Siege of Helmsley Castle

In the aftermath of the Battle of Marston Moor and the surrender of York, Lord Fairfax turned his attention to the remaining garrisons in Yorkshire. His first target was Helmsley Castle. In September 1644 his son Sir Thomas led a force to besiege the castle. Fairfax's plan seems to have been to starve the castle into submission rather than bombard and assault it. There is little evidence for the use of artillery at Helmsley but it must have been there as

Helmsley Castle, Tudor living quarters.

the Parliamentary forces at Knaresborough were unable to start a formal siege until the cannon from Helmsley had arrived. The garrison of about 200 men was commanded by Sir Jordan Crossland. Crossland was an ardent Royalist who converted to Roman Catholicism in later life.

Few details are available about the siege. The garrison made a number of sorties during the two-month siege. It is possible that Sir Thomas Fairfax was severely wounded during one of these sorties. There are two versions of how Sir Thomas received his wound, or possibly wounds. In one version Sir Thomas was leading his men in a counter-attack against sallying Royalist troops when he received two wounds from musket shot which fractured his shoulder blade and broke his arm. The other version has Sir Thomas visiting his lines and being shot by a marksman on the castle's keep. Frustratingly, all Sir Thomas says in his account is that he 'received a dangerous shott in my shoulder and was brought back to Yorke; All for sometime being doubtfull of my Recovery.' One of Fairfax's senior officers, Lieutenant-Colonel Forbes, was captured at some time during the siege, probably in another sally by the garrison.

By 6 November the situation in the castle seems to have become desperate. Crossland sent out a set of propositions to the besiegers' commander, John Lambert:

The remains of the Keep of Helmsley Castle. Its east wall was demolished after the siege as part of the slighting of the castle.

1. That the Governor of the Castle and all other officers shall march out with their arms, horses, and all the rest of their goods belonging unto them, and be safely convoyed to the garrison at Scarborough, without any molestation.
2. That the soldiers shall march out with their arms loaded, matches lighted, colours flying, and drums beating, and be safely convoyed to the said garrison.
3. That the gentlemen, or others the countrymen, that came hither for protection, may have free liberty to depart with their goods, unto their dwellings, and to have my Lord Fairfax's protection for their safeguard.
4. That the Lady Duchess of Buckingham's goods within the Castle, her servants and their goods, may remain safe within the Castle, or the town of Helmsley, under my Lord Fairfax's protection, as they have been formerly without interruption.
5. That any goods within the Castle belonging to any gentlemen in the country, or to any other whatsoever, may have three days' time after the surrender thereof for the disposing of them, and to have my Lord Fairfax's protection for their convoy.
6. That there may be carriages procured for the conveying of two little drakes [light cannon], arms and other baggage along with them, unto the garrison before mentioned.

7. That the Castle of Helmesley be absolutely demolished, and that no garrison hereafter be kept there by either party.

8. That in performance of these articles, Lieutenant Colonel Forbes, and all the rest of the prisoners, shall have their free liberty; and that Lieutenant Spright, and five soldiers belonging to me, now prisoners at York, shall likewise have their liberty.

9. And lastly, that there be time given until the 16th day of this month, for to consider of these articles, in case there might be relief had in that time from the Prince [Rupert], otherwise we shall perform these articles on our part.

It is interesting to note that Crossland stipulates that the castle be demolished. This is a little unusual as it was normally besiegers who decided to make a location indefensible. Crossland was obviously thinking to the future and a possible resurgence of Royalist fortunes and did not want the castle to be held against the King.

Whether Crossland had any foreknowledge of a relief attempt is not known but just such an attempt took place on 12 November. Sir John Mallory, the commander of the garrison of Skipton Castle, despatched a troop of horse to rendezvous with a force from Knaresborough Castle and then to relieve Helmsley Castle. The relief force was initially successful, surprising the besiegers and scattering them. The Parliamentary troops rallied and counter-attacked, driving the relief force away and killing and capturing a large number of them. A Parliamentary newssheet, *A Perfect Diurnall* (11–18 November 1644), gives the following list of prisoners:

Captain Richard Matterson	Lieutenant Edward Bradley
Lieutenant Will Richardson	Lieutenant George Johnson
Lieutenant John Wiose	Lieutenant William Hunderly
Lieutenant John Samson	Cornet Thomas Squire
Ensign Robert Burt	
Christopher Ward	Thomas Fletcher
Thomas Bussey	Richard Atkins
Edward Kiplin	John Wardroy
John Sherwood	Stephen Scameden
Edward Helme	Will Turner
Will Burton	Will Akin

Will Grames
James Greswick
Samuel Lupton
Thomas Bruce
John Walton
William Almsley
Robert Setle
Bernard Huet
Leonard Hodgson
James Harper
Richard Tankert
Thomas Williams
William Hodgson
Richard Southome
Marke Buller
Henry Barnet

Symon Burrough
Thomas Wright
Robert Wilkinson
Will Smith
Will Robson
John Dixon
Will Carre
George Short
Thomas Hart
Will Fairefax
John Price
Thomas Chappell
Thomas Boyle
James Smith
John Freeman
Thomas Stevinson

With the failure of the relief attempt the garrison had little choice but to yield. On 22 November Crossland and his 100 remaining men marched from the castle and on to Scarborough. Their service for the King was not yet over. Sir Thomas Fairfax was ordered to slight the castle. The curtain walls were partly demolished and the keep had its eastern wall blown down – today's visitor can still see the remains of this eastern wall lying in the ditch below the keep. Lord Fairfax now had the men and firepower available to turn his sights on his next target, Knaresborough Castle.

A selection of cannon balls found at Helmsley Castle and probably used during the siege.

Chapter 4

THE SIEGE OF KNARESBOROUGH CASTLE

The Early History of the Castle

Although the first mention of a castle at Knaresborough was not until 1130, it is very likely that the town, known as Chednaresburg in the Domesday Book, was a fortified settlement – 'burg' is Anglo-Saxon for a fortified enclosure. For most of its history the castle has been in royal hands or held directly from the reigning monarch. The first documentary evidence for a castle on the site comes from 1130 when an expenditure of £11 is recorded in the royal Pipe Rolls for work on the site. One of the early holders of the castle was Hugh de Moreville. In 1170 de Moreville and his followers took shelter in the castle after murdering Thomas Beckett in Canterbury Cathedral.

King John was a regular visitor to the town and spent a considerable amount of money on the castle. He also spent both time and money at Scarborough Castle. He often stayed in the town while hunting in the Forest of Knaresborough. John is thought to have spent more on Knaresborough and Scarborough Castles than on any other fortresses in the country. During the Barons' Revolt in 1215–16 the castle was held for the King. Little sign of King John's castle now remains, other than the moat.

Edward I carried out a programme of modernization on the castle during his reign. His son, Edward II, was a much weaker man than his father and continually advanced his favourites, much to the chagrin of the established nobility. In 1307 the Honour and Castle of Knaresborough were awarded to one of these favourites, Piers Gaveston. By 1311 the barons had had enough of Gaveston and put pressure on the king to banish him. Edward duly complied. By 1312 Gaveston had returned to England and was back in the King's favour. This time the barons took matters into their own hands and besieged Gaveston in Scarborough Castle. During the siege Edward remained at Knaresborough Castle. The King's proximity mattered little to

Knaresborough Castle: the remains of the main gatehouse.

the barons and Gaveston was forced to surrender. He was subsequently beheaded.

Friction between the King and his nobles continued. In 1317 John de Lilburn seized the castle for Thomas, Earl of Lancaster. There followed a three-month siege during which a large siege engine breached the wall and allowed the castle to be recaptured for the King. The town's tribulations were not yet over. In 1318 a raiding force of Scots burnt much of the town but most of the citizens were able to take shelter in the castle.

In 1331 Edward III's wife, Queen Phillipa, received the Honour and Castle as part of her marriage settlement. The Queen and her young family spent many summers at Knaresborough and it was during this period that the castle changed from a fortress into a royal residence. The Queen continued to be a regular visitor to the castle until her death in 1369.

In 1372 John of Gaunt, Duke of Lancaster, exchanged his possessions in Richmond for the Honour and Castle of Knaresborough and the castle became part of the Duchy of Lancaster. Following John's death in 1399, King Richard II confiscated all of the Duchy's holdings and banished his heir, Henry Bolingbroke. Henry returned and deposed Richard, assuming the throne as Henry IV. The deposed king was imprisoned and spent one night at Knaresborough Castle on his way to Pontefract Castle where he met his end. With Henry's assumption of the throne, Knaresborough Castle, and the remainder of the Duchy of Lancaster's possessions, came directly under royal control.

After the accession of Henry IV, the castle's importance in national affairs declined, although it was still an important regional centre. It remained under direct control of the crown, with the exception of a fifteen-year period between 1422 and 1437, when the dowager Queen Catherine held it after the

Knaresborough Castle: the King's Tower looking from the Inner Bailey.

death of her husband, Henry V. Although the castle had lost its importance to the crown it still continued to be maintained in the Tudor period. By the time of the Civil Wars it was still defensible.

The Castle's Defences

Any visitor to Knaresborough Castle can see why the castle was positioned where it was. On two sides the castle is defended by cliffs, dropping down to the River Nidd. The other two sides were defended by a deep, steep-sided dry moat. A solid curtain wall surrounded two wards, inner and outer, and was interspersed with towers. From the town the castle was approached through a barbican, across a bridge over the ditch and then through the main gatehouse into the outer ward. This area held most of the service buildings and stables for the castle. Two sally ports could also be accessed from the outer ward. Both exited into the dry ditch, one on the north side of the castle

Knaresborough Castle: view from the southern moat showing the remains of two of the curtain wall towers.

Knaresborough Castle: view from the outer bailey towards the Parliamentarian battery which breached the castle wall.

and one on the south. To enter the inner ward the visitor had to pass through another gatehouse. This area contained the domestic buildings, including the great hall and the King's Tower.

The castle's position posed a number of problems for any would-be attacker. It could be bombarded from the heights across the gully through which the River Nidd ran but even if the wall was breached the attacker would have to scale the cliffs to reach the breach and the defenders would have a distinct advantage. To approach the castle from the town, the town would first have to be captured. Although Knaresborough was not a walled town it may have had a substantial ditch around it, probably the old borough boundary. If the town was taken then the besiegers would have to mount their batteries close to the castle to have a clear line of fire against the castle walls.

The Siege

Knaresborough almost began the war as a Parliamentary fortress. In the autumn of 1642 Sir Henry Slingsby, the local MP, was informed that Lord Fairfax intended to seize the castle. At the same time Patrick Ruthven, the Earl of Forth, was passing through the town to join the King. Ruthven was a very experienced soldier, having served as a lieutenant-general in the Swedish army, and would assume command of King Charles's army. Slingsby sought Ruthven's advice and the Earl suggested that Slingsby should garrison the castle before the enemy appeared. Ruthven and his entourage departed and Slingsby followed his sound advice. Unfortunately, he does not seem to have had much local support and formed a one-man garrison. It can only be imagined what Sir Henry thought he could achieve had a force of armed Parliamentary troops arrived at the castle gate. His relief must have been immense when a force of the Yorkshire trained bands, the county militia, commanded by Sir Richard Hutton, arrived with a commission from the Earl of Cumberland, the Royalist commander in Yorkshire, to garrison the castle. Sir Richard carried out his orders and established a garrison from the trained

Knaresborough Castle: the exit of the southern sally port, from which the defenders carried out an attack on the Parliamentarian battery on 18 December 1644.

bands under Colonel Croft, a relative. The trained band garrison may have been replaced at some point in late 1642 or early 1643. A pamphlet published in 1643 does not give the garrison a glowing report and speaks of them raiding far and wide, and terrorizing the locals for many miles around. The same source also mentions a number of Londoners in the garrison, pointing to the Yorkshiremen of the trained bands having been moved elsewhere.

In December 1642, a force of Parliamentarians, commanded by Sir Christopher Wray, was billeted in the town overnight. It is possible that Wray was returning to Wetherby after the Parliamentary defeat at Piercebridge. The two sides opened fire on one another, possibly without orders from their commanders, and this forced the locals to take shelter in the fields around the town, not a very pleasant experience on a December night. Wray's force departed the next morning.

News of the Royalist defeat at Marston Moor (2 July 1644) reached the Knaresborough garrison very quickly. Two weeks later they saw the results of the battle when the remnants of the York garrison were marched through the town on their way to Skipton, closely escorted by Parliamentarian cavalry. The Knaresborough garrison made no attempt to assist them and watched as they marched away. The inhabitants of the town had formed a local militia force to maintain order in the town. When it became apparent that Lord Fairfax intended to take Knaresborough and its castle a number of them, under their leader John Warner, joined the garrison within the castle.

In November a force of Royalist cavalry left the castle and joined with a similar force from Skipton Castle. Their objective was to relieve Helmsley Castle. This relief force initially met with some success, driving the Parliamentarian besiegers away from the castle. Unfortunately, the enemy rallied very quickly and, in turn, drove the relief force away from the castle, pursuing it for some distance. The relief force lost many men killed and over fifty officers and men captured.

With the failure of the Royalist relief attempt, Helmsley Castle looked close to falling and Lord Fairfax was able to turn his attention on Knaresborough. He despatched Lieutenant-Colonel Lilburn with a force of between 500 and 600 men. This is one of history's coincidences, as the man who had seized and held the castle against King Edward II in 1317 was John de Lilburn. In the 1317 siege a Lilburn had held the castle and in 1644 another would attempt to take it. There is some debate as to which Lieutenant-Colonel Lilburn commanded at the siege of Knaresborough. Many historians have stated that it was John Lilburn. This identification is somewhat problematic as John Lilburn commanded the Eastern Association's dragoons and it is probable that he had marched south with the Earl of Manchester's army. It is more likely that Lieutenant-Colonel Robert Lilburn, John's brother, had been sent to Knaresborough by Lord Fairfax. Robert also served at several other sieges in Yorkshire, including Skipton and possibly Pontefract. Robert Lilburn's regiment of horse had two other brothers serving in it.

Initially, Lilburn blockaded Knaresborough and set up a small battery on Gallow Hill, across the River Nidd. How much use a breach made by this battery would have been is a moot point, as any attack against such a breach would have faced a 150 foot climb up the cliffs above the River Nidd.

The Royalist garrison comprised a mix of regular soldiers and townsmen. The presence of townsmen is illustrated by local tradition which reports that a boy from the town took supplies to his father in the castle by crossing the dry moat and passing them through a small opening. After making the journey on several consecutive nights, his luck ran out and he was spotted and captured by the besiegers. He was sentenced to be hanged in full view

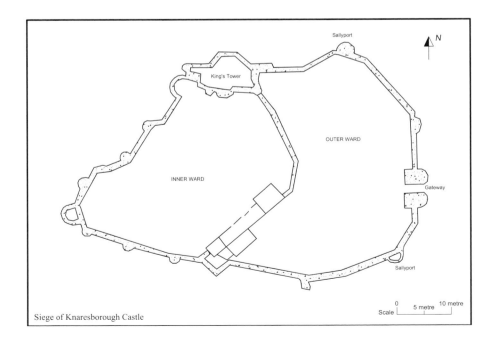

Siege of Knaresborough Castle

Knaresborough Castle's defences were reinforced by the gorge cut by the River Nidd.

of the castle and his father. The local women pleaded with Lilburn to spare the lad's life, a plea to which Lilburn agreed.

On 12 November Lilburn launched an attack against the town. The bulk of the defenders fell back into the castle but both sides suffered casualties during the assault. Parliamentary casualties are not clear. The Royalists lost twenty men killed, forty-eight wounded and forty-six taken prisoner. With the capture of the town and the arrival of heavy guns, which had been in use at Helmsley, Lilburn was now able to begin the siege in earnest. Initially, Lilburn placed his guns close to the tollbooth but these faced the strongest part of the castle, the King's Tower. A bombardment lasting from 28 November to 18 December made little impression.

Following the advice of a townsman – not all local inhabitants were Royalists – Lilburn moved his guns to a garden close to the top end of Briggate. His guns now faced a much weaker section of wall. The defenders realized this and launched a sally through the southern sally port during the night of 18 December to try and put the enemy guns out of action. The besiegers were driven from their works, having lost forty-two men killed and wounded and a further twenty-six taken prisoner. The besiegers rallied quickly and gathered a large force to counter-attack. At this point the Royalist garrison withdrew to the castle. On the night of the 19th the garrison sallied out again, this time from the northern sally port. The Parliamentarians were prepared for them and drove them back into the castle, killing twelve, wounding eight and capturing twenty-one.

On 20 December Lilburn began his bombardment from the new battery and quickly made a practicable breach in the curtain wall close to the southern sally port. As his men formed up for an assault, the garrison requested a parley. Rather than risk the lives of his men, Lilburn quickly agreed to this and the 120 men remaining in the garrison were allowed to depart.

Lilburn's men occupied the castle and found four cannon and a large store of gunpowder, arms and ammunition. They also found £100 in cash and £1,500 in gold and silver plate but little if any provisions. If the breach had not been made, the defenders may not have been able to hold out for much longer anyway. Lilburn had his men demolish many of the buildings within the two wards and much of the material was sold to the local inhabitants. In 1646 Parliament issued instructions that all castles which had been defended for the King were to be slighted. In 1648 it was Knaresborough's turn and

Knaresborough Castle: a view of the King's Tower from the northern moat.

The entrance to the southern sally port of Knaresborough Castle. A tunnel leads to the exit in the southern moat.

anyone who has visited the castle can see with what efficiency the work was carried out, although the King's Tower and the Courthouse were left intact, the latter to serve as its name suggests and the former as a local prison. With the fall of Knaresborough, Fairfax was now able to turn his attention to the biggest thorn in his side, Pontefract Castle. On Christmas Day 1644 his men occupied the town and blockaded the castle.

The Parliamentarians made a very good job of slighting Knaresborough Castle, as can be seen from the pitiful remains of the curtain wall.

Chapter 5

'O THOU BLOODY PRISON': PONTEFRACT CASTLE

A Brief History of the Castle

The town of Pontefract is not mentioned in the Domesday Book but areas of the present town were inhabited at the time of the Norman Conquest. One of Pontefract's railway stations is called Tanshelf and this name predates the arrival of the railways by almost 1,000 years. Tanshelf lies just to the north of the present town centre and was the site of a Saxon township. In 947 the English king, Eadred, summoned his Witan, or great council, at Tanshelf.

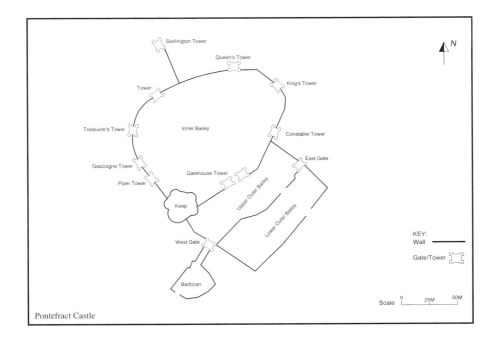

Pontefract Castle

There is also evidence for a fortified Saxon site where the remains of Pontefract Castle now stands. Archaeologists have found a substantial ditch and it has been suggested that this ditch may have been incorporated into the first Norman motte and bailey castle.

Ilbert de Lacey was awarded the Honour of Pontefract by William I around 1076. Although there is no evidence giving the date of the initial construction of the castle, it was in existence by 1086 and construction may well have been started by the time Ilbert de Lacey gained his estate. The castle would remain in de Lacey hands until 1194 when, for a brief period (1194–9) it became a royal castle. In 1199 the castle passed through the female line to Roger FitzEustace but a proviso of his inheritance was that he adopted the de Lacey name. The last of the adopted de Lacey line died in 1311 without a male heir. The castle then came into the hands of the House of Lancaster and with Henry Bolingbrook's usurpation of the throne, as Henry IV, the castle once again became a possession of the crown. It would remain so until 1649 when King Charles I was beheaded and, not long after, the castle was demolished on the orders of Parliament.

During its time as a royal castle, Pontefract was also used as a prison and place of execution. In the aftermath of Henry IV's usurpation of the throne, the deposed king, Richard II, was held and murdered there, possibly by being starved to death. In December 1460 the Lancastrian army marched from Pontefract to fight and defeat the Duke of York at the Battle of Wakefield. The Earl of Salisbury, one of York's main supporters and father of Richard Neville, Earl of Warwick, was captured and held briefly in the castle until he was

A view of the Barbican of Pontefract Castle showing the original guardhouse. An 'Iron Gun' was mounted in a small earthwork in the garden behind the building and bombarded the Parliamentary troops occupying All Saints' Church.

Pontefract Castle – The remains of the Round Tower. Signal fires lit on the top of this tower could be seen from the keep of Sandal Castle and from the tower of York Minster.

dragged out by the townsfolk and beheaded. His head joined that of the Duke of York in adorning Micklegate Bar at York. In late March of the following year, York's son, Edward IV, began his approach march from the castle to Palm Sunday Field which culminated in the Battle of Towton. His defeat of the Lancastrian army secured his place on the throne. On Richard III's accession to the throne in 1483 several of his opponents, including Earl Rivers, were held and executed in Pontefract Castle.

The castle was originally built of wood. In about 1177 reconstruction of the castle in stone commenced and improvements continued until the beginning of the Tudor period. Pontefract became one of the strongest castles in Britain. Under the Tudors the castle was allowed to fall into disrepair but this was reversed by Charles I who ordered the castle to be restored to its former glory. The castle would reward Charles's attention by standing three sieges between 1644 and 1649.

The Castle's Defences
Pontefract Castle's position was well defended by both man and nature. The castle sits on a rock outcrop which covers its eastern and northern sides. On the castle's western side, between it and the town, a deep, steep-sided ditch had been cut into the rock. To the southeast was a gentler slope, running down to the road to Knottingley and beyond that to Baghill. Two outer baileys had been built to cover this approach, the lower of the two reaching

down to the Knottingley road. These lower baileys are often referred to as 'the barbican' in contemporary accounts but this is incorrect. The barbican actually protected the West Gate, which was the main entrance to the castle from the town and allowed access to the Upper Outer Bailey. At the other end of the upper bailey was the East Gate which led to All Saints' Church. Another gate allowed access from the upper bailey into the lower one which, in turn, had a gate allowing access to the Knottingley road.

Access to the Inner Bailey from the Upper Outer Bailey was protected by the Gatehouse Tower, to the northeast of the main keep. The Inner Bailey was protected by a number of towers. Working in a clockwise direction from the Gatehouse, the first tower a visitor would have reached was the massive Keep, also known as the Round Tower. It was built on the original Norman motte and must have been a very impressive sight. Walking around the castle's remains, the next tower you come to is the Gascoigne Tower, close to which was a sally port which gave access into the ditch. Contemporary accounts of the first siege write of another tower between the Keep and the Gascoigne Tower, called the Piper's or Piper Tower. Archaeologists have been unable to find any sign of this tower's footprint and have put forward the possibility that it was not a tower but a turret built on the top of the wall, which from the outside would give the appearance of being a tower.

Continuing around the castle walls you will next reach the Treasurer's Tower. Running from the Gascoigne Tower, past the Treasurer's Tower, were the

A view of the ditch between Pontefract Castle and the town. The ditch was cut into the bedrock and was not flooded.

kitchens and bakehouse for the castle. At the north end of the kitchen range is evidence of another tower which was probably demolished when the kitchens were built. Next is the Swillington Tower. This tower is detached from the main body of the castle and joined to it only by a walkway. The remains of the tower were cut in half when Victorian town planners ran North Baileygate along the north side of the castle. Continuing around the castle's perimeter the final three towers are the Queen's, King's and Constable's Towers.

Although little now remains of the castle, what does remain gives a good impression of how formidable the castle was and this is reinforced by paintings and sketches of the castle. The one weakness the castle seems to have had was that the outer baileys were overlooked from Baghill and contemporary accounts report a number of casualties in the outer baileys caused by fire from the hill.

The First Siege of Pontefract Castle

With the fall of Knaresborough Castle on 20 December 1644, Lord Fairfax was able to turn his attention to the reduction of Pontefract Castle, which had been a thorn in his side since the Earl of Newcastle had garrisoned it in the aftermath of the Battle of Tadcaster in December 1642. On Christmas Day 1644 part of Fairfax's army occupied Pontefract town, while other elements occupied Newhall, Baghill and Monkhill, throwing a loose cordon around the castle. The garrison responded by firing three cannon shot towards the town, although no casualties are reported.

Few details are to be found on the size of the besieging forces. It is a fair assumption that they would have substantially outnumbered the garrison and must have been a substantial force to cover the four main positions they occupied. The first mention of Lord Fairfax at the siege is not until almost a month after it began and it is likely that Colonel William Forbes, one of his senior officers, commanded the besiegers until Fairfax's arrival.

We have a few more details of the composition of the garrison. It comprised two main elements: a force of regular horse and foot and a number of gentlemen and volunteers. It is difficult to ascertain the number or composition of the regular troops but Nathan Drake, whose diary is the main contemporary source for the first and second sieges, gives a list of 183 volunteers. These were split into four sections commanded by Colonel Grey, Sir Richard Hutton (High Sheriff of Yorkshire), Sir John Ramsden and Sir George Wentworth. Drake served in Sir John Ramsden's section. The garrison was commanded by Colonel Richard Lowther with his younger brother serving as his adjutant.

The Parliamentary forces were quiet during 26 and 27 December while they settled into their positions. The garrison continued to interfere with the besiegers' preparations by firing sixteen shot into their lines. On the 28th the besiegers made their first move. Close to the castle on its northeast side was All Saints' Church which had been incorporated into the castle's defensive perimeter and garrisoned by the defenders. In the early hours of 28 December a Parliamentary storming party took the church, driving the bulk of the defenders back into the castle. Eleven men and boys were trapped in the church and withdrew into the bell tower. All Saints' has a rare double helix staircase in the tower which is both steep and narrow. Having climbed the stairs it is easy to understand how the small Royalist party was able to hold out in the tower. The Royalists mounted several counter-attacks to retake the church but were unsuccessful, suffering eleven casualties, four of which subsequently died. Drake names Captain Waterhouse of Netherton as one of the dead.

As night fell the Royalist party were still trapped in the bell tower but had hatched an escape plan. First they cut the bell ropes and then crept along the church roof until they were at the end closest to the castle. They then

Pontefract Castle: the sally port was blocked up early in the first siege.

Looking up at the missing roof of All Saints' Church. A party of Royalist soldiers trapped in the tower, crossed the roof and lowered themselves down the wall in the foreground, using one of the bell ropes, before making their escape to the castle.

scrambled down the ropes and made good their escape. Unfortunately they were spotted by Parliamentary troops who fired a volley of muskets at their retreating backs, killing one of their number and wounding Captain Joshua Walker in the thigh. During the fighting for the church the Royalists had taken thirteen casualties, including five dead. Drake reports the besiegers removing forty wounded and leaving sixty dead around the church.

Between 28 December 1644 and 15 January 1645 things quietened down. The Parliamentary forces were awaiting the arrival of their siege guns which were in transit from Knaresborough. Both sides continued a desultory fire. Drake mentions both musket and cannon fire from the castle – several of the castle's towers were strong enough to have cannon mounted on their roofs. Although he mentions the besieging forces firing muskets at the castle he does not mention any cannon fire from them. Drake mentions a couple of casualties during this period. On 5 January a Mr Pattison was killed by a musket shot to his head while he was posted on top of the Round Tower (keep). On the 9th the Royalists fired a cannon at Newhall which punched through its wall, sending stone splinters in all directions, one of which struck Colonel William Forbes in the face. Local tradition has it that Forbes lost an eye but Drake states that he was struck but 'with little hurt'.

On 16 January the long-awaited siege train arrived. Drake states that all six guns were positioned in the Market Square which faced the side of the castle between the Round Tower and the Gascoigne Tower. Four of these guns were of large calibre, capable of firing shot weighing between 24 and 42 pounds. As the guns were positioned it became obvious to the defenders which stretch of wall would suffer the brunt of the enemy bombardment. Lowther order his men to reinforce the threatened stretch with four to five yards of earth – a similar tactic to that used by the defenders of Hull. Medieval castle and town walls were often high and thick but had never been designed to withstand cannon fire. Reinforcing the walls with earth on the inside could increase the wall's durability but sometimes at the price of the weight of earth on the inside of the wall causing damage, again as happened at Hull.

The 16th also saw the arrival of Lord Fairfax and his son Sir Thomas. The latter was still recovering from the shoulder wound he received at Helmsley. Now preparations had been made to bombard the castle it was time for the garrison to be summoned to surrender. Lord Fairfax sent Colonel Lowther the following message:

> In the performance of the trust reposed in me, by the parliament, for the service of the publick; and particular safety and preservation of this country, I have drawn here part of the forces under my command to endeavour the reducing of this Castle (which hitherto hath opposed the parliament, and infinitely prejudiced the country), to obedience of the King and parliament, which I much desire may be effected without the effusion of blood, and to that end, now send you this summons to surrender the Castle to me, for the service of the King and parliament. Which if you presently do, I will engage my power with the parliament for your reception into mercy and favour herewith. But your refusing or dissenting the same will compel me to the trial of the success which I hope will prevail for the public good. I shall expect your answer to be returned to me by Colonel Forbes, to whom I shall give further instructions in your behalfe.

Upon receipt of the summons Colonel Lowther gave a verbal reply to the messenger, Colonel Forbes, as Drake reports:

> The Governor upon the receipt of this Summons gave answer for the p'sent to the Messinger by word of mouth that the matter was of great

Consequence, & would require some time to Consider of it, that he would Call the Gentlmen of the Castle being many of good qualitie & Consult wth them about it, & upon Consultation wth them he would send him an answer wch should be sometime on the morruw at the Fordest.

Forbes accepted this and returned to the Parliamentary lines to convey Lowther's reply to Lord Fairfax. Lowther was stalling for time and the overnight delay in answering summons gave him chance to set 60 men working on raising a battery and reinforcing the walls opposite the Parliamentary guns in the Market Place. During the night he consulted with his senior officers and shaped an answer to Fairfax:

According to my Allegiance to wch I am sworne, and in pursuance of the trust reposed in me by his Ma'tie, I will defend this Castle to the

Pontefract Castle: a view from the gatehouse into the Upper Bailey. The castle's Lower Bailey continued beyond the trees in the background. A mound to mount a cannon on was raised close to this gate.

uttermost of my power, and doubt not by Godes assistance, the Justnes of his Ma'ties Cause, and the vertue of my Comrades, to quell all those that shall oppose me in the defence thereof for his Ma'ties service, for the blood that is like to be lost in this action, lett it be upon their heades who are the Causers of it. This is my resolution wch I desire you Certefie.

At seven o'clock in the morning, as Lowther prepared to send his reply, the Parliamentary bombardment commenced. During the course of the day they fired 400 shot into the wall around the Pipers Tower – this is now the area between the remains of the Keep and the Gascoigne Tower. After dark, two captains from the garrison, Munro and Laiborne, made their way into the ditch to examine the damage. The Parliamentary shot had penetrated up to one and a half yards into the wall. On receiving their report Lowther ordered the damaged section of wall to be reinforced with earth.

On the 18th the bombardment continued, with 548 shot being fired at the damaged section of wall. On the 19th another 286 shot were fired and the besiegers had their first success. At about nine o'clock in the morning the Pipers Tower collapsed, causing a breach in the wall. Two brothers called Briggs were manning the tower and were killed when it collapsed and several others were injured. The Briggs brothers were local lads and lived at Halfpenny House within a stone's throw of the castle's northern wall, close to All Saints' Church. How many of the garrison were within sight of their homes but unable to return to them? The Briggs brothers never would. The besieging forces were not free of casualties and Drake reports twenty-seven of them been killed in a powder explosion, possibly caused by a Royalist cannon shot.

Although the garrison had kept up a steady cannon fire on the Parliamentary lines, between 16 and 20 January they fired only sixteen shot. Drake gives a hint that they may have been running short of cannon balls. On the night of the 19th Lowther offered four pennies for every cannon ball his men could recover from the ditch.

On 20 and 21 January the bombardment continued apace with 144 and 189 cannon shot being fired at the area of the breach during that time. Sporadic musket fire was also taking place between the two sides while the bombardment continued. Drake reports two fatalities within the garrison on the 21st: Captain Browne was killed in one of the lower baileys by a musket shot and John Spence was killed when his overcharged musket exploded. At about eleven o'clock on the 21st a drummer approached the castle with a message from Colonel Forbes:

> Sir, I desire to have a positive answer of the Summons sent in upon Thursday last, that I may give an accoumpt to my Lord (who is now heare) of your resolutions, likewise I desire to know whether Mr Ogle exchanged for Leiutenant Browne, or for money, and if (for money) for what summe.

Lord Fairfax was based at York and visited the besiegers on a number of occasions. It is also interesting to note that prisoner exchanges were still been discussed. On receipt of Forbes's message, Lowther gathered his officers and gentlemen volunteers and held a council of war. They agreed unanimously to the contents of his original reply which was despatched to Forbes by the drummer sent with his message. When the drummer had been sent to the castle Forbes had ordered his men to arms, both horse and foot, and they remained on alert all afternoon until the drummer's return. On reading Lowther's refusal, Forbes ordered his men to advance on the castle. This does not seem to have been a deliberate assault against the breach but a general advance and exchange of cannon and musketry fire. It was during these exchanges that Captain Browne and John Spence were killed.

By 22 January it had become obvious to Fairfax that the castle was still very strong and an assault would be very bloody. Although the wall had been breached the ditch in front of it was still a formidable obstacle. Paintings and drawings of the castle show this section of ditch as deep and steep-sided. Even today it still gives an impression of what an effective defensive barrier it must have been. Added to that, the defenders had reinforced the breach with a barricade and a trench had been dug covering the area of the breach. Fairfax returned to York, leaving a detachment of troops under Colonel Poyntz to reinforce the besiegers.

Between 22 January and the end of February the bombardment slowed considerably. Drake lists the enemy firing six, three, two and fifteen shot on 22, 23, 24 and 25 January, respectively. In his entry for the 27th he notes that Parliament had fired 1,349 cannon balls at the castle. If one adds up his daily totals it comes to 1,594 shot and, interestingly, his original diary has 1,590 crossed out and replaced with 1,594. Between 28 and 31 January Drake reports no Parliamentary cannon shot but he does mention that James Elliot, a gun-maker from York, was injured in the arm by a stone splinter which caused his arm to be amputated, an injury from which he subsequently recovered. He also reports that between 22 and 31 January the garrison had fired only eighteen shot in return.

February began and continued with sporadic artillery and musket fire from both sides. By the 12th Drake reports 1,400 cannon shot from the besiegers, although his daily count totals 1,600. On the 15th he mentions the besiegers setting fire to a number of houses 'behind Mr Wakefield's house'. It is one of the frustrations of Drake's account that he mentions a number of houses belonging to local worthies, who were obviously well known, but it is difficult to pin down where they were. He also mentions five cannon shot being fired from the Swillington Tower at 'the hospital'. St Nicholas's Hospital was situated close to the King's Tower on the corner of Mill Dam Lane, and had been occupied by the besiegers.

Parliamentary troops had occupied a number of houses at the bottom of Northgate and were using them as sentry posts. On the 18th the garrison fired two cannon shot into these houses which were subsequently abandoned and set on fire. On the same day, five Parliamentary soldiers were killed in

Pontefract Castle: a view from the Inner Bailey towards Baghill. The Parliamentarians raised a number of trenches and earthworks on the hill. The view was unobstructed by trees at the time of the siege.

their works close to Mr Ward's house by musket fire from the Round Tower. It is likely that Mr Ward's house was close to the end of Micklegate as the Round Tower overlooks this street.

Intermittent skirmishing continued and on 20 February Drake reports that one of the garrison in the lower baileys had been shot through the cheeks but survived the wound. He also reports thirty Parliamentary soldiers been killed by cannon and musket fire on the 22nd. On the 24th things warmed up a little with a Royalist soldier being killed by a musket shot through the head and Captain Smith having his lip cut by a stone chip. Drake reports five or six besiegers killed. The main excitement of the day was when a body of foot was seen marching towards the town from the direction of Ferrybridge and Drake reports it having six colours, approximately 250 men. Half of them marched around the north side of the town to the Park (the area close to Pontefract Racecourse) and the remainder marched through the 'Frealles' to All Saints' Church. The garrison fired several cannon shot at the marching enemy but with no reported loss. At about seven in the evening two volleys of musket fire were heard by the garrison and Drake states that the Royalists believed this was the funeral service of a senior Parliamentary officer.

On 26 February a Royalist cannon shot landed close to one of the Parliamentary guns in the Market Place and Drake reports that many enemy around its point of impact were seen to fall. Captain Maullett was killed on the Round Tower by a shot to the head. The reader may have noticed that many of the Royalist casualties are reported as caused by shots to the head. The men manning the towers, such as the Round Tower, would have had little else but their heads showing to the troops firing from ground level below them.

On the 28th the garrison noticed that something was going on in the Parliamentary lines. The besiegers set fire to Elizabeth Cattel's house along with several others below Monkhill. The cannon in the Market Place were being prepared for moving and the garrison fired four cannon shot at them, causing 'great execution' according to Drake. During the night the enemy artillery were withdrawn from the town and across the bridge at Ferrybridge.

Drake reports a number of enemy guns bursting during their bombardment of the castle and this may be another reason for the intensity of the battery dropping after 21 January. He also mentions the enemy beginning a number of mines to undermine the walls of the castle. As the castle sits on a ridge of solid rock this mining must have been slow work. One of the mines was started close to Mr Ward's house and was to go under the ditch and the Round Tower. Another one started at St Nicholas's Hospital was intended to undermine the King's Tower. Usually mining during a siege was kept secret from the garrison. The ideal situation for the besiegers was that the first the garrison knew of the mine was when a section of wall or a tower lifted into the air and then collapsed back into the crater caused by the explosion. This does not seem to have been the case at Pontefract and Drake reports the besiegers openly boasting about the mines and the 100 barrels of gunpowder they had ready to use in them! The defenders sank eleven or twelve counter-mines within the castle, several of which have been found by archaeologists.

The garrison must have pondered the meaning of the besiegers withdrawing their guns during the night of 28 February. During the morning of 1 March the besiegers began to draw their troops together from the town and the positions around the castle. This must have also had the garrison wondering what was going on but did not prevent them from firing on the marching troops. At about three in the afternoon the reason for all this movement became apparent when several bodies of horse were seen cresting a hill towards Wentbridge. Sir Marmaduke Langdale and the Northern Horse had arrived to relieve the castle.

Pontefract Castle: the Round Tower seen from the Inner Bailey. The Norman motte can be clearly seen.

The Battle of Chequerfield and the Relief of Pontefract Castle

Langdale's force had left Banbury on Sunday 23 February 1645. Their mission was to relieve Pontefract Castle and then return to the Oxford area and rejoin the King's Army. Contemporary accounts do not give the strength of Langdale's force but at Naseby four months later the Northern Horse numbered about 1,700 men, so a similar figure for their march north would be close. Continuing their march on the 24th as far as Market Harborough they received news that Colonel Rossiter had gathered a sizeable force of horse from Leicester, Derby, Nottingham, Grantham and a number of other garrisons and was blocking their route at Melton Mowbray. On the 25th the two forces clashed close to the town and, after a hard fight, Rossiter's troops were routed. The Northern Horse then continued their march to the vicinity of Belvoir Castle. The 26th saw them march to a point about four miles north of Newark. Parliamentary forces were besieging Norwell House, one of Newark's outlying garrisons. News of Rossiter's defeat had preceded Langdale's men and on their approach the besiegers of Norwell House withdrew to Doncaster.

On 27 February the Royalist force continued its northward march, reinforced by 400 horse and 400 foot from the Newark garrison. The foot were probably musketeers as there is no mention of pikemen in accounts of the battle. The advance continued on the 28th and Langdale's men occupied quarters in Doncaster that night, having crossed the Don at Rossington. The relief force was now in striking distance of the castle. Early on the morning of Saturday 1 March Langdale drew his men into their battle order and began his advance towards Pontefract. The first clash with the enemy happened close to Wentbridge, where a force of 1,000 horse and 500 dragoons attempted, unsuccessfully, to halt the Royalist advance. Sir Gamaliel Dudley gives an account of the Northern Horse's march, from leaving Banbury to relieving Pontefract Castle, in a letter to Prince Rupert. Dudley gives a short report on the clash at Wentbridge:

> We marched without sight of Enemy, till we came neare Wentbrigge, above three miles short of Pontefract, where about 1000 Horse, and 500 Dragooners of the Enemies, attended that place, as much as possibly they could, to impede the speed of our course that way; but without much danger in the dispute, we forc'd the Passe, but yet they so retarded our march, as the besiegers had gain'd time to be all drawne together

both Horse and Foot in order, being in number about 2500 foot and neare 4000 Horse and Dragoones.

Dudley goes on to mention that the Parliamentary force comprised all the 'English' that Lord Fairfax could gather together, excluding the besieging forces at Scarborough and Sandal Castle. He also reports Lord Fairfax having arrived that morning with two regiments of horse and 500 musketeers, although this is not mentioned in any other accounts I have seen.

Drake gives a good description of the Royalist advance on to the battlefield:

> About 3 of the Clock, Sr Marmaduke's forelorne hope did appeare upon the top of the hill on this side of Wentbridge, and so marched, one Company after another, till his whole Army Came all into the Chequor field, where both Armyes mett, & faced one another till almost 6 of the Clock, the Parliament Armye allwaies giving ground (when Sir Marmaduke advanced) till they came to their foot wch they had placed, and lined the Long hedge from Englandes howse to the hill toppe.

There are some discrepancies between Drake and Dudley's accounts, typical of the same action being seen from different perspectives. The main difference is the time that the action started: Drake says that Langdale's force deployed on the hilltop at three in the afternoon, while Dudley tells us that it was between four and five. Dudley goes on to give an account of the opening clashes of the action:

> A good advantage was it to us, that our Forlorne Parties, seconded with severall Divisions of our Horse had beaten in that great Body of their Van-curriers in such disorder into their Main Battaile, as taking that opportunity with a continued charge, they had not time to recover themselves into any settled order, and though the suddainesse of the Actions gave not leave for each Division of our Horse to observe its proper time and place of their severall orders to Charge in, yet in the whole it was so fully done, as that there was not one Body of them all, but did foure or five severall times that day act their parts with very gallant Execution.

Langdale's men had followed up close behind the retreating Parliamentary horse they had defeated at Wentbridge, so close in fact that the enemy had been unable to rally and had been driven back onto their main body and a large body of musketeers who were lining a hedge. Both Drake and Dudley mention the Royalist troopers charging four or five times. Dudley notes that the fighting went on for almost three hours and by the time of the Royalist final charge only three bodies of about 120 men each could be gathered together. The Parliamentary foot still held the hedge and continued a brisk fire on the Royalist horse. By this time the Newark foot had caught up with the horsemen and these were used to flank the Parliamentary foot, while the Royalist horse charged and a number of musketeers sallied from the castle into the enemy's rear, as Dudley reports:

> The Fight continued without a cleare Victory, at the least three houres, until there was not left on our Party standing in order to Charge withal, more than three final Bodies, consisting of above 120 in each Body, which with some Officers and Gentlemen together rally'd, gave a seasonable Charge to the last of the Enemies strength, the Castle at the same instant making a gallant sally of 200 Musqueteers, who fell in the Reare of the Enemies Foot, our owne Foot firing upon them at the same time in their Flanck, and this totally cleared the Field.

With horse bearing down on their front, musketeers firing into their flank and a sally from the castle attacking their rear the Parliamentary troops finally broke. Many of them fled along the road to Ferrybridge, where a body of foot and dragoons, supported by one cannon, made a stand but were quickly beaten back. Both Dudley and Drake mention the capture of the enemy cannon at Ferrybridge. Drake mentions the pursuit continuing beyond Sherburn-in-Elmet towards Tadcaster.

Parliamentary losses in both men and equipment were high. Dudley mentions 300 enemy bodies on the field and many drowned in the river at Ferrybridge. Drake's figures are in close agreement with this and he mentions 160 dead on the field and 140 killed in the pursuit. Both state that a substantial number of prisoners had been taken: Drake 600 and Dudley between 700 and 800. A large quantity of powder, match and shot was captured and moved into the castle. A substantial number of standards and colours were also taken in the rout and again both Drake and Dudley give a similar figure, with Drake reporting 'above 40' and Dudley giving a more exact figure of twenty-two foot colours and twenty-six horse standards. He also mentions that the foot colours were all the enemy had.

After his account of the battle Dudley mentions an enemy plan to capture the castle by subterfuge:

> One remarkable circumstance I cannot omit to acquaint your Highnesse with; They [the besiegers] had some days before given out, that they would take the Castle with a Stratagem, which should be thus; They would make, as if reliefe were coming to it, and so they would seem to draw all off, as to fight the Reliefe, (leaving onely an Ambuscada in the Towne) and then they would skirmish together, and seem defeated by the Releevers, and so retreat disorderly as beaten, in expectation the Castle should make a Sally, and then their Ambuscada should surprise it; But I hope they were now taught the danger of jesting with edg'd Tooles, and will hereafter leave such mocking.

Dudley does not mention where he found out about this plan but it could well have been from one of the prisoners.

Drake reports that Langdale's men returned from their pursuit at between ten and eleven on the Saturday night. After resting his men overnight he sent parties of them into the surrounding countryside to gather supplies for the garrison as it was very likely that Fairfax's men would return to the siege once Langdale had commenced his return journey to the south. During the 2nd Langdale received news that Rossiter had once again gathered a force to oppose him and had reached as far as Doncaster. On the 3rd the Northern Horse departed from the castle and headed south. Rossiter had secured the bridge at Doncaster so Langdale had to look for another crossing point, which he found at Oldwark near Rotherham. By the 4th they had reached Newark, from where Dudley wrote his letter to Prince Rupert, which is dated 'Newark this 4. of March, 1644'. The date of the New Year had not been fixed as 31 December at the time of the Civil Wars. Many forward-thinking people did consider 31 December as the end of the year but others, of the 'old school', considered Easter to be the New Year. Dudley was obviously of the old school, hence his letter had been dated 1644. This can lead to confusion if the events in a document cannot be fitted into their context by other evidence. In this instance Dudley is writing about an event which we can firmly fit into 1645.

The Second Siege of Pontefract Castle

With the departure of the Northern Horse the garrison had a short period of grace to gather men and supplies before the enemy returned. Until the 10th the garrison concentrated on gathering provisions but after that they began to range further afield. On the 15th a party of horse from the castle raided towards Doncaster and routed Colonel Brandling's regiment, capturing three officers, sixty-seven men and 100 horses. During the same night another party attacked an enemy storehouse at Turnbridge and returned with forty new pairs of boots and a substantial amount of provisions.

Many historians set the start of the second siege as 11 March but this seems a little odd as Drake, a member of the garrison, does not mention the return of the enemy until the 21st, when he reports the enemy occupying the upper town, the area around the Market Place, at about two o'clock in the afternoon. Drake mentions the death of Captain Redman, although it is not clear where this took place, and of a soldier on the Round Tower. He also mentions three members of the garrison been captured. The defenders opened up a hot fire on the Parliamentary troops firing fourteen cannon shot during the afternoon and another two during the night. The enemy were not strong enough to occupy the lower town close to the castle and this allowed the defenders to gather wood and 'other necessaryes' from the burnt houses around the castle. It was Drake's opinion that the force which occupied the upper town was not intended to besiege the castle but to pin the defenders in place while Fairfax gathered additional troops to begin another complete siege.

On the 22nd the garrison fired fifteen cannon shot into various enemy positions, although no enemy casualties were reported. A woman and man standing on the Round Tower were both wounded by the same musket ball, the woman through the hand and the man in the thigh. Drake reports that both survived. The besiegers began to dig trenches in a number of places but most of the work seems to have gone on close to Alderman Lunn's house. For the next five days the garrison continued to fire the occasional cannon shot at the enemy positions, with little visible effect.

The 28th saw the garrison suffer what would now be referred to as a 'blue on blue' incident. A musketeer discharged his weapon accidentally and wounded a comrade in the thigh. In another incident a musket exploded in its owner's hands, injuring the unfortunate man. In neither case does Drake report the death of the victim, so it is probable that both men survived. On the same day the garrison also made a couple of sallies towards Monkhill and Baghill, claiming one enemy death at Monkhill and two on Baghill.

From 29 March to 3 April the siege continued very much as the first siege had with exchanges of musketry and cannon fire from the garrison. Interestingly, Drake does not report any artillery fire from the besiegers. On the 30th the garrison suffered another fatality when Nicholas Baune was killed by a musket ball as he stood next to a cannon mounted on a platform close to the Treasurer's Tower. From 4 April things began to escalate as the garrison committed more troops to attacks from the castle. Not only were these sallies larger but they were often more ambitious. To counter these attacks the besiegers began to dig siege lines to isolate the castle.

During daylight on the 4th the garrison continued to fire a small number of shots at the enemy position close to the end of Skinners Lane, Mrs Oates's house and Newhall. During the night a force of ninety men sallied from the castle, supported by artillery fire, to attack the Parliamentary guard positions close to Alderman Rusby's house, burning the enemy post and part of the house and killing one enemy captain and three soldiers. They also drove the enemy sentries from their posts in the lower town. The enemy deployed a large number of foot to prevent the attack pushing any further into their lines but the Royalist troops withdrew successfully into the castle with the loss of only one man who had been taken prisoner.

On the 5th Captains Washington and Beale led a small party of horse from the castle, supported by forty musketeers commanded by Captain Smith. A troop of enemy horse was driven back into the town. Shortly thereafter a larger force of Parliamentary horse, supported by 100 musketeers, who lined a hedge, opposed the Royalist party but Drake tells us that the Royalists, though heavily outnumbered, 'manteyned the field bravely'. During the sally the Royalists captured two butchers heading towards the town for the Saturday market, their horses laden with fresh meat, which Drake tells us came in very handy on the following day which was Easter Sunday.

Colonel Lowther, the garrison commander, had requested from Colonel Forbes, the commander of the besieging force, permission to send into the town for wine to celebrate communion on Easter Day and Forbes readily granted them protection to do so. Some of his soldiers had other ideas and the wine was prevented from been taken into the castle and Drake reports one Browne of Wakefield saying that 'if it were for our [the garrison's] damnation we should have it, but not for our Solvation [salvation]'. Lowther

All Saints' Church formed part of the defences of Pontefract Castle. Many local people still think that the damage to the church was caused by bombing in the Second World War. It was caused during the sieges, when both sides occupied or shot at it at various times.

determined that the besiegers should be taught a lesson and when the Easter sermon was over at eleven o'clock he ordered his men to arms. Once again Captains Washington and Beale led the horse from the castle. A body of fifty musketeers was led by Captain Munro from the Swillington Tower up Northgate while Captain Flood led another fifty from the Lower Gate towards Halfpenny House, close to All Saints' Church. Each body of musketeers was supported by twenty-five of the gentleman volunteers, drawn from all four watches. Both parties attacked and drove the enemy from their lines, before returning to the castle in triumph. Drake records at least twenty-six of the enemy had been killed in their works and one taken prisoner. The returning troops brought back 'divers muskittes & swords & drummes'. The Royalist sallying parties lost only two men killed and another two wounded. The castle's cannon fired twenty-six shots at the enemy in the Market Place, causing many casualties, although the 100 reported by Drake may be a little high.

Parliament's Easter tribulations were not yet over. At 10pm Captains Smith and Ratcliffe and Lieutenant Wheatley led 100 musketeers into Northgate and having crossed the enemy trenches moved on into Micklegate, which at the time ran all the way from the Market Place to the castle, where they 'gave fearce fire amongst them and did bloody execution for allmost one hower, where was very many of the besiegers killd'. The attackers lost only one man killed, Quartermaster Dawson, and another wounded. Once again the garrison's cannon fired in support of the attack and an enemy powder store near Mr Lunn's house was seen to burst into flames. Drake reports twenty of the enemy being badly burned in the incident.

The garrison continued to harass the besiegers over the following days. On 7, 8 and 9 April small sorties were made towards the enemy positions on Baghill. On the 7th a party of twelve horsemen had encountered an enemy patrol, killed one man and captured a Trooper Wilson. On the 8th a party of horse, commanded by Captain Washington, supported by forty musketeers commanded by Lieutenant Moore sallied out. After initially driving the enemy back, the Royalists were faced by a large body of horse which was supported by 100 musketeers. The Royalists carried out a controlled withdrawal to the castle and had only one man wounded, Lieutenant Moore, a wound from which Moore fully recovered. Skirmishing continued on Baghill on the 9th but the main event recorded on that day was the removal of a large number of the besieging force's wounded – Drake reports five wagons full.

The garrison remained within the castle walls on the 10th but continued a harassing fire into the enemy positions. Drake mentions two of the enemy being killed by cannon fire, five more killed by musket fire from the Round Tower and four men and a horse killed on Monkhill. The continual sallies and harassing fire from the garrison was causing a constant stream of casualties on the besiegers. Another five wagons full of wounded headed from the town towards Ferrybridge. The Parliamentary forces received a welcome reinforcement when Sir John Saville returned from Sandal Castle with a force of horse and foot. How good the morale of Saville's men was is debatable as they had lost almost 100 men to a sally by the garrison of Sandal Castle the previous day (see Chapter 7). The Parliamentary positions had come close enough to the castle for the garrison to fire two rounds of case shot, a short-range round that turned the cannon into a giant shotgun, into the enemy trenches from where the cry of 'O is me, O is me' was heard.

On the 12th Drake reports the death of one of the local worthies who had joined the garrison as a volunteer. Alderman Thomas Wilkinson was killed by a musket ball as he stood close to the barbican gate. While the bulk of the garrison attended a sermon on the 13th the besiegers deployed several troops of horse on the sand bed in front of Newhall. One of the gunners on the King's Tower considered this too good an opportunity to miss and fired a ball which dismounted a whole file of enemy horsemen, killing two men and horses and wounding four others. Standing cavalry in front of cannon was not a very good idea!

Through much of the siege the garrison was able to drive its horses and cattle into the fields close to the castle walls. On 14 April, at about 10am, a party of Parliamentary foot attempted to drive away a herd of cattle grazing close to the Swillington Tower but heavy musketry from the walls drove them off. At about the same time three wagons loaded with powder and other munitions were seen to arrive in the Parliamentary lines. For some reason this made the garrison conjecture that Prince Rupert was on his way to relieve them and that the 3,000 Scots in Leeds and other quarters in Yorkshire were gathering with local forces drawn from Knaresborough, Scarborough, York, Cawood, Selby and Pontefract. Drake does not give the reasoning behind the garrison coming to this conclusion.

Another incident occurred on the 14th which illustrates the aggressive spirit of the defenders. A party of twenty musketeers attacked a section of the enemy lines near Newhall. They drove the enemy from their works and then set about demolishing the enemy position until a body of enemy horse approached them, at which point they retreated. The interesting thing is that Drake tells us that they had made their attack without any command to do so or with any commander. One of their own number, William Wether, also known as Belwether, led them in the attack – as a quick aside, I wonder if Drake had misheard and written down Belwether when it was actually Bill Wether? Another small party of five musketeers became engaged with four enemy horsemen on Baghill. Seeing this, Lieutenant Perry and Jonathan, whom Drake describes as Sir Jarvis Cutler's man, mounted their horses and rode to the rescue. The enemy horse fell back and the musketeers were able to retreat to safety.

At six o'clock in the evening Belwether led another party of six firelocks against the enemy positions near the end of Broad Lane. It is interesting that Drake makes the distinction between musketeers and firelocks. Most muskets were matchlocks and were fired by the application of a lighted match to the powder in the pan. Firelocks were early flintlock muskets which used the spark from a flint to ignite the powder which fired the musket. Firelocks were often issued to artillery train guards – a lighted match was a real danger close to barrels of gunpowder! They were also very useful during night attacks as the lack of a lighted match helped to conceal the approach of an attacking force. Belwether and his comrades killed four enemy soldiers; one was described as a commander in a buff coat and black scarf, who Drake thought was Colonel Eden. The garrison's cannon continued to harass the enemy, with five rounds being fired towards the town during the day and another four during the night.

At about midday on the 15th a party of Parliamentary musketeers, thirty strong, lined an old hedge on Baghill and began a continuous fire into the castle until 1800. By this time the garrison had had enough and a round was fired from the 'Iron gunne' into the hedge bottom and, according to Drake, 'Caused them to make a great lamentation', although he does go on to say that they did not know how many of the enemy had been killed. Another incident on the 15th shows how much freedom the garrison still had and how loose the Parliamentary cordon around the castle was. One of the infantrymen from the garrison was having a walk, late at night, through the closes nearby the castle. An enemy horseman spotted and attacked him, wounding the footman four times, none of them seriously. The horseman didn't have it all his own way, with the footman stabbing him in the thigh, injuring his horse's nose and then running him through the middle with his rapier for almost half its length. The horseman, seriously wounded, beat a hasty retreat.

On the morning of the 16th the garrison launched another large sortie. Captain Hemsworth and fifty musketeers exited the lower gate and attacked the trenches close to Alderman Lunn's house, while another party of fifty musketeers, commanded by Captain Munro, attacked from the Swillington Tower up Northgate. These parties were seconded by fifty gentlemen and volunteers, drawn from all four watches. A smaller party of ten musketeers under Lieutenant Fevell, who was Captain Munro's lieutenant, followed the main attack and assaulted a small earthwork. The besiegers were driven from their positions with the loss of seventeen dead and many more wounded. As the musketeers advanced the Royalist cannon fired twenty shot in support. By the time the attackers had withdrawn to the castle they had inflicted fifty losses on the enemy, in dead, wounded and prisoners. Among the prisoners was one Captain Wade and another officer, a lieutenant, was among the dead. The garrison also captured sixty arms and seven drums.

While the foot attacked the enemy positions towards the town, Captain Washington and Cornet Speight led a force of thirty-eight horsemen onto Baghill. The enemy forbore to challenge them and the Royalist horse held its ground for some time. Washington and Speight, with two men, ventured forth again in the afternoon and captured Quartermaster Hill and his horse. The success of these continuous sorties must have had a very positive effect on the garrison's morale. A messenger arrived from Sandal Castle with a message from Colonel Bonivant, telling Pontefract Castle's defenders of his victory over Sir John Saville and Saville's subsequent withdrawal. Now the garrison knew the reason for Saville's reappearance at Pontefract on the 10th.

On the 17th the garrison targeted Newhall for its next attack, although Drake stated that the sortie did 'nothing wo'th the noting'. During the day the besiegers were seen to send seven wagon loads of wounded towards York, possibly casualties of the previous day's fighting.

It has already been mentioned that the Parliamentary blockade of the castle was quite loose and the 18th was to show this yet again. The garrison spotted a herd of forty-four oxen and milk cows grazing in the fields, although Drake does not mention which fields. Thirty horse, commanded by Captains Speight and Beale, and fifty foot under Majors Bland and Dennis, sallied out of the castle and brought the cattle in with little, if any, opposition. At the same time as the force sallied out to gather the cattle, one of the garrison, Sergeant Monks, was shot in the thigh but, as Drake put it, there was great hope of his recovery. As the day wore on the garrison spotted a force of Scots horse and foot, about 600 strong, arrive at Newhall. Drake says these were commanded men, i.e. drawn from several regiments, as they carried no colours. The Scots were commanded by Colonel Montgomery. The garrison gave the Scots a very hot welcome and fired twenty-four shot at them, causing ten casualties, several of which were officers. The besiegers drew a large body of horse and foot onto Baghill to prevent the garrison from sallying out in that direction and interfering with the 'markitt folkes' who were bringing their wares to the market. The garrison's cannon opened fire on the enemy force, killing and wounding several and causing the remainder to retreat. One of the Royalist gunners was hit and killed by a musket ball as he was about to fire the gun.

The garrison had sent a small herd of cattle into one of the closes on the Newhall side of the castle, guarded by thirty musketeers. A small force of the newly arrived Scots foot lined a hedge close by and opened fire on the Royalist musketeers. Two of the Royalist slipped behind the Scots and gave fire into their rear, causing them to beat a hasty retreat back to their positions, losing one man killed and another wounded in the process.

The remains of the Swillington Tower. The road was cut through the tower in Victorian times.

The next day, the 19th, was spent harassing the Scots before they had chance to settle into their positions, with small parties of foot attacking the Scots and driving them from the works. By the 20th the Scots had had enough of this and decided to reinforce their positions around Monkhill and Newhall. They burnt down a number of houses on Monkhill and set about raising a 'baricade' near Newhall and 'bulwarks in divers places to munkhill top'. Even though they had reinforced their positions it would seem that the Scots were still very nervous. During the night an alarm was given within the Scots lines and one of their officers, a major, was shot by a musketeer who mistook him for a 'Cavelear'.

On the 21st the garrison moved 'the Iron Gunne' into a new earthwork which had been raised for it before the main gate into the upper bailey. This may have been a little premature as the position was not finished, and the gun not able to fire, until the 24th. The besiegers sent a force of musketeers up onto Baghill that night and opened fire on the soldiers working on the new earthwork. Firing continued for two and a half hours with no loss to the Royalists and little delay to the work. During the afternoon the Scots had sent a drummer, as a messenger, to the castle and Captain Flood and a soldier went to meet him. Seeing the two Royalists, the Scots on Monkhill opened fire, wounding the soldier, Anthony Foxcroft in the leg, and grazing Flood's leg with another shot, at which point they fell back into the castle. Drake finishes his description of the day's fighting with a description of a far from savoury incident. The servant of Captain Grimstone had travelled to the castle to find his master, who had actually left with the Northern Horse several weeks earlier. Before he reached the castle he was captured by Parliamentary troops and tortured with lighted matches because he would not tell them his master's whereabouts, which he did not know and had come looking for him. This is a very rare account of such goings-on in the Civil Wars period.

The 22nd saw the Scots continue to reinforce their works around Newhall and Monkhill and Parliamentary musketeers on Baghill carried on their harassment of the parties working on the new platform for the 'Iron Gunne'. During the night the Scots forces gathered together at Newhall and marched away. They were replaced on the 23rd by Sir John Saville's contingent. Heavy musketry fire was exchanged between musketeers on Baghill and the garrison but the only casualty reported by Drake was a young maid, hanging out washing in Mr Tayton's orchard, who was shot in the head and died during the night.

On the morning of the 24th a body of forty musketeers deployed on Baghill and began a heavy fire on a small herd of cattle grazing in the closes adjacent to the castle. They then turned their shots on the castle itself. The defenders replied in kind and one of the Parliamentary soldiers was killed and the remainder withdrew. A small sally towards Monkhill killed one of Saville's men. In the afternoon the body of the young maid killed on the previous day was taken down to All Saints' Church for burial. A volley was fired over her grave and this caused a major alarm among the besiegers in the town who despatched a large body of horse and foot to Baghill. The besiegers and defenders opened a heavy fire on one another. While this was going on Belwether and his comrades captured a woman bringing a supply of ale to the town from Barwick-in-Elmet. The woman was led back to the castle, where the ale would have been most welcome. She also brought some news. The King had won a victory at 'Westchester' (Chester) and the besiegers were only to remain at Pontefract for another two or three days. This news must have been very welcome to the garrison but, unfortunately, it turned out to be false.

The besiegers continued to put pressure on the defenders from Baghill on the 25th when fifty musketeers and a troop of horse deployed there and the musketeers opened up a heavy fire on the castle, to which the defenders replied with enthusiasm with both muskets and cannon. The defenders were not sure how many casualties they had caused among the enemy troops but Drake says they 'saw either heads or hattes flye up at the fall of the Bullitts [cannon balls]' and heard 'great exclamations at one time'. Three or four of the garrison sallied out of the castle towards Monkhill and drove sixteen of the enemy from the houses back to their work, capturing one and bringing him back to the castle with them. Several more enemy were killed by musket fire from the Round Tower when they were changing the guards during the night.

Saturday the 26th was a very busy day for both the besieged and besiegers. Once again a large body of Parliamentary musketeers deployed among the hedges on Baghill and shot at the castle for five or six hours, causing no casualties on the garrison. The defenders replied in kind and opened up with cannon shot on the Market Place which was crowded with people. Drake reports a man being killed by a Mrs Jackson's door and cannon balls bouncing along the Market Place through the crowds, although he says the defenders were not sure how many casualties had been caused. At about noon a small party of defenders 'sallyd forth to Munkhill' and fought against a party of Sir John Saville's men, killing one and wounding another. The remainder withdrew to their trenches. A party of forty Parliamentary horse attempted to cut off the Royalist foot, only seven or eight men strong, but they withdrew into musket range of the castle and the enemy troopers refused to follow them. At around two o'clock another party of five men went up onto Monkhill and engaged the enemy, beating them back and killing one of their number. The same party returned up Monkhill and an enemy horseman attacked them. They quickly despatched the horseman and returned to the castle with his body and his horse.

At four o'clock another party of seven or eight men went up Monkhill. They decided to confuse the enemy by acting the part of Parliamentary soldiers. First they called to a horseman, possibly an officer, who rode over towards them. Realizing his mistake the horseman cocked his pistol but the Royalists fired two muskets at him, wounding him through the side. The rider's horse turned about and carried his wounded master back towards Newhall. When they got to the top of Monkhill they turned towards the castle and began to shout abuse at the defenders. Some Parliamentary musketeers were lining a hedge close by and the tricksters shouted for them to come forward with them and attack the castle, which one of the musketeers presently did. After he had approached the castle the Royalists disarmed the Parliamentarian and led him back into the castle as a prisoner. While all this was going on the garrison continued a stiff fire against the besiegers and fired several more shots into the Market Place.

During the evening a body of 150 foot came from Ferrybridge to reinforce Saville's men at Newhall. It seems that s decision had been made to make the blockade of the castle more secure. The Scots had already improved the works around Newhall and Monkhill, before their departure and replacement by Sir John Saville's men, and now the besiegers began similar work on Baghill. During the night at least 100 men went to Baghill and began work on a trench.

The day's fighting was not yet over. Close to midnight Captain Smith and Lieutenant Faivell led sixty musketeers out of the Swillington Tower into Northgate. The enemy sounded the alarm and called their men to arms. A heavy fire fight followed for about half an hour before the Royalists pulled back with no loss. At the same time Lieutenant Smith led twelve men into the lower town and attacked the enemy's sentry post, causing the guards to flee back towards Newhall. The garrison also fired two cannon shot at the work parties on Baghill, although Drake tells us that the defenders did not know if any casualties had been caused. Although many of the actions during this phase of the siege were on a small scale, they caused a continual drain on the besiegers' resources, through casualties and continual alarms.

Early on the 27th a large body of Parliamentarian musketeers deployed on Baghill and commenced a heavy fire on the castle. The fire was so heavy that the defenders could not put their cattle and horses out to graze. At some time during the morning the defenders spotted five 'very good hoggs' wandering up Broad Lane and a party from the castle sallied out to collect them. At about noon a kiln house belonging to Mrs Oates, situated close to the upper church, was seen to be on fire. Drake states that the garrison were unaware of the cause of the fire. As the besiegers gathered around the building trying to put out the fire, the Royalist guns opened fire on them. The Royalist musketeers kept up a spirited fire on the enemy in the nearby trenches, killing at least one and seeing several others carried away. At about eleven o'clock that night a soldier called Lowder led five of his comrades on a raid against the enemy position near All Saints' Church. The enemy sentries were driven back to Newhall and an alarm given, which spread through all the Parliamentary positions surrounding the castle. During the night work continued on the trench on Baghill. It was slow and laborious work due to the rocky nature of the ground.

On the following day, the 28th, work continued all day on the Baghill trench. At about six in the morning a party of 150 men relieved the night workers. Work continued apace and the diggers were covered by a party of musketeers. The fire from these troops does not seem to have been as hot as the previous day and the garrison was able to put their livestock out to graze for the whole day, not returning them to the castle until ten o'clock that night. At eleven in the morning a party of 200 horse was seen marching from the town towards Ferrybridge. At five o'clock Lowder, described as a 'good stout man', led a party of twelve musketeers towards Newhall. The enemy responded by sending a party of about 100 men from their lines to oppose the Royalists, probably believing that they would retreat in face of such numbers – they were wrong. Lowder and his comrades charged the enemy, killing two and wounding 'as many men (as is thought) of theirs as went up of oures'. The Parliamentarians fled back to their lines, taking one of the dead and all of the wounded. The morale of Sir John Saville's men must have been very low at this point. They had suffered a defeat at Sandal Castle (see Chapter 7) and had been continually harassed by the defenders since they had deployed around Newhall and Monkhill, taking a steady trickle of casualties along the way. Lowder and his men returned towards the castle, carrying one of the enemy dead with them. They gave him a decent burial at Denwell close to the body of another enemy soldier killed on Monkhill a couple of days earlier. Drake compares this treatment of the enemy casualties by the garrison to that of the enemy when they had captured All Saints' Church during the first siege. The bodies of the Royalist dead had lain in the open for ten days before permission had been given for the Royalists to recover and bury them. An even larger work party was sent to Baghill by the besiegers that night; possibly as many as 500. The garrison fired several cannon shots at the work parties, which were answered by heavy musket fire.

On the 29th work continued on the trench on Baghill which was very close to completion. The troops covering the work kept up a heavy fire on the castle and killed one cow and two horses grazing in the closes near the castle. The defenders replied in kind with both musket and cannon fire, killing two men on Baghill, one of whom may have been an officer. Another incident again illustrated the low morale of Saville's men. A party of nine Royalist musketeers went up Monkhill and drove a body of enemy troops from the trench, before withdrawing to the castle. Saville's men had fled from their position without suffering a single casualty. During the night four officers and their servants left the castle to ride to Newark. Twenty musketeers covered their breakout. Once clear of the enemy lines the mounted men clashed with an enemy scout and fired on him. The musketeers withdrew down Northgate and back to the castle, unimpeded by the enemy. At this point they decided their night's work wasn't done and went back up Northgate until they were close to the enemy trenches near Mr Rusby's house. They then fired two volleys into the enemy trench and fell back to the castle.

The last day of April saw the besiegers complete and occupy their work on Baghill. Their musketeers kept up a lively fire on the castle throughout the day, killing a horse in the lower bailey. The defenders were not slow in responding and caused several casualties on the enemy on Baghill and in the trenches between the castle and the town. During the day Saville's men burnt down two houses, one on Monkhill and another close to the castle near Halfpenny House. Drake makes an entry in his diary recording that the garrison had fired 315 cannon shot between the start of the second siege on

The Hope and Anchor public house. It is thought that this is the site of Halfpenny House. St Nicholas's Hospital stood on the other side of the road shown at the left of the photograph.

21 March and 1 May. He does not record a single cannon shot from the besiegers during the same period.

May began very much as April had finished. The Parliamentary forces had completed their works on Baghill, including a 'Triangle work' which Drake reports as being lined with stone and having a shelter within 'for officers to sit in'. The garrison had seen a large delivery of ale arrive by the work and assumed that its occupants were partaking in sampling it. A cannon was fired at the emplacement and a large number of men were seen to abandon it very quickly. With the completion of the works on Baghill and the arrival of supplies, it looked like the besiegers had decided to put a permanent presence on the hill. During the night the besiegers cut branches from the trees of Baghill and made them into screens at each end of the triangular work, to prevent the enemy seeing inside it. The garrison also observed a small cannon, a drake, been positioned within the work. This is the first mention of enemy artillery during the second siege.

On the same day, 1 May, skirmishing continued on the opposite side of the castle at Monkhill. Saville had drawn a force of between sixty and seventy musketeers and lined a hedge and ditch with them. An exchange of fire commenced between the musketeers and the garrison. Eight men sallied out of the castle towards the enemy position. The garrison saw two of Saville's officers fall and, at about the same time, the sally party charged the enemy position, causing the Parliamentarians to retreat to their trenches, or 'runne all away very basely' as Drake puts it. The Royalist party then fell back towards the castle where they received a resupply of ammunition. The besiegers drew out a large force of horse, supported by foot, but the horse would not come within musket range of the castle. The foot deployed into the same positions they had previously vacated. The Royalist party, supported by musket fire from the castle once more drove the enemy from their position. A little later another party of three men attacked the enemy positions. As they fell back towards the castle, after their foray, the enemy opened fire on them. Nathaniel Sutton, a barber, was shot through the body and killed but his comrades brought his body back to the castle. Captain Dent was hit in the head but the ball did not penetrate the skull and, according to Drake, he fully recovered. The final member of the triumvirate, a drummer carrying a musket instead of his drum, had a musket ball pass through the collar of his doublet without touching the flesh.

The 2nd was a little quieter. The besiegers relieved their guards on Baghill before eight in the morning and also fired the cannon from their earthwork. The besiegers on Monkhill, for once not harried by the defenders, shot an ox which was grazing near the Swillington Tower, although the garrison was able to recover the carcase with its precious meat. Exchanges of musketry continued for most of the day and Drake reports fourteen enemy being shot by musketeers on the Round Tower. Colonel Lowther had decided to send messengers to Newark to find out what was happening in the south and if relief was forthcoming. While the garrison gave an alarm to the enemy on Northgate Mr William Booth and Mr Thomas Bamforth, two of the gentlemen volunteers, set out for Newark. Drake also reports the death of a member of the garrison who was struck in the head by a musket ball while the guards were being changed in the lower bailey.

On the following day the besiegers continued a steady fire on the castle. An old mare and two oxen out grazing were killed but once again the garrison recovered the carcases and, as Drake tells us, made good use of them. He also reports that the boy who was watching over the cattle was hit in the thigh by a musket ball which glanced off, causing little hurt. As the besiegers changed their guards a number of casualties were caused by musketry from the castle. Welcome news was received by the defenders during the night when two letters from Newark arrived, giving 'very good newes from the South' which greatly heartened the defenders.

The 4th was a Sunday and the besiegers kept up a very slow fire on the castle. During the afternoon a deserter from the besieging force arrived at the castle and told Lowther and his officers how things stood in the enemy lines, although Drake did not elaborate on this. There was also a prisoner exchange where Royalists captured around Newark and Pontefract were exchanged for enemy captured during the siege.

For the next three days the besiegers seem to have changed the focus of their shooting from place to place. A much smaller guard was seen to occupy the work on Baghill on the 5th. For several days up to 150 musketeers had deployed on the hill and in the works but only thirty-four men and two officers replaced the night guard. A large body of Sir John Saville's men made their way through the burnt-out houses to the top of Monkhill, from where they opened a heavy fire on the Round Tower and the north side of the castle, causing no casualties among the defenders. The men on the Round Tower replied in kind and killed one man and wounded several others while the besiegers changed their guard.

On the 6th both Baghill and Monkhill were quiet with only occasional pot-shots being taken at the garrison. It was the turn of the men in the trenches between the castle and the town to open up a heavy fire on the defenders who in turn fired back. Drake does not report any casualties on the defenders but mentions one of the besiegers being killed in Paradise Orchard and another near Mr Lunn's house, along with several others wounded. The garrison seems to have had something against the defenders on Baghill having a supply of ale. Two women were seen to deliver ale to the triangle work and the garrison fired two cannon shots into the work. The first penetrated the earthwork and many of its occupants were seen to run out of it. The second knocked several stones out of its rampart. The garrison also spotted a horse litter arriving at the town which left again the following morning. The garrison assumed that it had removed a wounded enemy officer. During the night another deserter, this time a sergeant, arrived at the castle and gave the defenders news of the happenings within the siege lines. This is yet another illustration of the serious morale problems within the Parliamentary force. It is difficult to understand why anyone would desert to a besieged town or castle unless the besiegers held little hope of its imminent fall.

On the morning of the 7th the besiegers opened fire with their drake from the earthwork on Baghill. It was so close to the castle that it could fire case shot. The gunners' aim was not particularly good and Drake reported a hit on the stables, in the outer bailey, and another on the castle's ramparts, while the rest of the shot flew over the castle. Musket fire from the besiegers' lines was very slow all through the day, although they did manage to wound one man who was digging a trench in the outer bailey. During the afternoon ten of the besiegers advanced on All Saints' Church 'vaporing wth their Swordes' and eight musketeers came down from the castle and quickly drove them off – advancing on an enemy position, waving their swords, smacks of the Parliamentarians having had a little too much of their ale ration! Drake also reports several more of the besiegers had been killed or wounded by musketry as they changed their guards.

The next day, the 8th, was very quiet until the besiegers changed their guards, when a brief fire fight broke out, with several Parliamentary soldiers being killed or wounded. During the night the garrison sent out two parties.

Captain Horsfold and his servant set off for Sandal Castle while the ubiquitous Belwether left for Newark. They were escorted up Baghill by a small body of musketeers but when they were not challenged continued on their way while the musketeers withdrew to the castle. It would seem that, although the besiegers had guarded works on Baghill, there were still gaps in the blockade or they kept a very poor watch.

During the 9th the besiegers began to tighten their grip on the castle. The day started quietly with little exchange of fire during the morning, although the garrison did fire two cannon shots from the King's Tower into the Market Place, followed by a third shot in the afternoon. Yet again the changing of the besiegers' guards prompted a heavy exchange of fire. The defenders spotted the fall of one enemy soldier, standing by the cannon's embrasure in the triangular work on Baghill, and two others were killed in the works close to the end of Broad Lane. One of these was thought to be an officer as he was completely clad in red and carried a staff. At about four in the afternoon the

Looking up Horsefair towards the Market Place. This street was known as Micklegate at the time of the Civil Wars.

enemy began to burn down a number of barns and houses along Northgate and Micklegate, including the barns of the Mayor and Mr Robert Battley. The latter's house was also set alight, as was Mr John Wilkinson's along with a good many others. This was not an act of wanton vandalism but a means of clearing the buildings to allow earthworks to be built with a clear view of the castle. It also denied the defenders the cover of the buildings when they sallied out of the castle. At about nine at night a volley was heard from the Market Square which the defenders subsequently found out was part of an officer's burial.

On the following day the besiegers continued to raise new earthworks to surround the castle. This time a 'haulph moone' shaped work was raised on Monkhill with the intention of preventing the garrison from sallying out of the Swillington Tower. During the night another two men left the castle to make their way to Sandal Castle, although Drake does not name them.

On Sunday, the 11th, the garrison had two 'learned sermons', one given by Dr Bradley and the other by Mr Olley. Drake reports two of the enemy had been killed by shots from the Round Tower and one of the defenders was shot through the arm while looking through one of the embrasures on the tower. A 9-year-old boy from the garrison was outside the castle close to Swillington Tower, collecting fodder for the livestock, when he was shot through the 'belly' by a musketeer in the siege works on Monkhill. Drake mentions that the wound was dangerous but does not tell us whether the lad survived. In another incident that night, one of the gentleman volunteers was on the Round Tower talking to one of the besieging officers. Contrary to an agreement that had been made that neither side would fire while the conversation was going on, a Parliamentary musketeer fired at the gentleman. The shot ricocheted off the side of the embrasure and struck the man on his belt buckle, smashing it to pieces. The man was completely unharmed!

The 12th saw a resurgence of shooting between the two sides, although Drake was unaware of any casualties on either side. At nine o'clock in the evening the garrison drank toasts to the King and his friends with water from a new well. Their 'hallowes and Showtes' were so loud that the besiegers stood to throughout their lines and brought up horse in support which, as Drake put it, 'pleased us well'. With the enemy deployed waiting for a sally from the castle, the defenders beat tattoo and retired to their guard posts and beds.

The garrison's good cheer continued on the next day when several loads of goods were seen to be sent away towards Ferrybridge, which made the garrison think that the enemy might be about to break the siege and march away. This continued on the 14th when a large number of sheep and cattle were driven towards Ferrybridge. Fire was exchanged between the two sides with a number of the besiegers being killed and wounded, while the garrison suffered one casualty, Cornet Thurley, who was wounded in the arm while standing in the lower bailey. About five in the afternoon a troop of horse was seen approaching rapidly from the direction of Doncaster. Four of the riders split off and went into the town while the remainder continued on to Newhall. Following this all the Parliamentary horse was drawn up in the Park. Drake admits that the garrison had no idea why the enemy had done this. During the night Captain John Benson, his servant and two other men rode from the castle to Sandal. Benson would take an active part in the defence of Sandal Castle. Drake also reports a number of fires being seen 'abroade' during the night but the garrison did not know the reason why.

After two months of being besieged the castle must have been in a disorderly state. During the day of the 15th the garrison set to cleaning the castle. A drain was dug to run off the water from a 'Filthy pond' in the castle yard, which was covered in stones and earth. The garrison also set about cleaning the inner bailey which cleansed the castle of 'many noysome smelles'. In the afternoon a party of the garrison went into the lower town to collect wood and a pair of Parliamentary lieutenants came out of their lines to watch them. Thomas Lowther, a soldier, and two of his comrades spotted the enemy officers and attacked them. The first lieutenant struck at Lowther with his partisan, a halberd-type weapon which was use to signify his officer rank, but Lowther avoided the blow and ran his opponent through with his sword, while one of his comrades shot him in the thigh with his musket. While this was going on the other lieutenant took to his heels and ran back to the siege lines. Lowther and his comrades carried the wounded officer, called Thompson, back into the castle where his wounds were dressed. Within two hours a drummer appeared before the castle gate to ask for a prisoner exchange and Thompson was exchanged for a Royalist lieutenant who was being held at Cawood Castle, near Selby. At about midnight Belwether arrived back from Newark, along with a member of the garrison who had gone to Newark previously. As they arrived at the Swillington Tower they met with Thomas Hanson who was returning from Sandal Castle. Belwether carried letters from the King with 'Joyfull newes', although what that news was is not mentioned.

The news from Newark seems to have rejuvenated the garrison and on the 16th they launched three sorties against the enemy's works. At about one in the afternoon a party from the castle attacked the half-moon work on Monkhill and surprised the enemy sentries before they could give an alarm. The besiegers abandoned the work and fled to Newhall. The enemy then sent a large force from Newhall to attack the sally party on Monkhill, at which point the Royalists withdrew to the castle. At five o'clock a small party attacked the enemy position below All Saints' Church. The enemy moved a party of thirty men into the Grange Barn, opposite the Royalist party. The attackers took cover in a nearby orchard and the two sides continued to fire on one another for half an hour, before the Royalists withdrew to the castle with no loss. At ten o'clock that night Captain Smith led a party of forty men from the castle to attack the enemy positions at the bottom of the Abbey Close. Drake mentions that a woman had left the castle and informed the besiegers of the impending attack and they had manned their works ready to receive it. Rather than wait until Smith's party got close and then open fire on them the Parliamentary troops, in a fit of bravado, began calling challenges to the advancing enemy. Forewarned, Smith ordered his men to open fire and an exchange of shots continued for some time before the Royalists fell back to the castle, having had two men wounded. This foray may have been a diversion to cover Thomas Hanson leaving the castle and riding to Sandal Castle, once again.

The 17th was quiet. Drake claims that a Parliamentary soldier was killed in the Market Place by a shot from the Round Tower but does not say whether this was by musket or cannon fire. If it was by a musket shot then the soldier was very unlucky as the chances of being hit by a shot from the castle while in the Market Place were very slim indeed. Drake also reports one of the garrison been shot and wounded while exiting the Swillington Tower. Later in the day a drummer approached the castle from the town accompanied by a trumpeter from Lord Montgomery's brother. The trumpeter was escorted to Colonel Lowther's quarters and spent half an hour there. Frustratingly we have no idea what was discussed during this meeting other than the trumpeter telling Lowther that the besiegers had no more than 3,000 men in the area. This seems a very low number.

Whether it was in response to the message received from the trumpeter or had already been planned is not clear but on Sunday 18th Lowther launched another major sally from the castle. The plan seems to have been to isolate and attack the enemy positions on Monkhill. After the night attack on the 16th had been betrayed by a deserter from the castle, Lowther was taking no chances and sent Major Ward to the lower bailey to watch for any signalling from the castle to the besiegers on Baghill. After prayers the attack began. Captains Smith and Flood, Ensign Killingbeck (also referred to as Ancient Killingbeck) and Sergeant Barton led a strong party across the bridge on Mill Dam Lane towards Monkhill. Smith split off with thirty men and proceeded up Denwell Lane towards the enemy works on the back of Monkhill. On reaching the enemy works, Smith and his men turned right and attacked along the line, driving the enemy before them. Flood and Killingbeck led a party of fifty men up the main Ferrybridge road, setting fire to a number of houses and attacking the enemy works. Their attack had been timed to coincide with Smith's drive across the top of the hill and the two parties were once again united.

To cover the right flank of this attack a party of seventy men, commanded by Captain Munro, Ensign Otway, also referred to as 'Ancient', and Sergeant Copeland attacked through the closes by All Saints' Church and then drove the enemy from the Grange Barn, which stood between the church and Newhall. They then attacked towards Newhall, where they joined Smith and Flood's party close to the hall.

Lieutenant-Colonel Gilbraith and Lieutenants Willoughby and Ward took sixty musketeers to All Saints' Church to act as a reserve for the main attack and to prevent enemy troops from the town or Baghill supporting their comrades at Newhall. Major Ward and Lieutenant Fevell manned the walls of the lower bailey with forty musketeers whose allotted task was to interdict any enemy marching across or from Baghill towards Newhall. With the right flank of his attack secure, Lowther now sent a party of horse around the castle to advance up Monkhill. Captain Beale, and his twenty troopers, advanced as far up the hill as they were able but were unable to cross the enemy trenches.

The combined party under Captains Smith, Flood and Munro then continued their attack right up to Newhall, driving the enemy from their positions, as Drake puts it: 'The enemy Runne away Basely by 40 at a time over St Thomas Hill towards Ferry bridge.' With the enemy driven from their positions the Royalist sally parties began to withdraw to the castle, taking hats, shoes and money from the Parliamentary corpses.

Drake reports between fifty and sixty of the besiegers been killed. Two soldiers and two camp followers or 'leguer ladies' were captured. The ladies were duly released. A large amount of enemy weapons were also brought back into the castle, along with a substantial amount of powder and match which the attackers had found in the enemy positions. About nine o'clock that night the garrison saw two wagons of wounded depart from Newhall towards Ferrybridge. Later that night, about eleven o'clock, they also saw a bonfire on top of the keep of Sandal Castle.

The attack on the 18th had been well planned and executed. A part of the enemy works had been targeted and attacked quickly and with overwhelming force. The main attack had been supported and its flanks protected by other parties and had been so sudden, and carried out so quickly, that the enemy had little time to respond. It also shows the fragility of the morale of Sir John Saville's men manning Newhall, abandoning their positions at the enemy's first approach. The Royalists had only one fatality during the attack, Cornet Blockley, 'a gallant gentleman & brave Souldyer' as Drake describes him.

The attack on the 18th seems to have rattled the besiegers and during the morning of the 19th they remained in the cover in their trenches. The garrison became frustrated by the lack of targets and began to shout 'a prince, a prince'. Thinking that the garrison had spotted a relief force approaching the besiegers sounded the alarm. The bulk of the Parliamentary horse gathered in Grange Lane while forty-two men were sent from the town to reinforce the positions around Newhall and a similar number reinforced Baghill. These troop movements gave the Royalist musketeers ample targets and Drake tells us that three or four of the enemy were killed and as many wounded.

There seems to have been quite a lot of communication between the garrison and the besiegers, nothing official but chat between the men manning the trenches and those on the castle walls. One such example of this occurred on 20 May 1645. The garrison had heard that the enemy had a large body of foot at Ferrybridge that were heading towards Pontefract to reinforce the besiegers. At about noon this body of foot hove into view and turned out to be twenty-two men. Drake puts this forward as an example of how the

Parliamentary commanders tried to bolster their men's morale with lies, or 'bragges' as he puts it. Just after this, a body of 200 horse was seen approaching from Ferrybridge. They marched through Darrington and then into the Westfield, on the Wakefield side of Pontefract, before proceeding to the Park. They then marched up a lane towards Tanshelf. It was too good a target for the gunners by the Treasurer's Tower to ignore. After losing two men to a cannon shot the Parliamentary troopers turned about and rode back into the Park and took shelter behind a ridge out of sight of the enemy guns. During the night another large body of Parliamentary cavalry, possibly six or seven troops, arrived at Pontefract but then continued their march, possibly to Wakefield. Fire from the Round Tower continued to cause attrition on the besiegers in their positions on Baghill and between the castle and the town and two cannon shots were fired into the Market Place. The small cannon in the work on Baghill fired three times during the day. On this and subsequent days, Drake mentions that the garrison had no idea where these enemy cannon shots had landed and it is possible that they were overshooting the castle. If this is the case, it is possible that they might have landed close to the Parliamentary positions on Monkhill at the opposite side of the castle!

Both sides woke to heavy rain on the morning of the 21st and little happened until about two in the afternoon when half a dozen men from the garrison went into the lower town to gather firewood. Thinking this was an attack, the Parliamentary troops manning the trenches on Baghill and Monkhill opened a rapid fire on the wood gatherers. As this was going on, 500 men, with colours flying and drums beating, marched from the town to Newhall to replace the troops in that area. The garrison fired two cannon shots towards them and saw one man and his horse felled, probably an officer. With the arrival of the replacements at Newhall, 300 of Sir John Saville's men marched back to the town. Drake reports Saville's men having 'scarce ever beene in bed since they Came to newhall'. During the night Lowther decided to despatch the ubiquitous Will Wether (Bellwether) to Newark again.

The only incident of note on the 22nd was the wounding by a musket shot of a Mr Kirby's son, who had gone outside the castle to gather grass for his father's horse. During the day Colonel Lowther received letters from the King and Sir Marmaduke Langdale, although how these letters had arrived is not clear. Both informed Lowther that an army was marching north to

The earthworks shown in this photograph are the remains of St John's Priory. The Parliamentary siege works ran in front of the trees in the background.

relieve Pontefract Castle. During the night Thomas Hanson arrived from Sandal Castle with letters confirming the approach of a Royalist army. This must have been a great relief to the garrison but, sadly, their hopes would not be fulfilled. Drake reports that the garrison had no shortage of provisions and were fully resolved to hold the castle against 'all REBELLS whatsoever'.

The 23rd seems to have passed fairly quietly with a single shot from the Parliamentary gun on Baghill being the only thing of note. During the night Captains Washington and Lieutenant Wheatley were despatched to Sandal Castle. Later in the night the garrison observed a fire on top of Sandal's keep which they assumed to be news of the two officers' arrival. They promptly answered with a bonfire on top of the Round Tower. The garrison also received news of a sally by the defenders of Scarborough Castle. The message said that the Scarborough men had killed or captured 300 of their besiegers and spiked the guns in a battery close to the barbican, before pulling back into the castle (see Chapter 6).

During the early hours of the 24th the besiegers opened up a heavy fire on the castle. Drake states that the defenders had no idea why the enemy had opened fire unless it was in retaliation against the signal fire on the Round Tower, as that was the place most of the enemy shots were directed against. At about ten o'clock in the morning a woman from the castle was gathering herbs when she was hit in the thigh by a musket ball but the wound was 'not dangerous of death'. At about the same time the iron gun in the upper bailey fired a single shot into the town. Late in the afternoon four of the defenders made their way down to All Saints' Church, where a small party of the enemy were. The Parliamentarian soldiers fled back towards their trenches on the Royalist approach, with the exception of an officer who stood his ground and pelted the approaching Royalists with stones. For some time the Royalists were unable to approach the enemy officer until Thomas Lowther entered the church to try and capture the enemy officer. Drake says of Lowther that he was 'a man who, if his Judgement had beene according to his vallor, was as sufficient as most men'. Lowther's judgement does not seem to have been the equal of his valour and as he advanced on the enemy officer he received a musket shot in the leg which broke it. The enemy troops ran towards Lowther but his comrades were able to assist him back to the castle. At the time of the Civil Wars a wound causing a broken bone usually resulted in the amputation of the affected limb and this is exactly what happened to Lowther who had his leg removed. Drake assures us that, at the time of writing his diary entry, Lowther was well on his way to recovery.

The garrison received a message that the King's Army was still marching north. Part of the army, under Prince Maurice, had marched into Lancashire with the objective of relieving Carlisle, while the remainder of the army, commanded by King Charles, continued its march its towards Pontefract. This must have buoyed the defenders' morale considerably but, as events were to prove, was completely false. During the night the besiegers opened up a heavy fire on the castle which grew even heavier towards dawn on the 25th. Drake reports the enemy firing volleys towards the castle and shouting 'A Cromwell, a Cromwell' and says that the besiegers' commanders had put out the story that Cromwell was advancing north in pursuit of the King. Again, this was a fallacy. The besiegers then set fire to several houses towards the lower end of Northgate and a water mill close to the castle, possibly the one on Mill Dam Lane, along with several houses close to it. A tailor and his wife were taken prisoner but the rest of the residents were able to flee to the castle. The garrison opened fire on the arsonists and killed one close to the mill door, which Drake said 'was an officer for certain' and wounded another in the shoulder. The garrison could see no reason for these acts of wanton vandalism, unless it was to encourage the locals who were slow in paying their assessments, a tax raised locally to help support the resident military forces, to put their hands in their pockets more promptly.

After the musket fire and arson during the night, the remainder of Whitsunday, the 25th, remained quiet, with little shooting by either side and no casualties. The garrison listened to two 'very good' sermons. The defenders went quietly to their beds, while outside the castle the besiegers reinforced their guards – they were nervous of a repeat of the previous Sunday's sally by the garrison.

Whitsuntide Monday saw the garrison reorganize some of its cannon. The iron gun was moved to a platform just outside the upper gatehouse, where it had been previously positioned. Once in place a shot was fired against the enemy's sentry house close to Alderman Rusby's. The shot was on target and the house's occupants, between forty and sixty, abandoned the house. At the same time a drake was raised to the roof of the Swillington Tower, where it promptly opened fire on the enemy troops manning their works at the Paradise Orchard.

During the day a number of parties left the castle to gather grass for the cattle and horses. Among them was one William Jubbe, who, accompanied by a boy, strayed too near the Parliamentary lines. The boy was shot through the cheeks, although the wound was not mortal and the lad escaped, while Jubbe was captured by the enemy and led into the town. His captors seem to have treated him well and many of them came to speak to him and plied him with 'strong Ale', thinking to befuddle him and gain intelligence from him. During the night Jubbe was escorted towards Newhall where he was to be questioned. He may not have been quite as drunk as his captors thought and, when his escort became a little negligent, he slipped away and returned to the castle.

Jubbe was not the only member of the garrison to return that night. Captain Washington returned from Sandal Castle with good news for the defenders. The King was still advancing northwards with the intention of relieving Pontefract Castle and the defenders of Scarborough Castle had managed to drive off their besiegers. The garrison was so overjoyed with this news that a bonfire was lit on top of the Round Tower. Unfortunately, neither piece of news was correct.

The bonfire was not the only fire to be seen in the vicinity of the castle on that day. Drake reports a fire in the enemy's works in Northgate. He puts the cause of the fire down to an accident and the enemy managed to put it out during the night. Three captains from the garrison held a short parley with three Parliamentary captains during the night. Unfortunately, Parliamentary musketeers opened fire on the group, which then caused the defenders to open fire. Needless to say, the two parties cut their discussions short and headed back to their own lines.

During the day on the 27th the fighting was low key. The garrison fired a couple of cannon shots: one into the Parliamentary positions close to Mr Rusby's house and the other through Mrs Oates's house which stood close to St Giles's Church in the Market Place. The occasional musket shot was also fired by both sides. Captain Joshua Walker, one of the castle's defenders, killed one of the besiegers in Primrose Close at the bottom of Baghill. The unfortunate soldier had gone into the close to have a quiet pipe of tobacco. The besiegers in turn wounded 'a little poore wench' who was tending a cow close to the Swillington Tower. The girl was hit in the thigh but the wound was not fatal.

The night of the 27th saw the next major sally from the castle. Lieutenant Wheatley, who had gone to Sandal Castle with Captain Washington on the previous Friday, set off back to Pontefract Castle with between forty and fifty horsemen from the Sandal garrison. On the way they captured two enemy scouts and their horses. They then came across a herd of between 120 and 130 cattle and decided to take them along with them to Pontefract Castle. If the Royalist force did capture the cattle on their journey, as Drake reports, rather than the cattle drive being a planned event, then Wheatley must have sent a messenger to the castle as by the time his men arrived in the vicinity of Chequerfield a major sortie had been prepared to support them. In fact, Drake states that the sortie was in place in the upper and lower baileys an hour before Wheatley's arrival.

As the cattle were been driven over Chequerfield, Wheatley became concerned that their lowing would alert the enemy sentries in their works on Baghill. Spurring his horse forward he galloped over Baghill and towards the closes underneath it, crying 'Armes, Armes, to your Armes, a prince, a prince' which was the signal for the sally to begin. At this signal all three 'Great Gunnes' fired and the garrison began to sally from the castle.

Captain Flood with Captain Ogleby, Ancient Killingbeck and fifty musketeers advanced up Baghill but were not to attack the enemy lines. Their task was to fire on the enemy should they leave their works and try to intercept Wheatley and his men. Lieutenant-Colonel Gilbraith with Lieutenants Smith and Ward and forty musketeers occupied a small enemy work in Primrose Close, under Baghill. The besiegers were driven back to the large triangular work on Baghill. Captain Smith, Lieutenant Ogleby and thirty musketeers went up Monkhill to Elizabeth Cattel's house and burnt houses around it. Smith and his men would prevent troops from Monkhill marching to the relief of their comrades on Baghill. Captain Munro, Captain Barthrome and Sergeant Barton, with an unspecified number of men, attacked past the All Saints' Church towards the enemy's works below and prevented the enemy within the works from reinforcing Baghill. Captain Joshua Walker with twenty musketeers moved through the houses on the south side of All Saints', through the closes to the top of Baghill, where he met with Wheatley. The various Royalist parties had isolated a section of Baghill through which the cattle could be driven to the castle's lower gate. It is interesting that these parties had orders not to enter the enemy works but simply to stop their occupants moving towards Baghill.

The Parliamentary forces manning their positions on Baghill during the night were so ashamed of the night's events that in the morning, according to Drake, they told their commander, Colonel Overton, that 500 enemy horsemen had escorted the cattle. In reprisal the besiegers opened a heavy fire on the castle for much of the day, with no loss to the defenders. Overton sent a drummer, accompanied by three women who owned some of the cattle which had been driven into the castle, with a message, haughtily demanding their return or the payment of compensation by the besiegers. Lowther's reply was hardly surprising: if they could take the castle they could have them back and he would not sell the cattle back to the besiegers for less than £40 for the worst cow brought in to the castle.

During the night of the 28th a party of ten or twelve men arrived from Sandal Castle. Having delivered their messages they began their return journey almost immediately. The Sandal men were to be escorted up to the enemy works on Monkhill by a party of musketeers, who would return to the castle once the Sandal party had passed through the enemy lines. As the party approached St Nicholas's Hospital the lighted match of the musketeers was spotted by an alert enemy sentry and the Parliamentary troops manning the works on Monkhill opened a rapid fire on the Royalists. One of the Sandal men was struck in the cheek by a musket ball and the Sandal men and musketeers then withdrew to the castle.

By 29 May the besiegers' grip on the castle had tightened to such an extent that sending horses and cattle out of the castle to graze had become very difficult. Colonel Lowther resorted to paying his men a bounty of 4d a trip when they went out of the castle to gather fodder for the animals. Drake reports one of the defenders, whom he describes as a covetous man, going out of the castle six times on the 29th and returning successfully. On his seventh trip he refused to return with the rest of the men and was shot and captured by the Parliamentarians. The party who captured him granted him quarter but another soldier ran him through with a sword and killed him.

During the afternoon a large party of Parliamentary soldiers marched from the town to Newhall to relieve the troops who had been positioned there for the past ten days. The Royalist guns on the King's Tower took the opportunity to open fire on Newhall while both bodies of enemy troops were there. About seven o'clock in the evening a party of 480 Parliamentary troops, the relieved guard, marched from Newhall back to the town through the Abbey Close. On other occasions the Royalist guns had bombarded troops marching to and from Newhall, and it seems that the besiegers had learnt their lesson well as they marched in single file. It would have been a waste of a cannonball, and the powder to fire it, to shoot at troops in single file as it was unlikely that more than one enemy soldier would have been hit with each shot. Another smaller party of Parliamentary troops marched in single file from Newhall to the town at about three o'clock in the morning.

The besiegers continued to tighten their grip on the castle during the night. A small triangular work was erected in the closes above Denwell, close to the Swillington Tower. The new work was intended to restrict the Royalist ability to sally out of the tower. When they spotted the new work on the morning of the 30th the defenders opened fire on it with a drake positioned on the Swillington Tower and caused the enemy to abandon it, but they returned during the night to repair and reman the position. Drake reports heavy fire from the Parliamentary positions all round the castle and the defenders fired the iron gun into the enemy works between Mr Rusby's and Mr Lunn's.

The last day of May saw heavy fire exchanged between both sides, mainly musketry but the Royalists fired six cannon shots, most of them towards the Market Place. Three wagons had arrived there during the night and the

Royalists observed enemy soldiers loading goods from Bonny Coup's and several other shops. After a couple of near misses from cannon fire the wagons hastily departed towards Ferrybridge. During the musketry exchanges one of the defenders killed a woman in the Market Place. At the distance between the castle and Market Place it is highly unlikely that this was intentional. Colonel Overton, the Parliamentary commander, sent a letter to Colonel Lowther to discuss a prisoner exchange and 'other matters', although Drake does not give any further details. He also mentions Lowther receiving letters containing 'very good newes'. Frustratingly, he does not say where these letters arrived from, although he does mention a couple of pieces of the good news. The first was that Sir Marmaduke Langdale had summoned Derby, which was incorrect. The second piece of news told of the breaking of the siege of Scarborough Castle, with the capture of a number of senior Parliamentary officers and the death of Sir John Meldrum, the Parliamentary commander. Meldrum was a professional Scots officer who had served Parliament faithfully since the start of the Civil Wars. Parliament seems to have used him to fight fires in the North, sending him wherever a steady hand was needed. He commanded the besieging forces at Scarborough and his death was correctly reported, although the siege had not been broken and would continue into August (see Chapter 6).

The first day of June was a Sunday and Drake reports the garrison having two good sermons. He also mentions a musketeer asleep on top of the Round Tower been struck in the thigh by a musket ball, probably a ricochet. The ball did not touch the bone and the soldier was expected to make a full recovery.

The morning of the 2nd saw a meeting of Parliamentary officers in their trenches behind Mr Rusby's and Mr Lunn's houses. The defenders took the opportunity to fire a round of case shot – fourteen large musket balls according to Drake – from the iron gun at the group. This shows how close the besiegers' trenches were to the castle. The Parliamentary officers dispersed quickly but the Royalists did not know whether any casualties had been caused among them. Following up on Overton's letter of 31 May, Lowther sent Mr Massey from the castle to the town to discuss an exchange of prisoners. The discussions were fruitful and an exchange was agreed, with Overton sending messages to Hull, and several other places where Royalist prisoners were being held, for the prisoners to be brought to Pontefract. Massey also heard enemy officers within the town telling their men that he had come to Colonel Overton to discuss the castle's surrender. This was definitely not the case and the castle's defenders put this lying down to the Parliamentary officers trying to improve their men's spirits. While Massey was with Overton another incident occurred which amply illustrated the parlous state of the besiegers' morale, when an officer entered the room and told Overton that he could not prevent his men from mutinying. Overton was 'not well pleased' that this had been said in front of Mr Massey who, no doubt, was eager to pass this intelligence on to the garrison!

During the night the besiegers continued to reinforce their lines around the castle, building a 'haulph moone' work in the closes below Baghill, close to All Saints' Church. Drake reports that at this stage of the siege the Parliamentarians had twenty-six works and trenches around the castle. He also states that, due to a lack of men, the besiegers were having difficulty in manning all their works.

On the 3rd Colonel Lowther received news from Newark that the King had stormed Leicester, killing and capturing many of the garrison. The King's intention was then to march to Derby and, once that town was captured, move north and relieve Pontefract. This news must have been very welcome to the garrison. Men continued to risk their lives going from the castle to gather fodder for the livestock held within. One soldier had gathered a load of grass and was crossing the drawbridge at the Lower Gate back into the castle when he was hit in the leg by a musket ball which did not break the bone and his full recovery was expected. Drake reports another soldier had been wounded on the 3rd. He was going from prayers to his watch position and was leaning on a gun close to the Upper Gate when a musket ball came through the embrasure and struck him in the arm. Passing through the arm it continued into the soldier's back and continued under the surface of the skin but did not break the bone. The soldier subsequently had the bullet cut out and was expected to make a full recovery. A large body of Parliamentary troops was seen gathering in the Market Place and a gun on the King's Tower was fired at them. Three or four casualties were seen being carried away. Cannon from the castle must have also been fired at the new half-moon work under Baghill. Drake does not mention this but does report a party of the enemy carrying out repairs to it.

On the following day another member of the garrison had a lucky escape. The soldier was sleeping in the lower bailey when a bullet ricocheted off the wall and struck him in the arm but, fortunately, did not break the bone and by the time Drake made the entry in his diary the soldier was well on his way to recovery. For most of the day the besiegers were quiet. Then, at about seven in the evening, as their guards changed they opened up a heavy fire from all around the castle which made the garrison think that an assault might be about to take place. Drake says that the Parliamentarians' 'fury lasted but a little' and the firing quickly abated with no casualties caused on the garrison. The cannon on the King's Tower attempted to bombard the half-moon work under Baghill but it was found that the gun's barrel could not be depressed low enough to hit the work. The besiegers carried on constructing new field works when they began another close to Zachary Stables's orchard. This work was probably close to the Knottingley road and about 100 yards from All Saints' Church. During the night a signal fire was seen on top of the keep of Sandal Castle and was replied to with a beacon on top of the Round Tower.

The 5th saw the garrison suffer another casualty while gathering fodder for the livestock, this time a boy who was an apprentice of Mr Richard Stables. The musketry between the two sides intensified and went on for most of the day, with the garrison causing at least two enemy casualties, one being an ensign. Having had no success on the previous day firing on the new Parliamentarian field works below Baghill with the gun on the King's Tower, the Royalists decided to use the iron gun in the upper bailey. Will Ingram, its gunner, shot three rounds into one of the enemy works, which the garrison thought had caused many casualties among the work's occupants. Although firing had gone on all day, it intensified as the Parliamentarians changed their guards, as it had on the previous day. The firing was so heavy that Drake reported that 'the muskittes and firelocks on both sides spared not any powder'. The Royalists caused at least two enemy casualties, one in Primrose Close below Baghill and one on top of the hill. As an illustration that life went on for the local population during the siege, Drake also reports the theft by Parliamentary troops of a number of hides from Peter Redman's tannery.

During the morning of the 6th a number of troops Parliamentarian horse were seen around the town. The garrison spotted four enemy soldiers stealing iron from the mill below Monkhill. One brave, or foolhardy, soul ran towards the mill, calling for his comrades to follow him. Three of the four thieves ran as the Royalist soldier approached but the fourth was too late and was captured and taken back into the castle. The prisoner explained that the troops of horse the garrison had seen earlier were newly arrived from Doncaster. He also said that part of the King's Army had reached as far north as Tuxford, between Newark and Doncaster and probably no more than a couple of days' march from Pontefract, but the Parliamentarian commanders had concealed it from their men until that morning. The prisoner confirmed that Will Ingram had killed two men in the work he had fired the iron gun into the previous night, one was an officer. He also gave news of how desperate the besiegers were for men. Overton, the Parliamentary commander, had given orders for all military-aged men in the villages within four miles of Pontefract to be woken from their sleep and brought to the town, where they were then conscripted into the Parliamentary Army. This was a measure to try and make up for the constant stream of deserters from the besieging forces.

Once again, the area of Baghill does not seem to have been a healthy one for the Parliamentary troops, with two more being shot on Baghill and a shot from the iron gun once more hitting one of their field works, this time the work close to Zachary Stables's house. Will Ingram also fired a shot from the iron gun into the Market Place where a crowd of enemy soldiers was gathered. At about midnight a strange incident took place. Five drummers left Newhall and spaced themselves between Newhall and the town side of the Abbey Close. They then began to beat a march in a similar manner to the Scottish army. Two further drummers in the town joined in the performance and a trumpet was heard sounding in the Park. Drake puts this elaborate charade down to an attempt by the enemy to fool the garrison into thinking that a force of Scots horse and foot had arrived to reinforce the besiegers. Far from been fooled, Drake tells us that the garrison 'never regarded it'.

The 7th was quiet until the Parliamentarians changed their guards in the evening when both sides began a heavy fire on the other. The Royalists initially opened fire to cover twenty of their men who were outside the castle foraging. The garrison made such a commotion with shouting and firing their muskets that the besiegers sounded the alarm and some of their troops advanced from their trenches close to the end of Broad Lane. The garrison drove the enemy back into their works, killing one and wounding another but in return one of their foragers was slightly wounded in the side.

Drake reports another incident on the 7th. At about ten in the morning a lone Parliamentary soldier was seen coming down Monkhill towards the mill. Two members of the garrison, Jonathan, Sir Jarvis Cutler's servant, and

Richard Laipidge, left the castle to intercept him. Jonathan captured the enemy soldier and escorted him back to the castle where he 'eased him of his money'. The soldier was then questioned but gave up little information as he was very drunk.

The following day was Sunday and the garrison were given two 'exceeding good' sermons by Mr Key and Mr Hirst. Nine Royalist prisoners were seen being escorted towards York but none of them had come from the garrison. The day was quiet with only sporadic exchanges of musketry. About six in the evening a large body of enemy horse appeared from the direction of Wenthill. Close to the town they divided and five troops marched towards Knottingley, almost coming with cannon range of the castle. The garrison later learnt that the horse had been part of a Parliamentary force quartered around Tickhill, Rossington and Doncaster but had marched north on hearing of the approach of a Royalist army, which seems unlikely unless it was a force from the Newark garrison. For some reason the Parliamentarians did not change their guards on Baghill at seven, the usual time, but at nine and both sides opened a heavy fire. The garrison killed one man and wounded another making their way down to one of the works below Baghill.

A lieutenant-colonel from the garrison sent his horse, a mare, and a foal to a close near the Swillington Tower to graze. A Parliamentary soldier crept down to the close, unobserved by the garrison, cut the mare's rope, jumped on her back and rode her away, calling to the garrison to collect the foal. Nine or ten Parliamentarian firelocks were concealed close by, waiting for members of the garrison to leave the castle and bring in the foal. The firelocks carried flintlock muskets and, therefore, did not have a glowing match to give their position away. This incident suggests a preplanned ambush by the Parliamentary troops but the Royalists did not leave the safety of the castle.

On the morning of the 9th one of the Royalist sentries standing on the Lower Gatehouse was struck in the back by a spent musket ball fired from Monkhill and dangerously wounded. The ball was not removed until four days later but the soldier recovered. During the night a strong body of horse had relieved the guard at Newhall and two riders were seen galloping towards the town, who the garrison assumed were messengers from York. A Parliamentarian drummer came to the lower bailey wall and reported that the King's Army had captured Derby. This seems a little strange. Even if the committee at York believed that Derby had been captured by the enemy, and passed the intelligence on to their field commanders, why would Colonel Overton have then passed the morale-boosting information on to the garrison? Drake also reports that cannon fire was heard several times in the distance during the day and the garrison supposed that it was the guns at Welbeck and Sheffield they could hear.

At about eight o'clock in the evening the besiegers opened fire from all around the castle and the garrison replied. Will Ingram shot his iron gun into the Market Place, where a large number of enemy soldiers had gathered as their guards were changed. The cannon ball bounced twice as it travelled along the Market Place. The garrison could not tell whether any of the enemy were injured but did see a 'great running away'! At about eleven o'clock one of the Sandal soldiers left Pontefract Castle to return to his home garrison and an hour later a signal fire was seen on the keep of Sandal Castle and replied to in kind from the roof of the Round Tower. It was thought that the signal fire presaged good news but it is unlikely it signified the arrival of the returning soldier.

A view of Baghill from the churchyard. The Parliamentarian siege works ran along the hill, below the houses in the background. The castle's Lower Bailey ran down as far as the road in the foreground, so it can be see how close the two sides were to one another.

On the morning of the 10th the garrison spotted the Parliamentary forces working on two new works, one at Moody's Close on Baghill and the other close to the Swillington Tower on the opposite side of the castle. The guards on the Swillington Tower opened fire on the enemy party and caused them to abandon their work. The garrison suffered another two casualties while taking livestock out of the castle to graze: a boy was shot in the cheek and a man was slightly wounded in the neck. During the night a number of bodies of Parliamentary horse were seen arriving and departing from the area. First, eight troops came from the direction of Doncaster and formed up near Carleton. They were then seen to march away in the direction of Hardwick. A troop came from the direction of Darrington and marched into Pontefract while a second troop came from Ferrybridge and marched to William Booth's in the Park. This troop then despatched half a dozen riders into town. Shortly afterwards eight men rode from the town back to the troop, which then split into several bodies and departed in four different directions.

On 11 June there was a major sally by the Royalist garrison. The morning passed quietly with only sporadic exchanges of musketry. Colonel Lowther, the garrison commander, ordered his men to arms at two in the afternoon. As the men formed up a heavy shower began to fall and the men took shelter. By four o'clock the rain had stopped and Lowther ordered his men to attack. Captain Munro, Lieutenant Moore and Sergeant Barton led a party of thirty musketeers to All Saints' Church. The church stood between the castle's defences and the besiegers' works. Munro found the church empty and his party pushed on to Mr Kellome's house, which stood close to the Knottingley road. Munro's party covered the right flank of the attack.

Following in Munro's wake came a party of eighty musketeers commanded by Captain Smith, Captain Flood, Ancient Killingbeck and Ancient Otway – Killingbeck and Otway both held the rank of ensign. Flood's task was to lead half the party in an attack on an enemy work close to Zachary Stables's house, again close to the Knottingley road about 100 yards beyond All Saints'. Smith took the other half of the party close to the enemy trenches to prevent a counter-attack against Smith's men. To prevent the Parliamentary troops at Newhall interfering a party of forty musketeers, commanded by Lieutenants Willoughby and Middleton, and Sergeant Parker occupied the Starre public house on the street running along the north side of the church. At the same time Lieutenant-Colonel Gilbraith and Lieutenants

Wheatley and Ward led a party of forty volunteers and musketeers into an orchard between the church and the enemy siege lines to form a reserve.

Flood led his men against the enemy work but had difficulty breaking into it. The work's only entrance was narrow and so low that a man had to stoop to pass through it. Frustrated at the entrance, Flood and his men then began to fire through the work's embrasures at the enemy troops inside, who fought bravely to hold their position. After a hard fight, eight or nine of the Parliamentary garrison climbed out over the side of the work and fled back towards Newhall. The Royalist musketeers opened fire on the fleeing enemy, wounding and capturing two of them. Captain Flood was now able to enter the enemy work as the remaining enemy troops were either dead or wounded. Inside the works the Royalists captured a captain, a sergeant, a corporal and eight other ranks, all 'soare wounded' according to Drake. Having cleared the enemy position the Royalists began a steady withdrawal to the castle, taking their prisoners with them.

While the main attack had been in progress beyond the church, Lieutenant Monks and Sergeant Barton led a party of twenty musketeers up Monkhill

At the time of the Civil Wars, the Starre inn stood opposite the All Saints' Church, where the modern houses are shown in the centre of the photograph.

to occupy the enemy in that area. Monks manoeuvred his men in such a way that the enemy thought several companies of Royalist troops were attacking them, which prevented the Parliamentarians from sending reinforcements towards Newhall. Monks kept this up until the drums in the castle beat the retreat.

The remainder of the garrison had not been idle. The remaining musketeers within the castle had manned their positions, ready to fire on any enemy troops attempting to relieve the assaulted position, and the remaining officers and volunteers formed a reserve in the lower bailey, ready to sally out should the need arise. The cannon within the castle opened up on the enemy positions. Will Ingram fired three rounds into a work on Baghill about 80 yards from the position Flood and his men were attacking. Ingram fired two cannon balls and then a round of case shot. The gun on the King's Tower fired a single shot towards Newhall.

It is possible that the attack on the enemy earthwork was a diversion for the reoccupation of All Saints' Church. Captain Joshua Walker with twenty firelocks was ordered to occupy the church and hold it for twenty-four hours. Once this had been done the drums were sounded for the attacking parties to withdraw. Walker's party occupied the steeple and opened a brisk fire on the Parliamentary troops who came to reoccupy the work Captain Flood had taken, killing or wounding twelve in the process.

For the loss of two wounded men, one of whom subsequently died, the Royalists had killed forty of the enemy and captured eleven. They had also captured a substantial amount of arms, ammunition and powder. After things had quietened down a number of the garrison went down to the area around All Saints' to gather fodder for the livestock – this may have been the main reason for the occupation of the church – and one of the party was killed and another wounded.

On the 12th Colonel Overton was visited by Lord Fairfax, the commander of Parliament's Northern Association, and General Poyntz, his soon-to-be replacement. The purpose of the visit was a tour of inspection as part of Fairfax's handover to Poyntz. The pair of generals was escorted by four troops of horse. Later in the day the generals, and their entourage, rode away in the direction of York.

There was little shooting from either side during most of the day but this changed as the Parliamentary sentries were being changed. The Parliamentary troops opened up a heavy fire from all of their field works and the garrison replied in kind. The Royalists were shooting so quickly and shouting so loudly that the besiegers suspected another sally was in the offing and deployed a number of troops of horse on the far side of Baghill, although once it was realized that the enemy was not about to sally from the castle, the horse returned to their quarters. The musketeers deployed in the church continued to harass the enemy in the nearby trenches, killing four during the course of the day. On the Royalist side, Drake reports Lieutenant Ward been wounded in the arm while he was going from the castle to All Saints'. Later in the day Captain Walker's party in the church was relieved with a similar party commanded by Captain Munro.

General Poyntz returned to Pontefract on the 13th. The Royalists thought that this was to gather all the Parliamentary horse in one place. Throughout the day the garrison worked on a trench from the castle's East Gate to All Saints' Church. The trench ran through Mr Taytom's orchard on the lower side of the Booths, where the present car park for the castle is situated. Blinds were erected between the church and Mr Kellome's house from boughs and earth sods, to give shelter to the men gathering fodder from the area. The Royalists were able to gather almost 100 man loads of grass behind the shelter of the blinds and covered by musket fire from the church steeple. The men in the steeple killed one enemy soldier and wounded four more on Baghill, close to Mr Kellome's. During the evening Lieutenant Willoughby and twenty-four musketeers relieved Captain Munro's party. During the relief the enemy opened a heavy fire on the church but the Royalists suffered no casualties.

An incident on the 14th illustrates how stretched the besieging Parliamentary forces were. Although the siege lines surrounded the castle, a single Royalist soldier was able to leave the castle and approach the enemy trench behind Mr Rusby's house. Finding only two sentries there he shot one of them while the other fled. He was then able to return to the castle unmolested. Willoughby's musketeers in the church continued to harass the enemy in their trenches, killing a woman who was delivering ale to the Parliamentary soldiers and wounding several of the enemy.

Every ten days the Parliamentary troops at Newhall were relieved. The garrison watched a body of about 320 men march from the town to Newhall. The relieved troops then marched back towards the town. Their march was interrupted by a shot from a cannon mounted on a roof close to the

Treasurer's Tower which killed all three men in one file. The iron gun also fired a shot into the town near Alderman John Wilkinson's house. The shot passed through several houses and, although the Royalists did not know if any enemy had been killed or injured, a number of Parliamentary troops were seen running from the houses. During the evening Captain Hemsworth, with twenty-six men, relieved Lieutenant Willoughby's party at the church.

Sunday the 15th seems to have been quiet until afternoon when a troop of Parliamentarian horse was seen marching down Bondgate by the gun crew on the King's Tower. It was too tempting a target not to fire at. The cannonball bounced among the horsemen, killing three men and horses and wounding several others. Several horses were seen galloping away without riders. Another cannon was fired at the houses close to Mr Rusby's. During the day two loaded wagons were seen moving through the Park, heading towards Ferrybridge, and another two heading for the same destination but via Chequerfield. The garrison suspected that all four wagons were loaded with wounded. As night approached the Parliamentarians relieved their guards and a heavy musketry exchange took place, although Drake says he did not hear of any casualties on either side. The besiegers were not the only ones to relieve their guards as Captain Cartwright, with twenty-six men, relieved Captain Hemsworth. During the night the Parliamentary troops dug a trench to the south of Mr Kellome's house in an attempt to stop the Royalists from gathering grass in the area.

Further south momentous events had been taking place. On 14 June 1645 Parliament's New Model Army, commanded by Sir Thomas Fairfax, had clashed with the King's Army at Naseby, near Market Harborough. In a hard-fought battle the Royalists were soundly beaten and the King's Army routed, losing most of its infantry in the process. The besieging forces at Pontefract received news of the great victory on the 16th. Drake tells us of 'great shooting, showting & rejoycing' by the enemy, who happily boasted of Fairfax's victory to the Royalists in the castle. General Poyntz sent a drummer to Colonel Lowther summoning him to surrender the castle. Lowther promptly gave a verbal answer to the drummer 'that he neither feared his [Poyntz's] forces not vallued his mercy' and bade the drummer to be gone and tell his master so. Later in the day Lowther received a letter from Colonel Washington at Newark. The letter was dated the 14th and told Lowther of the King being at Melton Mowbray and marching north. The Royalist army would be at Pontefract within ten days. By the time Washington had sent his letter the King had been defeated but the garrison assumed that its contents were true and that news of the King's defeat was merely a ploy by Poyntz to trick the garrison into surrender.

Prior to the besiegers receiving news of the victory at Naseby, a number of Royalists had gone out of the castle to gather fodder for the livestock. The boy who was shot in the cheek about a week before was among them. Having had one lucky escape, he decided to risk another. He approached the Parliamentary lines and began to abuse the enemy soldiers asking them why 'durst they not shoot'. A musket ball through the body was their reply! The same ball hit another of the Royalist foraging party in the thigh. It was doubted that the boy would recover but the surgeons expected the man to make a full recovery.

During the day a number of troops of horse arrived at the town and settled into quarters. The cannon on the King's Tower fired three shots at the Parliamentary cavalry: two of them at two troops of horse on Baghill and another at a troop of horse in the Market Place, although the garrison was unsure whether the shots had caused any casualties. Four or five loaded wagons were seen departing from the town and heading towards Ferrybridge. It was now Captain Smith's turn to man All Saint's Church, along with twenty musketeers. The besiegers continued their attempts to prevent the Royalists from gathering fodder in the area by Mr Kellome's house by digging a trench through two small closes near the house.

On the 17th the Parliamentarians continued to work on their positions beyond the church. They attempted to enlarge the work that had been attacked by Captain Flood on the 11th but were driven into cover by musket fire from the men in All Saints' Church and, so Drake reports, 'durst not looke whilst it was light'. Throughout the day the garrison observed a large number of loaded wagons leaving Pontefract in the direction of Ferrybridge. This must have reinforced their belief that the King was on his way to relieve them and Drake tells us that by about eight in the evening the Royalist soldiers were 'disposed to be very merry' having been told that the letters the enemy had sent into the castle the previous day were all lies. The commotion made by the Royalists, both in the castle and the church, caused the besiegers to stand to their arms. As a number of Parliamentary troops formed up in the Market Place, the garrison took the opportunity to fire the iron gun through 'a howse upon the bridge' into them. It is possible that the 'howse upon the bridge' was the castle's guardhouse which stood in the barbican. The building still stands today. During the evening Lieutenant Wheatley and twenty musketeers assumed responsibility for guarding All Saints' Church.

The 18th saw the arrival of two letters from Newark. Once again these letters said that the King would be at Melton Mowbray on the Sunday and at Newark by Tuesday, from where he would march to the castle's relief. This false information buoyed up the garrison's morale. They also heard that General Poyntz and his senior commanders, including Colonel Overton, were holding a council of war close to Doncaster. A convoy of wagons – Drake says thirteen to fifteen – was seen leaving Ferrybridge and heading down the road to Doncaster. As the convoy was escorted by four troops of horse and 'some foote' it was assumed that it was carrying arms and ammunition. The fact that the local Parliamentary commander and his senior officers were near Doncaster and an arms convoy was seen heading towards the same town, may have reinforced the Royalists' belief that the King was on his way to relieve them and the Parliamentary forces were preparing to block his march from Newark to Pontefract at, or close to, Doncaster.

The rest of the day was quiet with little firing by either side. Drake does report a cow grazing in the churchyard being hit by a musket ball. It was immediately driven back to the castle and slaughtered. The men manning the church were relieved by Captain Kitchen and twenty musketeers. About eleven at night a bonfire was lit on top of the Round Tower and was replied to from Sandal Castle's keep. The garrison took this to mean that the garrison at Wakefield had also heard news of the King's supposed advance.

On the 19th Drake reports the return of General Poyntz and Colonel Overton to Pontefract. The convoy which had passed through Ferrybridge towards Doncaster on the previous day was also seen to retrace its route. The Parliamentary troops spent most of the day mustering and making 'great posting up & downe, never resting' but there was little firing on either side. Drake does mention Will Ingram firing one shot with the iron gun at a body of enemy troops forming in the Market Place. The cannon ball landed just in front of them and then bounced through them, a perfect shot but the garrison could not tell if any casualties had been caused.

The evening saw Captain Joshua Walker, and his twenty firelocks, assume responsibility for All Saints'. Walker's men shot and killed two Parliamentary soldiers shortly after their arrival at the church. At about eleven o'clock that night Captain Washington and Lieutenant Emson left the castle to try and reach Newark. They went up Denwell Lane and then through the closes. The garrison listened intently for any shots which would mean that the pair had been spotted. No such shots were heard. Once again a bonfire was seen of the keep of Sandal Castle and replied to from the Round Tower.

The mystery of the King's defeat or advance, depending on which letters one believed, continued on the 20th. It is worth quoting Drake's entry at length:

> This day we had newes brought us of the Battell wch the enemy gott against the Kinges force neare Harborow as they was Coming from Oxford, upon Fridday night & Saturday the 13th & 14th of this Instant. But upon Sunday morning, Genrall Goring wth Genrall Jarett Came in the Rescue, & plaid theire p'tes bravely, both that Day & the day following, and recovered all the 12 peeses of Cannon was lost before, & all the forces the enemy had taken, wth all theire ammunition, where (it is said) that Gen. Cromwell was slayne, & we gave them Chase to Northampton from whence the enemy had drawen allmost all the Forces was in the Towne to the Battell. Thus the newes Came to us.

Although this letter does admit to the King having lost the initial battle, losing twelve cannon and a large number of men captured, it then goes on to say that Goring and Jarett recovered both guns and prisoners and Cromwell had been killed. Unfortunately for the Royalist cause, neither of the latter two pieces of intelligence was true. Goring was in the West Country and Cromwell was far from dead. The remnants of the King's Army, mainly cavalry, were in full retreat.

Jumping forward to the next day, Drake reports a Parliamentary deserter coming to the castle and telling his interrogators that the King had lost a battle but had recovered and routed the Parliamentary forces opposing him. It is difficult to ascertain whether the besieging forces at Pontefract had received similar intelligence to the castle's garrison or whether a member of the garrison had shouted the information to someone in the siege lines and the rumour had spread from there.

During the afternoon of the 20th the Parliamentary commanders put the next part of their plan to take All Saints' Church into action. The Royalists had noticed a new work being raised on Monkhill during the past two nights. Several wagons were seen to arrive at Newhall and then continue on to the new work. The wagons had come over St Thomas's Hill and had been fired on once, but not halted, by the cannon on the King's Tower. One of the wagons was carrying a cannon and the others powder and ammunition. Towards nightfall a wagon full of planks went from the town, through the Park and on to Monkhill, where it was unloaded at the new earthwork. The Parliamentary troops continued to build the work during the night and into the 21st, ready for the cannon to be mounted in it. The convoy of wagons was accompanied by a body of ninety foot, newly arrayed men according to Drake. They too had been engaged by the gun on the King's Tower but it was not known by the garrison whether any casualties had been caused by the two shots. The footmen continued past Newhall, through the Park and into the town. They marched from Newhall to the town in single file, seemingly taking notice that they were in range of the enemy guns. It was the turn of Lieutenant Smith to assume command of the church with twenty musketeers. Once again both Pontefract and Sandal Castles lit bonfires on their highest points to signal the other.

Earlier in the siege, the besiegers had burnt a number of houses on Monkhill and some of their inhabitants had come to the castle for shelter. One of these unfortunates, a man, left the castle to gather grass for the livestock on the morning of the 21st. Close to the mill below Monkhill he was shot and killed. Members of the garrison went out that night and brought his body back for burial. The cannon on the King's Tower shot at the new gun position on Monkhill and a man working on the earthwork was shot by a musketeer in the castle. Other than these two incidents the day passed quietly. News arrived from Newark that the Royalist garrison had carried out a raid on a large force of enemy horse and had captured or killed 500 – this smacks of another piece of misinformation to buoy up the garrison's spirits.

The besiegers continued their work on the gun position on Monkhill, chivvied on by a visit from their commander, Colonel Overton. By nightfall the position was finished and the gun readied for use on the next day. In answer to this the Royalists began to build a new work by the East Gate. Lieutenant Willoughby and twenty musketeers prepared to occupy the church for the next twenty-four hours. As has already been mentioned, a deserter came into the castle during the night. Not only did he confirm the intelligence the garrison had received of the King's defeat and victory but he also confirmed that the Parliamentarians had conscripted all the able-bodied men from the villages around Pontefract.

Lieutenant Willoughby and his men in All Saints' had a rude awakening at about two in morning of the 22nd when a force of about 100 Parliamentary troops carried out a surprise assault on the church. Part of the assaulting force advanced up the trench between the church and the Castle's East Gate and others moved up the Booths. Willoughby's men in the church and steeple put up a brave fight, blasting the enemy with musketry and throwing stones down onto them. The men in the castle were alerted by the gunfire and by the ringing of the church bell. Musketeers manned the walls and opened fire on the enemy advancing up the Booths, the street running between the church and the castle, and the trench, driving them back towards the churchyard. Other members of the garrison sallied out of the East Gate and at this point the Parliamentarians broke and fled back to their siege lines, taking their dead and wounded with them. Some of the Parliamentary troops took shelter in Mr Kellome's house but soon abandoned it for the safety of their trenches. The fight had lasted only half an hour and at least four or five of the assault force had been killed and numerous others wounded.

With the failure of the attack, the gun in the earthwork on Monkhill began to fire on the church, using the lantern on the steeple as its aiming point. It kept up a steady bombardment for one and a half hours, firing thirteen shots during that time. The gun on the King's Tower opened fire on the enemy gun position and with its fifth shot dismounted the gun from its carriage, preventing it firing for the rest of the day. With this the firing quieted. Little movement was seen in the siege lines. During the afternoon a body of 400 foot marched from the town to Newhall to replace the troops manning the lines in that area, who promptly marched back to the town. The Royalists also changed their guards at the church, with Lieutenant Fevell and his men relieving Willoughby's tired party. During the night Drake reports that 'the enemies Officers from all theire workes neare the Castle tould us so many abominable & apparent lyes as is a shame to heare them related'. Although Drake does not elaborate on what their 'lyes' were, it is likely that the Parliamentary officers were merely shouting news of the King's defeat at Naseby, which, if this was the case, was far from lies.

At two o'clock in the morning of the 23rd the repaired Parliamentarian gun on Monkhill opened fire on the church once more. It fired once but could not tell whether it had hit the church or not. It then fell silent until it started getting light, when it started up a steady bombardment of the church. After sixteen shots a hole had been made in one side of the church's lantern. The gunners then changed their aim to hit the steeple below the bell. They fired eight shots at the steeple and then a single shot at the castle's East Gate. At just before 6am the gun ceased fire and remained silent until just after noon when it again opened fired on the church and steeple. The gun fired sixty rounds during the course of the day, fifty-nine of them at the church. Other than the cannon fire, the day passed quietly with little musket fire, although one unfortunate Royalist soldier sleeping in what he thought was a safe place, in the lower bailey, was struck in the arm by a ricocheting musket ball. During the day a cannon and seventy-four newly conscripted foot soldiers were seen coming from the direction of Ferrybridge. The foot soldiers marched in single file through the Park to the town.

It was Lieutenant Moore's turn to guard the church. Expecting another enemy attack during the early hours of the next morning, Colonel Lowther had given him orders to leave only two sentries in the church and to take the rest of his men to occupy the houses on the north side of the church, where they could engage any attackers from an unsuspected direction. During the night the iron gun was moved from its position in front of the upper gatehouse to a new position in the garden of the guardhouse, where a small earthwork had been raised to shelter it. From here it had a good line of sight to the church. At one o'clock in the morning of the 24th a single shot was fired from the Parliamentary gun on Monkhill, which was the signal for the attack to begin. As the Parliamentarians attacked the churchyard, Lieutenant Moore's men opened fire on them from their right flank and the iron gun, which had been sighted on the church and loaded ready, fired into the church. The attackers had hoped to take the Royalists by surprise but had themselves been surprised by musket fire from their flank and cannon fire from their front. The Parliamentary troops quickly withdrew to their siege lines, taking their casualties with them.

The remainder of the 24th was quiet until about five in the afternoon when the iron gun fired a single shot into the Parliamentary works below the church. The enemy responded by firing a single shot from the gun on Monkhill at the church steeple. As the besiegers changed their guards during the evening a heavy musket fire was opened up by both sides, with little hurt to either except for a Royalist soldier outside the castle gathering apples, who was shot in the leg. During the evening Ancient Otway took two files of musketeers to relieve the guards at All Saints'. Lowther had decided that the enemy would attack the church again during the night and had given Otway orders to abandon the church and bring his men back to the castle once tattoo had sounded at ten o'clock, when it would be dark enough to carry out the manoeuvre unobserved by the enemy.

The early hours of the 25th would see Lowther proved right. The Parliamentarian assault force attacked at one in the morning and entered the church and the houses about it. In the castle Royalist musketeers manned the walls and waited for the enemy to occupy the church, before opening a heavy fire on them. The gun on the King's Tower fired five shots into the steeple and the iron gun fired five shots into the church. With sunrise, the Parliamentary troops were seen to be raising an earthwork in the churchyard, between the church and the castle – Drake mentions them 'digging up dead men's Corpses'. He also reports the death of Sir Jarvis Cutler, who had been ill for some time. Drake laments that the enemy would not allow any fresh meat to be brought in to the knight while he lay ill, except for one chicken and 'one poore Joynt' which his wife had brought in with her two days

St Giles's Church stands in the Market Place. It was often referred to as the Upper Church in Civil Wars documents.

earlier, and that the enemy would not allow Sir Jarvis to buried in the churchyard or to be taken and buried with his ancestors. During the night the iron gun fired a single round into the church but the enemy made no reply.

Little military action took place on the 26th. The garrison, denied permission to bury Sir Jarvis Cutler outside the castle, committed the knight's body to the ground in the chapel inside the walls. The body had first been prepared and laid in a coffin, then the coffin was wrapped in a lead sheet. Three volleys were fired over the grave to honour 'such a brave souldyer as he was'. It was hoped that Cutler's friends would be able to retrieve the coffin and bury Sir Jarvis somewhere more appropriate when the siege was over. The besiegers refused to allow Lady Cutler to leave the castle and return to her family home and children. Two of the remaining Sandal men left the castle during the night to return to their own garrison.

Drake tells us of a rogue leaving the castle during the night and deserting to the enemy. The man's name was Metcalfe and he had been attending to Alexander Metcalfe, who was bedridden with gout – Drake does not elaborate on whether the two were related. The deserter stole a riding coat, a doublet, a pair of breeches, a pair of stockings, a pair of shoes, a hat and a rapier. Metcalfe's company had the watch that night and he climbed over the barbican wall to escape. Metcalfe's mischief for the night was not yet over. A surgeon and drummer from the Parliamentary army regularly visited the castle to tend to the wounded prisoners and to take rations in for them. Metcalfe told the besiegers that the surgeon and drummer had also passed news on to the garrison and taken tobacco in for them. The pair were immediately imprisoned.

On the 27th the garrison saw a number of troops of enemy horse form up close to the town and by Newhall. The troops near the town marched along the high road to Carleton and those at Newhall marched around the back of Baghill to the same place. Once the troops had arrived at Carleton they were seen to retrace their steps. The garrison took this to be a ploy by the Parliamentary commanders to fool the Royalists into thinking that a number of fresh troops had arrived to reinforce the besieging force. Drake reports that the ploy did not work and was 'little respected'.

The Parliamentarians were also seen to hold at least two thanksgiving sermons during the day, at both the town and Newhall. The garrison assumed that the besiegers had received news of a great victory. As part of the celebrations, the soldiers in their field works fired two volleys of musketry at the castle – if they were going to fire two celebratory volleys they might as well point their weapons in the direction of the enemy! The besiegers also fired two cannon at the castle's lower gate. After this a desultory exchange of musket fire continued. Two men in the lower bailey were struck and lightly wounded by the same musket ball, fired from Baghill. The Royalists manning the Round Tower opened fire on the enemy in the trenches behind Mr Rusby's house, killing one of them. During the night a signal fire was seen on the keep of Sandal Castle and was replied to from the Round Tower.

News reached the garrison on the 28th that the Scots had begun to blockade Newark in preparation for a formal siege of the town. The message went on to say that the Newark garrison had sallied out of the town and driven the Scots off with heavy loss (500 horse and foot). The Scots had withdrawn and were camped between Doncaster and Rotherham. During the evening Colonel Overton sent a drummer down to the castle with a message that Lady Cutler could leave and return home. Her chaplain and one of her tenants came down to the castle's sally port to meet the lady and a maid and accompany them back to the town. When Lady Cutler's party reached the first Parliamentary guard they were stopped, forced to strip down to their undergarments and searched for any letters they were trying to bring out of the castle. They were then held at the guard post until noon on the following day and not allowed to continue up into the town. Although Overton had given her permission to leave, his direct superior, General Poyntz, had countermanded Overton's instructions. One of the garrison's horses had been driven out into the moat to feed. Not been satisfied with the grass in the moat it had strayed a little further and the Parliamentary musketeers opened a heavy fire against it. Several Royalists ran from the castle to recover the horse and the enemy turned their fire on them. They reached the horse and brought it back into the castle, all unmolested. The Royalist musketeers opened fire to cover their comrades and killed an enemy soldier.

Sunday the 29th was mainly quiet, being a Sunday. At about noon, General Poyntz sent Lady Cutler back to the castle with her waiting maid. Neither of the women had eaten in the last twenty-four hours. Colonel Lowther refused to let her back in as the besiegers had sent for her and said they would allow her to return home. The poor women, and Lady Cutler's chaplain, remained in no-man's-land, without food or water, until ten o'clock that night, when

Poyntz sent for her to come up into the town. She then sent for two horses and returned home the following day. During the night two fires were seen on the keep at Sandal Castle, which were answered by a single fire on the Round Tower. The garrison took the two fires to be a signal of good news.

The last day of June saw a large number of Parliamentary horse passing to and fro in sight of the castle. Troops came from all directions and gathered at a general rendezvous at Brotherton Marsh. The Royalists thought there were at least 1,000 horsemen. One troop had passed over St Thomas's Hill and the cannon on the King's Tower fired a single shot at them but failed to cause any casualties. After the rendezvous the troops of horse went their separate ways. Four hundred horsemen rode up Baghill and faced the castle, before about facing, riding down the rear of the hill and camping there. Others rode through the Park towards Featherstone, while another body camped on the western side of the town close to Clay Dyke. Still more marched to Carleton and the villages close to it and the remainder camped at Ferrybridge and Knottingley. The influx of cavalrymen led the garrison to believe that most of the Parliamentary forces in Yorkshire had gathered close to Pontefract and took this as a sign that they had gathered to block a Royalist force on their way to relieve the castle.

Drake recounts another attempt by the besiegers to fool the garrison into thinking they had more men available than they had. Six hundred foot marched from the town to relieve the guards on Monkhill and at Newhall. A similar size force was seen marching back to the town shortly afterwards. Drake is certain that this was a ploy and the enemy had only left about 300 men at Newhall. During the evening a convoy of seven or eight wagons was seen to arrive at the town. For some reason, which Drake does not state, Colonel Lowther expected an assault on the castle during the night and doubled his guards. The Royalists kept a close watch on the enemy but instead of an assault they heard a large number of axes chopping wood. The enemy had spent the night chopping boughs to make faggots with which to build barricades and one such barricade had been built close to William Farrow's house.

On 1 July the besiegers continued to put the boughs to good use. A barricade was built across Baghill Lane and from the end of the barricade a trench was dug running along the line of the hedge behind Zachary Stables's house. The Parliamentary musketeers manned the new trench and barricade, which had loopholes cut in it to allow muskets to fire through, and opened a heavy fire on the castle, which was replied to in kind, with a number of Parliamentary soldiers seen to fall within their works. The Royalists also fired the gun on the King's Tower into the Market Place but were unable to see if any casualties had been caused. During the evening the besiegers were seen to bring a number of ladders and faggots down into the lower part of the town, which made the Royalists suspect an assault was imminent. Colonel Lowther ordered the guards to be doubled and that the bulk of his remaining men were to stand to in the inner bailey at midnight – Drake says that this was done willingly.

The morning of the 2nd saw one of the garrison on top of the Gatehouse Tower in a shouted conversation with one of the besiegers in a nearby trench. Another Parliamentary musketeer spotted the Royalist soldier, shooting him through the head and killing him instantly. The Parliamentary cannon on Baghill fired a single shot at the East Gate, missing the gate and striking the wall close to it. The spent cannonball rolled underneath the gate's drawbridge. The Royalists also fired several cannon shots. The 'Dutchman' fired his cannon, mounted on a roof near the Treasurer's Tower, into the Market Place. Several of the enemy were seen to fall and the remainder ran for cover. The gun on the King's Tower fired a shot among a troop of Parliamentary horse in Baghill Lane. How many of the horsemen had been hurt was difficult to ascertain but one horse was seen galloping away without its rider. Another shot was fired by the same gun at another troop of horse in the Frealles an area of closes running along the Knottingley road which had originally belonged to St John's Priory, with no discernible effect.

Once again, towards nightfall, a large number of enemy horse were seen moving and encamping all around the area, at least fifteen troops. The enemy movements made Colonel Lowther suspect an assault, as he had the previous night, and he ordered the guards, both of soldiers and volunteers, to be doubled. Drake puts forward a very plausible reason for the Parliamentary horse's comings and goings. He suggests that Poyntz and Overton were not trying to surround the castle but were, in fact, surrounding their own foot soldiers, to try and stem the stream of deserters from becoming a flood.

The following morning, the 3rd, a large body of horse was seen leaving the town and at about noon more than twenty troops of horse returned. Towards nightfall the horsemen dispersed to their various encampments in preparation for a night of patrolling for deserters. General Poyntz despatched a trumpeter to the castle, requesting that Captain Clarke's mother could visit him. Clarke was a prisoner in the castle. His mother was accompanied by Dr Oyston. Poyntz also asked if he could send provisions to his men held as prisoners in the castle. Colonel Lowther granted permission for both requests to be carried out.

At some point in the day a heavy exchange of musketry broke out between the two sides, which went on for some time. The Royalists suffered no casualties but musketeers on the King's Tower shot several enemy soldiers in their works close to All Saints' Church. Although the enemy soldiers had been seen to fall the Royalists were not sure whether they had been killed or wounded. During the night two men were despatched to Sandal Castle, from where they would continue on to Newark. These two were not the only ones to leave the castle that night as a man from Captain Cartwright's company deserted to the enemy.

On the morning of the 4th the garrison saw that an alarm had been raised among the besieging force but not through any action of the garrison. All the horse that had been seen about the area on the previous day gathered together close to the town and a body of about 400 foot stood to their arms in the Market Place. The foot were carrying their knapsacks, as though they were about to march away. About noon the horse marched off in the direction of Wenthill and were seen formed in two bodies on a hill between Pontefract and Wenthill, where they remained for about half an hour. They then rode back towards Pontefract and halted at the Westfield, close to a stone windmill, where another large body of horse met them. Drake thought there was over 2,000 horse gathered together. They remained in the Westfield until six in the evening, when they began to disperse. Those who remained lit large bonfires. At eight o'clock a body of 100 foot marched from the town towards Ferrybridge and en route they were joined by fifty men from Newhall. Drake writes that the garrison supposed the enemy footmen were to act as a guard at Ferrybridge and prevent deserters crossing the river. After dark another two men were despatched to Sandal Castle.

The morning of the 5th saw the Parliamentary cannon on Monkhill turn its attention on the castle's East Gate. The cannon ball hit the ground about 20 yards short of the gate and caused no damage. Around three o'clock in the afternoon the cannon fired another round, this time with more accuracy. The ball struck and penetrated the raised drawbridge but did not have enough power left to penetrate the gate behind, falling to the floor between the two. Another cannon was seen by the garrison passing through the town into the West Field. Drake describes it as a 'small dimiculvarin [demiculverin] or some other smaule feeild peese'. The Parliamentarian horse gathered in the West Field and remained there for much of the day. Later in the day several troops of horse were seen to march through the Park and on to Newhall, before returning by the same route to the West Field. The garrison supposed that the enemy horse spent the night encamped in the field. Once again Colonel Lowther doubled the guards within the castle, expecting the Parliamentary troops to try an assault. No such assault took place. A pair of bonfires was seen on top of the keep of Sandal Castle and replied to with two bonfires on the Round Tower. The garrison took the two bonfires at Sandal to mean that a relief force was expected in two days.

The 6th was a Sunday and the garrison had two 'exceeding good sermons': one in the morning by Mr Key and another in the afternoon by Mr Hirst. There was little shooting between the two sides all day. Once again the Parliamentary horse drew up in the West Field, where they remained for most of the day. During the evening some troops left the field for various guard posts around the town. About nine o'clock an alarm was given by six trumpets and the horse gathered in the West Field before marching off in the direction of Doncaster. The foot soldiers in the town also stood to, fully armed and with lighted matches, ready for a fight. A Welshman in the Parliamentary trenches near the castle told one of his fellow countrymen inside the castle that the horse had marched towards Doncaster to fight 'the prince' (Prince Rupert). Unfortunately for the garrison, this was not true and the Parliamentary horse had returned to the West Field before morning. During the night the garrison had noticed a number of bonfires between Wentbridge and Doncaster and supposed that these were the campfires of enemy horse guards. The two men sent to Sandal on the 2nd returned during the night bringing a letter with 'very good newes'. Frustratingly, Drake does not illuminate us to what this news was, although, judging by previous messages to the garrison, it probably was news of the impending relief of the castle.

On the following morning a body of 200 Parliamentary horse marched through the Park and drew up in the Westfield. The Royalists thought these horsemen had come from Sandal Castle as the siege there had been raised.

The local Parliamentary forces were also reinforced by an undisclosed number of Scots horse and foot. The garrison seems to have got news of the Scots' arrival from conversations with enemy soldiers. All of the Parliamentary horse formed up in the West Field, where they remained, at arms, for most of the day. Towards nightfall seven or eight troops of horse were despatched in the direction of Carleton and Wentbridge and a number of other troops moved to a number of fields around the town. About ten o'clock an alarm sounded and the Parliamentary horse gathered in the West Field while the foot around the town lighted their matches and stood to arms. The garrison had little idea of why their opponents had stood to arms for the second consecutive night.

The Parliamentarian movements continued through the night. At about 4am on the 8th, a body of approximately seventy foot left the earthwork close to the Swillington Tower, marching through the town towards the West Field. A couple of hours later more than 1,000 foot marched from the West Field to the town. As the Parliamentarian foot had been stood to arms for most of the night, the garrison suspected that they were marching back to their quarters.

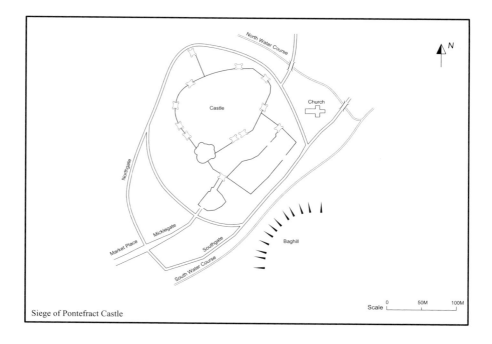

Siege of Pontefract Castle

The garrison heard that the foot had initially been drawn out from all the Parliamentary positions around the town to march to the West Field and the men seen marching into town had returned to the field. Most of the Parliamentary horse remained out of sight of the Royalists, behind a hill in the West Field. Towards nightfall several troops rode to the town where they quartered, while a number of troops marched away in the direction of Wentbridge. The Parliamentarians kept a strong guard close to Wentbridge which had an alarm during the night of the 8th. The remaining enemy horse was observed, by the Royalists, to encamp in the West Field, where two large bonfires were lit.

The 8th was also the tenth day since the besiegers had relieved their guards at Newhall, which they consistently did on a ten-day cycle. At about nine that night a large body of foot was seen to leave the town and make their way to Newhall and a similar sized body returned to the town. Drake also comments that the enemy's guards in their earthworks were changed later than usual. During the night General Poyntz, the Parliamentary commander, approached the barbican gate and asked to speak to Colonel Lowther. Lowther was not present but his son, a captain in the garrison, was and apologized for his father's absence. Poyntz then demanded the surrender of the castle and said that if it capitulated within three days the garrison would be given the honours of war. If they did not surrender for ten or fourteen days, then the garrison would be prisoners. Drake reports that Captain Lowther replied that the castle was kept for the king 'and if they stayd 14 daies & 14 daies more after that, there was as many Gentlemen wthin the Castle as would make many a bloody heade before they p'ted from it' – Drake adds 'or words to the like effeckte' after Lowther's reply. Poyntz began to get angry at the reply and the abuse of the Royalist soldiers watching the exchange. Captain Lowther replied that neither he nor his father could 'rule the Souldyers Tounges'. At this, Poyntz bade the captain goodnight and returned to the Parliamentary lines. This was not the only communication the garrison had with the enemy that night. Drake reports a number of Parliamentary soldiers speaking to their friends within the castle, telling the Royalists that the relief of the castle was impending and that they, the Parliamentary soldiers, intended to desert to the garrison before the Royalist relief force arrived. Yet again this shows how low the besiegers' morale was.

During the 9th the Royalists saw little movement within the enemy lines. They suspected the bulk of the Parliamentary horse was hidden behind the hill in Westfield but did see continuous cavalry patrols riding between the town and Newhall, both by Monkhill and Baghill. The patrols covered the full circuit of the siege works and may well have been watching for deserters among the foot. Both sides continued a heavy musket fire throughout the day. Drake says that the garrison did not know whether any of the enemy had been killed but doubted that casualties had not been caused by the weight of fire put out by the garrison. He does confirm that the Royalists had suffered no casualties even though members of the garrison had ventured outside the castle to collect grass and parsnips, as they had done on a regular basis for the past three weeks. Colonel Lowther despatched five men from the castle during the night, some to Sandal Castle and the remainder to the King's Army, if it was approaching, or Newark if it was not.

The heavy firing continued throughout the 10th. Drake expresses his surprise that the garrison was still able to collect grass from outside the castle, even though the enemy had dug numerous trenches to prevent them from doing so. The Parliamentary musketeers lay 'lurking' within their trenches to shoot at the Royalist foragers. Drake goes on to mention two casualties suffered by the garrison during the day. One of the garrison had climbed an apple tree to collect apples, where he was spotted and shot at by the enemy musketeers. The Royalist soldier was hit in the arm but only lightly wounded. The other Royalist casualty was not so lucky. As the garrison changed their guards, one of the first sentries to arrive on top of the Round Tower stood on a stone and looked out of an embrasure. A Parliamentary musketeer spotted him, fired and struck the Royalist in the head, killing him instantly.

The remainder of Drake's entry in his diary for the 10th is taken up with various pieces of information received from outside the castle. First he reports a letter arriving at the castle telling of a great victory by the West Country Royalists, commanded by George Goring, over the New Model Army, under Sir Thomas Fairfax. The Royalists had then gone on to capture Taunton. As heartening as this news was to the garrison, it was completely false. A Royalist drummer, from the Newark garrison, had arrived at Pontefract during the night to verify the story being put about by the Parliamentary forces that the castle had been surrendered. The drummer was not allowed to approach the castle, so it must have been obvious to him that the castle still held firm for the King. The drummer spent the night at Mr Washington's house, where he persuaded Mrs Washington to take a message to her husband who was a volunteer in the garrison. Mrs Washington was provided with a Parliamentary drummer as an escort and met her husband at the barbican sally port. While another Royalist carried on a conversation with the drummer, Mrs Washington was able to pass on the information that a relief force was only four or five days away. As she shook the hand of another member of the garrison of her acquaintance, she was able to pass two letters to him, unobserved by the drummer. During the evening two members of the garrison were despatched to Sandal Castle or the King's Army, whichever was most convenient. That night four bonfires were seen on Sandal Castle, which the garrison took to signify that the men who had left the castle on the 9th had arrived safely. The number of bonfires also agreed with the message delivered by Mrs Washington and was taken to mean the number of days before the relief force arrived. The garrison replied with a single bonfire on the Round Tower.

The Parliamentarians continued to manoeuvre their horse on the 11th. Four large bodies of horsemen formed up in the West Field, at about eight in the morning, with a smaller body some distance away. It appeared to the garrison that the enemy were exercising their men and this continued for about three hours. At this point most of the horse disappeared from view, some behind the hill in West Field and others, it was supposed, to Sandal Castle. Two of the Royalists sent to Sandal Castle two days earlier returned during the night of the 11th and reported that a large body of Parliamentary horse rode from Pontefract to Sandal each day. About nine o'clock four heavily loaded wagons, pulled by eight oxen each, were seen progressing through the Park to the town and then on to the West Field. Drake says that the garrison did not know whether the wagons carried rations or ammunition but were sure they carried one or the other. The Royalists also saw a number of enemy officers gathering for a council of war but had no idea what was being discussed. There was very little fire between the two sides, which Drake ascribes to it being a Friday which was a fast day – this is the only time this is mentioned. During the evening a pair of bonfires was spotted on top of Sandal Castle, to which the garrison replied with a single fire on the Round Tower. Two of the men who had been despatched to Newark ten days earlier returned to Pontefract. Unfortunately, the pair was unable to gain access to the castle but was able to signal to the garrison, which was taken as a sign of good news. Two men arrived from Sandal, as has already been mentioned, and were able to get to the castle.

Much of Drake's entry for the 12th is taken up with discussing the communications brought into the castle. The letters brought in by the two men from Sandal Castle informed the garrison that they could expect relief shortly. The two men who had arrived back from Newark had finally managed to get the letters they carried to Colonel Lowther. Unfortunately, the letters were in code and the key to their encryption could not be found initially. Once the letters had been decoded they were found to contain very good news for the garrison: the date and time when Sir Marmaduke Langdale intended to relieve the castle. They also confirmed that Sir Thomas Fairfax's Parliamentary Army had been soundly defeated by George Goring's Royalists in the West Country and Fairfax was nowhere to be found. Although both items of news must have raised the garrison's spirits, they would both prove to be false.

The day passed quietly, with little sign of the Parliamentary horse and little shooting between the two sides. Drake states that neither army suffered any casualties. The Parliamentarian forces began to fortify Ferrybridge and raised a number of works, including a gun mount, close to the bridge. It was thought by the garrison that the enemy was fortifying the town as a precaution against the approach of the expected relief force. During the night an alarm was raised in the besiegers' lines and Drake reports that the enemy 'Sounded theire Trumpitts, lighted theire matches and Calld to horse'. The besiegers stood to their arms through the rest of the night.

At four o'clock in the morning of Sunday the 13th, the Parliamentary horse was seen formed up in several large bodies in the West Field. The garrison also saw that a large part of the enemy army was now encamped in the West Field, including General Poyntz, and many of the foot in the siege works were moved back to the West Field during the night. Sixty foot were seen marching along the road from Ferrybridge and the Royalists assumed that these were newly conscripted men. The garrison also spotted the enemy moving a gun, a drake, through the Market Place, where it was positioned out of sight of the castle. The Royalists also had a report of a body of horse from Skipton Castle marching past Sandal Castle, possibly on their way to join with Langdale. Once again the Parliamentarian forces raised an alarm, which put the garrison into very high spirits. Drake reports the Royalists giving a great shout from the castle yard and then another three from the top of the Round Tower.

Monday saw the Parliamentary troops continue to build field works and raise their tents in the West Field. They also raised an earthwork to join the two triangular works close to the Swillington Tower, with numerous embrasures to fire through. The besiegers kept up a heavy fire on the castle for most of the day and the garrison replied in kind, although Drake was unaware of any casualties on either side. Two large bodies of horse were despatched to Doncaster and Sandal by the besiegers. As things quietened towards evening, the reason for the Parliamentary Army moving its quarters from the town into the West Field was communicated to the garrison by enemy troops. Plague had broken out within the town and earlier that day five soldiers, who had died in houses in the Barley Market, had been buried. One or two signal fires, Drake was not sure which, were seen on top of Sandal Castle's keep and a single fire was lit on the Round Tower to reply. Another bonfire was seen in the direction of Doncaster. Two men left the castle during the night to go to the King's Army but both failed. The first was betrayed by a boy who knew him at Knottingley and the second was spotted and pursued back to the castle by five enemy soldiers.

By the 15th the garrison was starting to get short of food. Twelve Royalist soldiers left the castle at about five in the morning to collect apples from an orchard in Northgate, close by the enemy's trenches. As they climbed the trees they were spotted and had to drop from the trees among the watching Parliamentary troops. Two of the Royalists were taken but the remainder escaped back to the castle unscathed, with the exception of one man who had received several blows before escaping. The besiegers dared the garrison to come out and recover their dead but it was later found out that the two had not been killed but taken prisoner. Another man left the castle to gather pears and was wounded in the cheek while climbing a tree. The fruit was not being gathered for the men to eat but to be sold to the women within the castle for anything up to sixpence each.

The Dutchman, who is not named in Drake's diary, was down in the lower bailey when a musket ball cut through his stockings but did not touch his legs. He then returned to his gun, close to the Treasurer's Tower. He was not having a good day as shortly afterwards a splinter of wood, caused by a musket ball, hit him on the leg but caused only a bruise. He observed four troops of horse marching through the Park towards Newhall. Expecting them to return along the same route he decided to get his own back on the enemy. He prepared his gun to fire and waited for the enemy to return. As they marched through the Park he fired a single shot which killed one man and his horse. Some of the Dutchman's comrades said they had seen three or four enemy fall but could not be certain of it.

In the afternoon a Parliamentary drummer approached the castle, first having stopped at the siege lines to give good news to the besieging soldiers. He announced that aid was coming soon as the New Model Army, commanded by Fairfax and his lieutenant-general, Oliver Cromwell, had routed both George Goring and Sir Marmaduke Langdale. The drummer then continued on to the castle and passed his message on to the garrison. Later in the day General Poyntz sent a trumpeter to the castle with a letter from himself and the committee in York. Drake reports the contents of the letter and Colonel Lowther's response:

> That whereas they had heretofore sent to sommone the Castle wch was still rejected, but now taking into Consideration the great Care & love to soe many Gentlemen and Souldyers wch weare wthin the Castle, and the miserye we lived in, and the effusion of so much innocent blood, wch there was likely to be made, and many a sackles man in it, they thought good once more to Sommond us and to give us to understand that if we pleased to Come to a treatye about the surrendering of the same, they would Treate wth us upon honourable tearmes, and wth Conditions fitting for such a garrison, & give hostages for the same, whereupon

The octagonal 'lantern' on top of the tower of All Saints' Church is a replacement for the one damaged by artillery fire from Monk Hill during the second siege.

Answer was given by the Governor, that it was a matter of too great a Consequence to treate or give answer at the First, but he would Conferre wth the knights and Gentlemen of the Castle, & returne answer as speedily as he Could (or words to that effeckt), whereupon the Trumpitt was sent away.

Lowther's response to the summons gives us an impression of how close the garrison was to running out of provisions. Previously, Lowther had rejected such summons out of hand but this time he agreed to discuss it with the knights and gentlemen of the garrison.

On the morning of the 16th another Royalist soldier was wounded while getting apples. The soldier fell from the apple tree after been struck in the head by a musket ball. At first he was given little chance of survival but by the afternoon had come round enough to speak and eat. Drake thought it was possible that he would survive. A Royalist musketeer on the Round Tower shot and killed an enemy soldier close to Mr Rusby's house. During the afternoon Colonel Lowther appointed Sir Richard Hutton, Sir Thomas Bland, Major Copley and Mr William Tindal to meet with four Parliamentary officers close to the castle, although they did not have authority to treat with the enemy, only 'to drink & be merry'! The weather was hot so the parties took shelter in the semi-ruined Halfpenny House close to All Saints' Church. The meeting continued for two hours and 'Sack & Ale' was sent from the town and, no doubt, consumed. While this was going on Colonel Lowther called a meeting of all the gentlemen, captains and volunteers to discuss what should be done. It was decided to send a deputation to treat with the besiegers, which would comprise Sir Richard Hutton, Sir John Ramsden and Sir George Wentworth for the gentry, Mr Hurst and Mr Key for the clergy, Mr Hodgson and Mr Hare for the volunteers, Mr Auspice and Mr Lunn for the townsmen and Lieutenant-Colonel Wheatley, Captain Hemsworth and Captain Munro for the soldiers. During this meeting a truce had been declared around the castle and members of the garrison and the besiegers mingled together to talk. Drake also reports a raid on an orchard by a mixed group of at least twenty men from each side.

Before noon on the 18th Colonel Lowther sent a drummer from the castle with a letter for General Poyntz, stating that the garrison was prepared to discuss terms, at a time and place appointed by Poyntz. The drummer was returned without an answer from the Parliamentary commander. There was little, if any, firing between the two sides and Drake reports the soldiers walking in the open and conversing with one another. About four o'clock Colonel Overton sent a drummer to the castle telling the governor that they would take their time to agree on whether or not to open discussions. An unnamed captain from the garrison had been outside the castle during the truce on the previous day and had told an enemy officer that the castle had only five days' provisions left, so it is hardly surprising that the Parliamentarians felt in no hurry to discuss terms. This seems to have become general knowledge among the Parliamentary forces and their soldiers told the garrison that they would starve them out, strip them of all their possessions when they were forced to surrender and pillage the castle.

The garrison was in dire straits but in the nick of time news arrived which raised their spirits and hardened their resolve. A letter arrived from Newark telling Lowther that Sir Marmaduke Langdale, with his horse and 4,000 Irish troops, had begun his approach march to the castle on the 12th and Mr Gervase Neville had been sent from Newark to Langdale to hasten his march. The letter also contained good news from the West Country and Scotland. From the West it was the old story of Goring defeating Sir Thomas Fairfax and had as little truth to it as previously. In Scotland James Graham, the Marquess of Montrose, had defeated a Scots Covenanter army and its commander, General Baillie, had been killed. Montrose was the King's commander in Scotland who had, with a rag-tag army of Irish and highlanders, carried out a highly successful campaign, tying up large forces of Covenanters in Scotland and preventing them from marching south to support Parliament in England. On 2 July 1645 Montrose clashed with Baillie's army and defeated it at Alford, so this part of the Newark letter was true. Lowther decided on a drastic measure to eke out the garrison's meagre remaining supplies and gathered all the supplies together, including the gentlemen's and volunteers' own private supplies, so that the remaining food could be rationed in equal measure between all members of the garrison. Drake goes on to mention that the rationing would keep the garrison on a reasonable diet but leaves a blank between 'for' and 'dayes'.

Lowther then requested Sir Richard Hutton and Sir George Wentworth to gather the garrison together in the castle yard and read out the letters from Colonel Overton and Newark. The two knights also explained that food would be rationed and that the gentlemen and volunteers were satisfied with their lot and would not surrender under the conditions set by the enemy.

Indeed, if relief did not arrive and the supplies ran out they would set fire to the castle and attempt to break through the enemy lines. The soldiers were of one accord with Hutton and Wentworth and gave three great cheers and threw their hats into the air. At this Lowther ordered 'flagges of defiance' to be raised, one on the King's Tower and the other on the Round Tower, a command which was quickly carried out.

The flags were not the only gesture of defiance Colonel Lowther ordered. His gunners were commanded to open fire on the enemy. The Dutchman was the first to open fire and his shot landed among, and bounced through, the enemy troops gathered in the Market Place. This was followed by a shot from the cannon on the King's Tower at Newhall. It was not known whether either of these shots had caused any casualties. Will Ingram's iron gun was moved from the inner bailey to its old position on the platform close to the Upper Gate, from where Ingram fired a round into the nearest enemy position. This time casualties were caused as a number of dead or wounded were seen being carried away. Ingram fired another round into the enemy works and then the Royalist musketeers opened a heavy fire on any targets they could see.

Poyntz and Overton had expected Royalist resistance to crumble once they had refused to discuss terms. The cheers from the castle and the heavy fusillade which followed them, pointed to their refusal having had the opposite effect. The Parliamentary commanders sent down a drummer with provisions for the Parliamentary prisoners held within the castle but his entry was refused. At about nine o'clock Colonel Overton sent down another drummer with a letter saying that he was sorry that his first drummer had not been allowed into the castle and requesting the Royalists to maintain the ceasefire until Poyntz, who had gone to York, returned. As another defiant gesture the Royalists lit a fire on top of the Round Tower.

Before ten in the morning of the 19th, General Poyntz sent a trumpeter with a letter to Colonel Lowther, informing him of the time and place for a parley. Poyntz would let Lowther know when things were ready. The trumpeter remained in the castle while a service was held and then returned to his own lines with Lowther's reply. A tent was set up in a close at the bottom of Baghill, near to the end of Broad Lane. At about four in the afternoon, Poyntz, Overton and nine of their officers came to the Barbican Gate where they were met by the Royalist deputation and then both proceeded to the tent. Drake gives the names of the representatives for both sides: Sir Richard Hutton, Sir John Ramsden, Sir George Wentworth, Lieutenant-Colonel Gilbraith and Mr Hirst for the Royalists and Mr Wasthill, a lawyer, Colonel Bright, Lieutenant Colonel Fairfax and Lieutenant Colonel Copley for Parliament. The meeting tent was surrounded on all sides by a guard of musketeers, positioned about 100 yards away. Discussions continued until nine in the evening without any firm agreement, other than that the two sides would meet again at nine in the morning. Poyntz and Overton joined the representatives and had a drink with them before the two sides returned to their own lines.

At about eight in the morning of the 19th the Dutchmen, having his gun primed and ready, fired a shot into the Market Place. Drake states that he did not know whether the Dutchman had been ordered to fire or not. This was the only cannon shot of the day and little musketry fire took place. Poyntz sent a trumpeter to escort the Royalist committee back to the meeting tent. Discussions did not go well initially and the Royalist committee made it clear that they would continue to fight unless an honourable agreement could be reached. The Royalist commissioners left the meeting to return to the castle but were intercepted by their Parliamentarian counterparts and asked to meet again on the 20th. On the following day the Parliamentarian commissioners reduced their demands and a concord was reached. The Royalist garrison would march out of the castle on 21 July 1645, with the full honours of war: their flags flying, matches lit and a musket ball in each musketeer's mouth. Every musketeer would also be allowed to carry six powder charges and musket balls.

And so the five-month second siege of Pontefract Castle came to an end. The Royalist garrison was far from beaten and seems to have had the better of the fighting. It was a shortage of rations which forced them to yield. Drake reports the garrison having lost 99 men, women and children to enemy action and disease during the seven months of the two sieges. The enemy had lost 762 men, women and children during the same period, dead and wounded. Unbowed, Lowther's men marched from the castle to join the garrison at Newark.

This would not be the last time that Pontefract Castle would be besieged. In the Second Civil War the castle would stand an even longer siege, from May 1648 until March 1649, and would be the last Royalist fortress to fall. The local inhabitants had had enough. While the castle remained defensible another siege was a possibility. A petition was sent to Parliament requesting the dismantling of the castle, which was agreed to. The work was carried out efficiently and the castle could no longer be defended. The locals must have heaved a sigh of relief.

Chapter 6

THE SIEGE OF
SCARBOROUGH CASTLE

The Early History of the Castle

Scarborough Castle is superbly situated on a headland surrounded on three sides by precipitous sea cliffs. Humans have inhabited the flat top of the headland for thousands of years. Fragments of Beaker pottery have been found dating to between 2100 and 1600 BC. Evidence of human habitation has also been found from the ninth and sixth centuries BC. In the fourth century AD the Romans built a signal station on the headland, the remains of which are still visible. It was thought that this was one of a series of signal stations running down the East Coast to act as an early warning system against Angle and Saxon raids, allowing time for the Roman land and naval forces to react. More recently doubts have begun to creep in as to the extent of the line of signal stations and their use. There are large gaps between the stations that have been found and it may be that the stations had a much more local use, simply warning the inland settlements of an impending raid.

The name Scarborough probably comes from Norse and means 'the man with the hare lip'. One candidate for this epithet was a Viking raider called Thorgils. The town was founded by the Vikings and it was also destroyed by the Vikings in 1066. In September 1066 King Harald Sigurdsson led a Norwegian invasion of the north of England. Part of his army landed close to Scarborough but was attacked by the local inhabitants. In reprisal the Norwegians built a large bonfire on the headland and threw bales of burning straw down onto the houses below. The destruction was so complete that the town is not mentioned in the Domesday Book.

The castle was founded during the 1130s by William le Gros, Count of Aumâle. Aumâle was created an earl in 1138 by King Stephen and became a major power in the area. The castle had been built in a royal manor and when Henry II acceded to the throne in 1154 he demanded the return of all royal property. Aumâle initially defied Henry but when the latter marched an army to York, the earl was brought to heel. At this point Scarborough became a royal castle and would continue to be so for many years. Henry began a phase of rebuilding at the castle and the royal Pipe Rolls show that £650 was spent during a ten-year period. It was also during Henry's reign that the town was refounded.

King John continued the improvements to the castle with a series of alterations and additions between 1202 and 1212. John spent more money on Scarborough than on any other castle in England, spending £2,291 according to the royal accounts. During John's rebuilding the curtain walls were extended, a hall was built in the inner bailey and a new royal residence in the outer bailey. During the civil wars in the latter part of John's reign the castle was garrisoned by a force of less than 100 men, including knights, footmen and crossbowmen, under the command of Geoffrey de Neville.

Henry III, John's son, continued to maintain the castle throughout his reign. The castle's position was defensibly superb but also left it open to the weather rolling in from the North Sea. Throughout the thirteenth century repairs had to be made to roofs and the curtain walls due to storm damage. Henry also made improvements to the barbican by building the gate tower with its two drawbridges. By the end of his reign the castle was one of the strongest in the country.

Edward I continued to use Scarborough Castle as a royal residence and Scots prisoners captured during his campaigning north of the border were held there. During the reign of Edward's son, Edward II, Scarborough Castle saw its first siege when one of the King's favourites, Piers Gaveston, was besieged there. When the castle was close to surrender, due to lack of provisions, Gaveston agreed safe conduct to the south with his besiegers. On his journey he was seized by one of his enemies, the Earl of Warwick, who had him beheaded in front of a very appreciative crowd.

During the later medieval period the castle seems to have gone into decline, not helped by unscrupulous guardians selling off parts of the castle's material. The last king to stay at the castle was Richard III, who spent time there during the summer of 1484 while he gathered his fleet to oppose Henry Tudor's expected invasion. The invasion was aborted but Tudor landed in Wales in 1485 and defeated, and killed, Richard at Bosworth on 22 August 1485. Henry was crowned as Henry VII and the Tudor dynasty was founded.

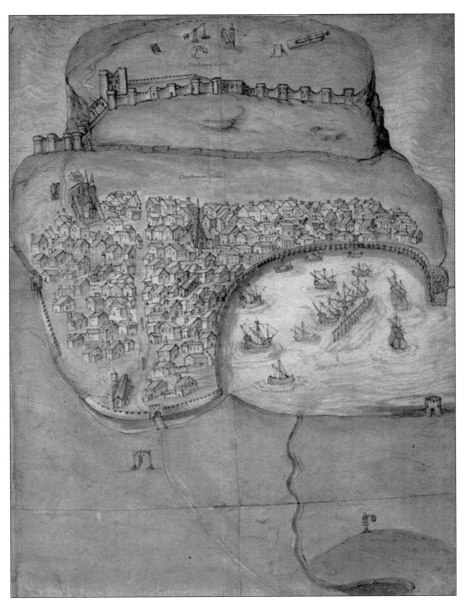

Plan of Scarborough from a 1547 survey.

Scarborough saw its next military action during the Pilgrimage of Grace in 1536 and 1537, when the northern counties of England rose against Henry VIII. Sir Ralph Eure held the castle for the King during this period and was besieged by local rebels. The rebellion eventually petered out and the siege ended. For his services Eure was awarded the guardianship of the castle for life. A survey carried out during 1538 reported damage to the castle caused by artillery fire. This would not be the last rebellion against a Tudor monarch which would result in military action at Scarborough Castle. On 25 April 1557 Thomas Stafford attempted to raise a popular revolt against Queen Mary and seized the castle. It is possible that the castle was so poorly guarded that Stafford's men simply walked through its gates and seized it. A short siege followed, only six days long, and Stafford was captured, taken to London and convicted of high treason. He was hanged, drawn and quartered at Tyburn on 28 May – his rebellion had lasted less than one month. His supporters were tried and executed at Scarborough and their bodies displayed. In 1569 a number of northern Catholic lords rebelled in support of the captive Mary, Queen of Scots. The rising failed but Queen Elizabeth garrisoned the castle and maintained the garrison until 1602.

With the accession of James I a new era of peace began. The king saw his royal castles as a drain on his often stretched finances. James was king of both England and Scotland and the likelihood of war between the two nations was much reduced, as was the need for northern fortresses A number of previously important castles were sold to private individuals. Scarborough Castle was purchased by an important local family, the Thompsons, who rented out most of the headland for grazing.

The Castle's Defences

Scarborough Castle had formidable defences. The headland is virtually surrounded by cliffs, both on the seaward and landward sides. The cliffs to the land side of the plateau had been further augmented by man into what were known as the Castle Dykes. A curtain wall was built along the full length of the Castle Dykes but was not continued along the sides of the plateau facing the sea – there was little need for defences as the sea cliffs were so precipitous. The curtain wall was reinforced by a number of towers.

The only approach to the castle was through the barbican. First, an attacker would have to break through the barbican's formidable gatehouse. From the gatehouse it was about 100 metres to the castle gate. The roadway between the two was sheltered by 5.5 metre high walls, complete with walkways and embrasures which allowed the defenders to fire into the flank of any attacker rash enough to try crossing the Castle Dykes. About 30 metres along the roadway sat a tower with drawbridges on either side, forming yet another layer of defence. If an attacker managed to cross the first drawbridge, take the tower and then cross the second drawbridge, he would still be faced with a 60 metre dash to the castle's gatehouse, flanked all the time from the keep, towering to the attacker's right, before the gatehouse itself could be assaulted.

The castle's medieval defences were further supplemented by two gun batteries. The first was below the southern end of the curtain wall and was approached through a sally port. The South Steel Battery, as it was known, was built to cover the harbour and the town. Another battery had been raised to protect the barbican gatehouse. This battery was called Bushell's Battery, after Captain Browne Bushell, a cousin of Sir Hugh Cholmley, the Royalist governor of Scarborough.

Just down the hill from the castle stands St Mary's Church, sections of which can still be seen lying in ruins. The church could act as an outlier to

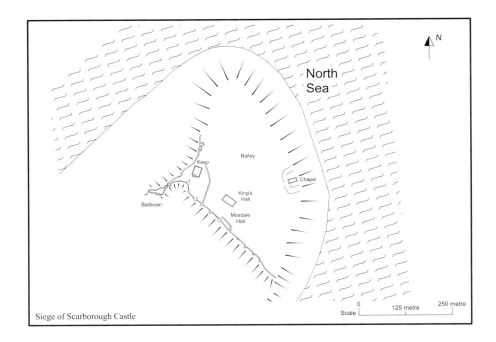

Siege of Scarborough Castle

the castle's main defences and had to be taken before an approach could be made on the barbican. It was defended briefly by the Royalists and once the Parliamentarians had captured it, used to site a battery to bombard the castle's keep.

Scarborough also had its own defences. The town had two main gates, each with a section of wall. The wall was not continuous and a large gap existed between the two sections. The town moat covered the whole south and west sides of the town, while the east was covered by the harbour and the sea and the north by the castle. The town's outer defences were not particularly strong but would have to be overcome before an attacker could approach the castle.

The Siege

In the aftermath of the Battle of Marston Moor (2 July 1644) the Marquess of Newcastle and Prince Rupert, the defeated Royalist commanders, both abandoned York. Rupert marched into North Yorkshire and then over the Pennines into Lancashire. He hoped to raise a force of sufficient strength to oppose the victorious Allied army and relieve York once again. It was not to be. Newcastle was of a very different mind. His army had nigh on been destroyed, with the exception of the cavalry which would continue to serve the King. The Northern Horse, commanded by Sir Marmaduke Langdale, became part of the King's Oxford Army. Newcastle had also exhausted his not inconsiderable fortune in financing the war in the North. His honour would not allow him to face the jibes of the king's courtiers and so he decided on an honourable exile on the Continent. Sir Hugh Cholmley tried to persuade Newcastle to fight on but the Marquess, and his entourage, departed for Hamburg. He would not return to England until after the restoration in 1660.

The garrison of Scarborough had not played a large role in the war up to this point. As both a Parliamentarian and Royalist commander, Sir Hugh Cholmley had led raids into the North and East Ridings. Troops from the garrison had also taken part in the abortive Siege of Hull in September and October 1643. As far as the war on land was concerned, Scarborough was a backwater and of little importance. Scarborough's importance, in Parliament's eyes, was as a base for Royalist privateers and as a port of arrival for arms shipments. The privateers played havoc with the coal trade between the northeastern ports (Newcastle and Sunderland) and London. In October 1644, twenty-two colliers were taken by privateers sailing out of Scarborough. Any interruption of the coal trade could cause major unrest among the chilled inhabitants of the capital. The worst of these privateers was Sir Hugh's cousin, Captain Browne Bushell, who operated across the North Sea and well into the English Channel. The only way to stop the Royalist attacks was to capture Scarborough and its harbour.

With the fall of York the Parliamentarian commander, Lord Fairfax, could turn his attention to the few remaining Royalist garrisons in the county and Scarborough was high on his list. Sir Hugh Cholmley was in an unenviable position. His garrison comprised only 300 foot and 200 horse, along with a number of gentlemen and volunteers. After the fall of Helmsley Castle on 22 November 1644, Sir Jordan Crossland and his remaining 100 men marched to Scarborough and were incorporated into the garrison. As well as a shortage of men, Sir Hugh was also short of powder and match, having only twenty-three barrels of powder and three bundles of match. Lord Fairfax was preparing to march to Scarborough and lay siege to the town. To forestall this Sir Hugh offered terms for the surrender of the town and castle to Parliament but insisted that he would only discuss terms directly with Parliament. Lord Fairfax granted a twenty-day truce while the terms were sent to London, discussed in Parliament and their answer returned. The terms offered were as follows:

1. That the Burgesses and other inhabitants of the Towne of Scarborough may enjoy all their privileges which formerly they did before the beginning of these troubles, and have freedom of trade both by sea or land, paying such duties and customs of other places do under the command of the King and Parliament.
2. That in all charges the Burgesses and inhabitants of Scarborough shall beare only such part with the country at large as was formerlye used in all other assessments.
3. That the garrison placed here be at least two parts of three, Yorkshire men.
4. That such officers and soldiers both of the Horse and foote, and all others who shall desire it, may have libertie to march with their horse and arms, colours flying, trumpets sounding, drums beating, matches lighted at both ends, to the Prince's army, or the next garrison which they shall make choice of, being allowed accommodation for their quarters, and not to march above ten miles a day, and every soldier to have 12 charges of powder with bullets and match proportionate.

5. That all persons who have any goods in the Town and Castle may have liberty to dispose of them in what place and in whose hands they will in the towne or carry them to what place they desire within the Kingdome or beyond the seas, and to have protection and passes for their securitie and better conduct of their said goods.

6. That all and every person of what quality or degree so ever, which is with in the towne or castle at the rendition thereof, may have free power and liberty to remove himself and family, and to live att his own house or else where as he pleaseth and to pass and travel quietly about his occasions with out molestations, and to have protections and passes from the three Generals at York for his and their better security.

7. That all officers, soldiers, Gentlemen, Townsmen and every other person which shall be in the towne or castle at the rendition thereof, may have power and liberty to depart with their arms, and dispose of their estates reall and personall as they please, and shall not be charged with other taxes and payments than is charged upon the country in general, and paid in a proportionate way by those who are of the Parliament's side and party.

8. That all and every person that hath interest in any ship now lying in the harbour or belonging to the towne, may have power and liberty to dispose of the said ship and ordnance tackling and all things belonging to her, as they please to their best advantage.

9. That all clergy men which are now in the Towne and shall be at the rendition thereof, and are now dispossessed of there spirituall or temporall livings by reasons of these troubles, may be restored to them, and enjoy their estates, real and personal and dispose the same as they please, and that they may live quietly at their own houses and have protection from the three Generals in York for that purpose.

10. That no man with in the town or castle at the Rendition thereof be enforced to take any oath other than such as is settled by Act of Parliament, not troubled or molested for refusing any oath not settled by Act of Parliament.

11. That neither the Governor nor anie under his command be questioned for any matter or thing that hath been done or acted by them or any of them either by sea or land.

12. That the votes passed against the Governor in the House of Commons be revoked, and that he be put in the same capacity he was before they passed.

13. That the Governor may have liberty to pass to what country he please beyond the seas, and power to dispose his estate reall and personall as he pleases, and protections from the three Generalls for himself and his servants for better security in this point.
14. That the Governor's wife may have liberty to live at his house in Whitby without molestation, and that the soldiers there may be removed and noe other put in their place.
15. That when the town and castle be rendered, Sir Henry Cholmley, brother to Sir Hugh may be governor of the place and have command in chiefe.
16. That in case these articles be agreed on, Colonel John Belasise be released.
17. That the Governor may have assurance from the Committee for both Kingdomes and the Lord Fairfax that these articles shall be punctually observed without any breach or violation, and that they will promise to obtain an order in the House of Commons for the confirmation of them in one fortnight after the surrender of the Town and Castle.
18. That between this and the 4th of September the Governor may receive and answer how far the Committee for both Kingdomes and the Lord Fairfax do consent to these articles after the receiving of which the Governor desires and reserves two days time to consider before he returns a conclusive answer, and after he shall declare his assent to the articles who shall be condiscended to the Committee and the Lord Fairfax, he promiseth in the word of a Gentleman within five days to render it into the hands to such person as the Parliament or the Lord Fairfax shall appoint and authorise for that purpose, the Towne and castel of Scarborough, with all victualls, armes and ammunition and ordinance but such as was formerly excepted in these articles.
19. And whilst these articles are in agitation there may be a cessation of all acts of hostility, and under this the Governor subscribes his name.

After consideration, the Committee of Both Kingdoms was unable to agree to all the articles and rejected Sir Hugh's terms, which is exactly what Sir Hugh had expected to happen. The negotiations had gained him time to continue preparations for a formal siege and stock up on provisions and armaments.

In late January 1645, a Parliamentary force under Sir John Meldrum arrived before Scarborough to begin a formal siege. Meldrum was a professional Scots soldier who had served Parliament well in the North. He was often sent

A Parliamentarian's eye view of Scarborough Castle, looming above the town.

to 'hot spots' to steady local commanders. He had served under Lord Fairfax in Hull during the Royalist siege in September and October 1643 and had been instrumental in the garrison keeping up an active defence. He had led the major sally on 11 October (see Chapter 1) which, in combination with the Royalist defeat at the Battle of Winceby on the same day, led the Marquess of Newcastle to withdraw his army from Hull and into early winter quarters. He had also been despatched to shore up the defences of Manchester during Prince Rupert's campaign in Lancashire before his march to Marston Moor.

Meldrum's selection by Parliament, and the size of the force assigned to him, 1,000 horse and 2,000 foot, is a good indicator of the importance attached to Scarborough's capture by the Committee of Both Kingdoms. Another pointer is the time of year that the campaign took place, January, the midst of winter. Meldrum positioned several guns on high ground ready to bombard the town should it become necessary.

Sir Hugh Cholmley was well aware that he did not have enough men to hold the town's outer works, should Meldrum put in a determined attack. To try and delay Meldrum's preparations for such an attack, Cholmley ordered two sallies from the town, which destroyed earthworks and delayed the enemy's preparations. Meldrum was having other problems, which he outlined in a letter to the Committee of Both Kingdoms:

> I cannot determine when the service before Scarborough shall allow me time for my journey. I doubt not to be master of the harbour and town

within a short time, if the defects of men, money, victuals, ammunition, arms, and mutiny of the soldiers for want of supplies do not enforce me to abandon the service and deprive the public and myself of the fruits of my hopes.

A want of supplies, men and money was a perennial problem for Parliamentary commanders in Yorkshire. To alleviate some of these problems Colonel William Stewart and a Scots foot regiment raised in Galloway were sent to reinforce Meldrum. On the financial front, Meldrum was voted money from King's Lynn and Ipswich, two towns that were happy to contribute to protect their shipping which was continually attacked by privateers based in Scarborough.

Tuesday 18 February 1645 was Shrove Tuesday. At ten in the morning the Parliamentarian forces began a two-pronged attack on Scarborough. The town's defences were attacked by four columns from the land and by a number of blockading ships sailing into the harbour. It must have come as a great surprise when their attacks were not opposed and the town and harbour fell within a couple of hours. Sir Hugh Cholmley had gotten wind of the attack and had withdrawn the bulk of the garrison to the castle during the night. He had also warned the townsfolk of the impending attack and the Parliamentarians advanced along empty streets as the locals, wisely, stayed in their homes. Sir Jordan Crossland and his men, the survivors of the Helmsley garrison, were ordered to hold St Mary's Church, below the castle. The church saw the only serious fighting of the day. It was stormed by Parliamentary foot, which captured Sir Jordan and eighty of his men for the loss of eleven of their own. With the capture of St Mary's the approach to the castle was cleared and the garrison firmly penned inside. Meldrum's men also captured the South Steel Battery.

In the harbour 120 ships were secured, the bulk of which belonged to supporters of Parliament and had been captured by privateers. In response to a letter from Sir John Meldrum sent with news of the taking of Scarborough and its harbour, the Committee of Both Kingdoms responded on 27 February:

By yours we received the good news of your taking Scarborough town and harbour, which being in your hands we hope the castle will not be of much concernment to the enemy, nor the harbour be any more a den of thieves, either to interrupt the coasting trade of our small vessels, or a refuge for them to escape the pursuit of our ships or the danger of an eastern storm, they having now no place left them on our whole eastern shore.

Sir John was also instructed to ensure that any ships taken in the harbour, belonging to Parliamentarians or Scots, should be returned to their rightful owners. He had also been awarded £1,000 by the House of Commons.

Within a week of the taking of the town and the harbour, Sir John Meldrum commenced a series of attempts to persuade the Royalist defenders to yield the castle. His initial method of communication was to shoot messages over the walls with bows. This seems to have had some success and up to forty men deserted but once the faint-hearted members of the garrison had departed the remainder prepared for a long siege. Meldrum also wrote directly to the officers of the garrison with little success. On 25 February Meldrum wrote directly to Cholmley with a very high-handed demand to

Scarborough, the Barbican Gate: Bushell's Battery stood to the left of the gate.

surrender the castle. Sir Hugh responded in a similar manner and there followed an acrimonious exchange. It is possible that Meldrum's lack of civility was caused by a rather painful wound 'neere the tenderest partes' – Sir Hugh mentions the wound being in Sir John's 'cods'! Meldrum recovered in due course.

By the beginning of March Meldrum had come to the conclusion that the castle would not fall without a formal siege. He requested siege guns to be sent from Hull and York to Scarborough. By the middle of March two of the largest guns available had arrived. The pair was known as the Queen's Pocket Pistols and had been captured from the Royalists during Meldrum's successful sally from Hull on 11 October 1643. The smallest of the pair was a demi-cannon which fired a 32lb ball. It had the intriguing nickname of 'Sweet lips', evidently named after a well-known Hull prostitute. The other gun was one of the largest in Britain, a cannon-royal which fired a 64lb ball. These guns formed the core of a battery Sir John mounted inside St Mary's Church to fire through its eastern windows at the barbican and Bushell's Battery. Other batteries were raised on the North and South Cliffs.

During the raising of one of the batteries on the North Cliff, Sir John Meldrum had a serious accident. On 24 March Sir John was standing close to the edge of the North Cliff when a gust of wind blew his hat off. This was just the start of his troubles, as Sir Hugh Cholmley reported:

Beeing to plant these ordnance neere to the sea cliff for more advantage to matter, Meldrum there in person giving directions about them, his hatt blowes of his head, and hee catching to save that, the winde being very great blowes his cloake over his face, and hee falls over the cliff amongst the rockes and stones att least steeple height; itt was a miracle his braines were not beaten out and all his bones broaken, but itt seemed the winde together with the cloke did in some sorte beare him up, and lessen the fall; yet hee is taken up for dead, lyes 3 dayes speechless, his head opened and the bruised blood take out, though a man above threescore years old, recovered this soe perfectlie that with in six weekes hee is on foote againe, and begins to batter the Castle.

Shortly after Meldrum's injury, Cholmley ordered a sally against the South Steel Battery. Captain Wickham, with fifty men, attacked the battery and quickly drove the Scots troops manning it down the hill towards the harbour. Wickham continued his attack as far as the harbour side, before withdrawing to the castle with twenty prisoners. Over 100 Scots had been killed and wounded or had drowned trying to swim across the harbour to get away from the Royalists.

The next major event in the siege took place in early May, although the exact date is difficult to ascertain. The Queen's Pocket Pistols continued to bombard the barbican and the castle's keep. Although the keep had fifteen-feet-thick walls it could stand the pounding of 32lb and 64lb balls only for so long:

> In 3 dayes the great Tower splitt in two, and that side which was battered falls to the ground.

Twenty men had been in the tower at the time of the western wall's collapse but only two failed to make it to safety in the standing half of the tower. Not only had the collapse made the keep uninhabitable but the debris had clogged the route to the castle gate and beyond that the barbican, cutting off the men stationed there.

Now was the time for the assault to go in but, at about six in the evening, Meldrum sent in another demand for the Royalists to surrender and stated that there would be no quarter given if they did not. Cholmley set his men about clearing the debris around the gate and returned his refusal just before nine, three hours after the demand. Cholmley's reply angered Meldrum who immediately ordered an assault on the barbican. Bushell's Battery was quickly overrun but the attackers failed to breach the walls or gate of the barbican. To save their powder and ball the Royalists threw stones from the collapsed tower at their enemies. The Parliamentarian assault was driven off with substantial loss – up to 200 dead and wounded according to Cholmley's account.

Having captured Bushell's Battery, the Parliamentarians moved up two demi-cannon into the earthwork. These guns, along with those positioned in St Mary's Church, commenced a heavy bombardment of the barbican. So hard-pressed were the defenders that they withdrew across the drawbridges, part way up the barbican. The two guns mounted in Bushell's Battery could also bombard the castle yard. Cholmley decided that something had to be done about this. During the night of 10 May he ordered Major Crompton, an

Scarborough Castle: the wall of the Keep collapsed after several days' bombardment. The rubble blocked the main gate into the castle and provided the Royalist defenders with a ready supply of missiles.

experienced officer, with sixty hand-picked men to attack Bushell's Battery and spike the guns. Crompton succeeded in his task, driving the Parliamentarians from their position, dismounting the guns and smashing their carriages. The Parliamentary leaders rallied their men and brought up reinforcements to counter-attack.

Fighting continued into the 11th as both sides reinforced and continued to fight over the ruins of the barbican, with heavy casualties on both sides. Sir John Meldrum was in the thick of the fighting and suffered his third injury of the siege. A musket ball struck him in the lower abdomen, passed through and out of his back. This time the wound would prove to be fatal, although Parliamentary newssheets tried to hide the seriousness of Sir John's wound. Meldrum lingered on in pain for six days.

After Meldrum's demise, Sir Matthew Boynton assumed command of the Parliamentarian forces. He was cut from a different cloth to Sir John and decided on starving the Royalists out, rather than risking the lives of his men in assaults. One of the reasons for this was that the Scots infantry had been withdrawn and Boynton was reinforced by only a smaller number of Yorkshire foot.

St Mary's Church was partially ruined during the siege of Scarborough Castle. The Parliamentarians mounted a battery of heavy guns in its nave, firing through the windows. It was these guns which caused the collapse of the Keep's facing wall.

The siege continued into June and then into July. Towards the middle of July it became apparent to Sir Hugh Cholmley that his men could not hold out for much longer. Due to the poor rations remaining in the castle, many of Cholmley's men had gone down with scurvy. So few of Cholmley's soldiers were fit enough to carry out their duties that officers were assisting in grinding corn and manning guard posts. The garrison was also short of water. One of the castle's wells had failed and the other was under bombardment from the Parliamentary squadron stationed off the headland. Sir Hugh also reports that the garrison was very low on powder, although some of the Parliamentarian accounts of the surrender of the castle cast some doubt on this. Added to this was the news, which the besiegers were very happy to share with Cholmley and his men, of the King's defeat at Naseby on 14 June. Cholmley must have realized that there was little, if any, chance of relief.

On 22 July Boynton and Cholmley agreed the following terms for yielding the castle:

1. That the Castle be surrendered upon Friday next being the 25th day of this instant July 1645, by twelve of the clock at noon: That all the Armes, Ordinance, Ammunition, Provision and goodes of whatever sort soever, now in, and about the castle (except what is hereafter excepted) shall be delivered to the Commanders in Chief in Scarborough, or to whome they shall appoint, to the use of the King and Parliament.

2. That all prisoners now in the castle be set at liberty within six hours of the sealing of these articles.

3. That the Governor Sir Hugh Cholmley and those officers and Gentlemen soldiers, if he desires it shall have a safe convoy from hence to Holland or be safely convoyed to Newark, whether they shall choose, and if any after their coming to Newark shall then resolve to go into Holland, giving notice thereof to the Committee for Military Affairs at York, they shall have passes from thence to take shipping at Hull, Scarborough or Bridlington key and be there Accommodated, paying small rates so that they take the first opportunity of wind and shipping. And such other who desires them, shall have Passes from the said committee to go to the King's Army, or any of his garrisons, as they please; they travelling not above twenty in a company, where the governor or colonel shall be in person otherwise not above ten in a party, the time permitted in their several passes, as the distance of the places they go to shall be require none of them passing through any garrison for the King and Parliament if there be another way.

4. That no person whatsoever going from this Castle be plundered, Arrested, or staid upon any ground or pretence whatsoever, and in such case upon complaint made to the aforesaide Committee in York, to be speedily redressed.

5. That the Lady Cholmley shall have liberty to live at her own house in Whitby, and enjoy such part of her estate, as is allowed by Ordinance of Parliament: That she may have two men servants, and two horses to carry herself and such necessary things as shall be granted her.

6. That all inferior officers, Common Soldiers, and others, who have desire to live at home, shall have passes granted them for that end and shall not be forced to take up Armes against their mindes: That the sick and wounded shall be provided for until their recovery, and then have Passes to travell to what place they please, having such time allowed for their journey, and two persons permitted to take care of them.

7. That the Governor march on his own horse, with Sword, Pistolls and defensive Armes, and all Field Officers upon their owne Horses, with their Swords and Pistolls, all Captains whatsoever, Lieutenants, Cornets of Horse in like manner, Three servants of the Governor, and one for every Field Officer as aforesaid, and all other Officers and Soldiers whatsoever of foot, without any other armes than their Swords, and not be compelled to march above ten miles a day.

8. That all Officers and Soldiers may carry upon their persons what is really their owne, that nothing be carried in cloth-bags or snapsacks, but their owne wearing apparel, writings, Evidences and Bills.

9. That all Officers, Gentlemen and Clergymen may have liberty to buy or lawfully procure a travelling horse for himself and his servant, that all sick and lame men may have the same privilege.

10. That all Gentleman of Quality and Clergymen shall have liberty to march, Gentlemen with their swords, that none of them carry above the value of £1 in money or plate about their persons, and nothing in cloth bags, but as is expressed in the eight Article.

11. That there be no fraud or deceit whatsoever used, in spoiling or embezzling any thing before mentioned, or comprised in the Articles; and if any of them shall be violated, the party offending shall bee delivered to the Commander in chiefs where fact shall be done, to give satisfaction to his offence, and his particular act shall not be understood as a breach of these Articles, not be prejudicial to any others.

On 25 July 1645 the pitiful remnants of the garrison marched from the castle. Unfortunately, the road from the castle to the barbican gate was still blocked by rubble from the collapsed keep. A gap had to be cut in the curtain wall to allow the Royalists to exit the castle. Over 100 of their number were too sick to walk and had to be carried from the castle. Captain Richard Legard's company amply illustrates the dire conditions suffered by the garrison during the siege. Legard and his lieutenant were both wounded and the company's two sergeants were killed by cannon fire. The captain's two servants were the two unfortunates killed in the collapse of the keep, the only two casualties of the event. Of the fifty soldiers in the company at the start of the siege only three were in a fit state to march from the castle on 25 July. The remainder were dead, wounded or too sick to walk.

Scarborough: looking across the headland towards the Keep. This area was swept by cannon fire from Parliamentary ships stationed in the North Bay.

Sir Hugh Cholmley, and most of the garrison who were fit to march, chose to go to Newark. Sir Jordan Crossland and his men were also released and allowed to join Cholmley. Sir Hugh only made it as far as Selby before he had a change of heart. Having received leave to do so, he rode to Bridlington, where he boarded a ship for the Continent. He returned to England in 1648 and compounded for his estate. During the Third Civil War in 1651 he was imprisoned for several months while the Scots and Royalist army marched south to their defeat at Worcester on 3 September 1651. Sir Hugh spent his final years living with his family in Kent and passed away in 1657.

Chapter 7

THE SIEGE OF SANDAL CASTLE

A Fortress in Miniature

In 1106 William de Warenne began construction of a motte and bailey castle on a sandstone ridge overlooking the village of Sandal and, in the distance, the town of Wakefield. The area on which the castle was built was originally part of Sandal's field system. As the ditch, or dry moat, was cut into the Oaks Rock, the local sandstone, the debris was piled in successive layers to form the motte on which the castle's keep was built. The bailey, in which the domestic buildings were situated, was surrounded by a wooden palisade.

Sandal Castle's gateway. A drawbridge crossed the gap shown in the photograph.

Between 1240 and 1270 another de Warenne, John, replaced the wooden castle with a stone one. The design of the castle was a little out of the ordinary. The four-storey keep still occupied the motte, as its wooden predecessor had. Separating the keep from the bailey was an internal barbican, something of a rarity. The new stone-built domestic ranges, including a great hall, kitchen and bakehouse, formed the outer edge of the bailey, which was surrounded by a 20-foot-high curtain wall. The wall continued across the ditch and joined to the outer walls of the keep. The main entrance to the castle was through a gatehouse which was further defended by a drawbridge and portcullis. The gate faced onto the main road towards Wakefield, now a quiet suburban street called Manygates Lane. The real surprise at Sandal Castle is its size. The whole castle would fit into Pontefract Castle several times over.

Successive owners of the castle continued to make improvements, both in its defences and decoration. Richard III ordered building work to be carried out in 1483 on his accession to the throne, or usurpation depending on your

An English Civil War earthwork at the eastern end of Sandal Castle. Although this has the look of a position for artillery pieces, there is no evidence for the garrison having any cannons. It is possible that cattle and horses were corralled within the earthwork as there was little space in the castle to hold them.

A view from the keep to the Barbican Tower. Sandal Castle is one of the few castles to have an inner barbican.

way of thinking, after the death of his older brother, Edward IV. During the Tudor period the castle went into decline, although early Tudor sketches of the castle give an idea of how impressive it must have been in its heyday.

In 1566, a report on the state of the castle talks of leaking roofs, rotting timbers, missing floorboards and cracks in the walls. In 1592 a survey of the castle stated that 'the residence of this castle is near ruinous and in great decay'. During the early decades of the seventeenth century the castle was unoccupied. Just how bad its state was when the Royalist army garrisoned it in the early 1640s is not recorded but a hint is given by the fact that the Royalists put up lean-to stables and a smithy where the original bakehouse had stood, pointing to the bakehouse having collapsed or been in such a bad state that the garrison had to demolish it.

The Battle of Wakefield 1460

Many of the castles in Yorkshire had seen little, if any, military action until they were garrisoned during the Civil Wars. This was most definitely not the case with Sandal Castle. On 30 December 1460, during the Wars of the Roses, Richard, Duke of York, marched from the castle down the hill towards Wakefield, where in the open fields between the castle and the town he fought a desperate action against a much larger Lancastrian force. Within a couple of days the heads of York, his son, the Earl of Rutland, and a number of his allies adorned Micklegate Bar at York. Why Richard marched from the castle to fight a much larger army has never been fully explained and, barring new documentary evidence, probably never will be. It is beyond the scope of this book to go into depth about the causes of the battle, but Richard's defeat led directly to what was quite possibly the largest and bloodiest battle on British soil and certainly in the Wars of the Roses, the Battle of Towton (29 March 1461), where Richard's son, Edward, smashed the Lancastrian army and cemented his right to the throne.

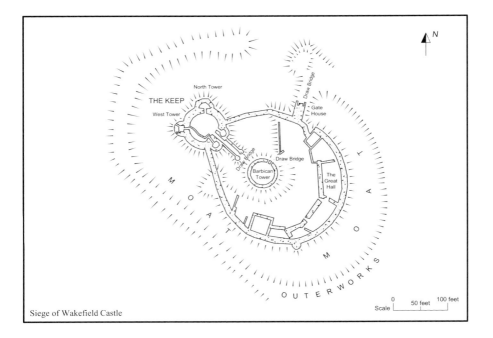

Siege of Wakefield Castle

Sandal Castle Besieged

It is not certain when Sandal Castle was first garrisoned for the King. Wakefield had been garrisoned at various times since early 1643. Sir Thomas Fairfax with a force of about 1,500 men stormed the town in the early hours of 21 May 1643. Military intelligence, a contradiction in terms if ever there was one, gave the strength of the garrison as about 800. Once the shooting had finished Sir Thomas had captured close to 3,000 Royalist troops; his men had stormed a town held by twice their number. His father, Lord Ferdinando Fairfax, summed up the action as more a miracle than a victory.

The first mention of a garrison in the castle comes in June 1644, prior to the Battle of Marston Moor (2 July 1644), when Parliamentary forces captured twelve Royalists marching from the castle to Sheffield. A small force was left in the area to pen the garrison inside the castle. The garrison's first recorded commander was a Major Ward, who had been sent to command the garrison by Major Thomas Beaumont, the commander of the garrison of Sheffield

Sandal Castle had a dry ditch running round its full perimeter. It was cut into the rock on which the castle was built.

Sandal Castle: a view of the base of the Well Tower, which formed part of the Keep. The tower was one of the main targets for the Parliamentary bombardment and suffered heavy damage.

Castle. Ward did not last very long in his command. While descending a staircase within the keep he slipped and broke his neck. It is possible that his was one of the nine Civil War burials found by archaeologists inside the castle's bailey. His place was taken by Colonel George Bonivant, who commanded the garrison until its surrender.

In early April 1645 Sir John Saville was despatched by Lord Fairfax to blockade Sandal Castle, while the main Parliamentary force concentrated on besieging Pontefract (see Chapter 5). On Thursday 10 April Saville had the drums sounded to call his men to prayer. Bonivant also ordered his drums to sound, lulling the Parliamentarians into a false sense of security. While Saville's men sang psalms and listened to a sermon, Bonivant's soldiers prepared to attack. In two short, sharp sorties the Royalists killed forty-two of their opponents and captured a further fifty, including a captain. *Mercurius Aulicus*, a Royalist newssheet, reports that Sir John 'packt up bag and

Sandal Castle's Keep was built on top of the original Norman motte. It was so heavily damaged that a trench had to be cut across the top of the motte.

Sandal Castle: the stairs leading down from the Keep to the Barbican Tower were protected by a pair of drum towers, the bases of which can be clearly seen. The gap between the Keep and the Barbican Tower was crossed by a drawbridge.

This photograph illustrates how small Sandal Castle was. The view is from the Keep, looking over the Barbican Tower. The arc of grass between the inner ditch and the walls is the full extent of the castle's courtyard.

Sandal Castle: this view of the Civil War earthwork clearly shows the ditch and a raised platform for cannon. There is no evidence for the garrison having artillery.

baggage, raised the seidge and went quite away, with a small number in comparison of those he brought and lost before Sandall Castle'. Nathan Drake, a member of the garrison of Pontefract Castle, reports the arrival of Saville's beaten force at Pontefract.

The next mention of the garrison comes in early May when a force of horse left the castle to gather May blossom, although the reason for collecting the blossom is not given. The Royalists clashed with a larger Parliamentary force and suffered losses as they were driven back to the castle.

On 14 May Captain John Benson was despatched from Pontefract Castle to assist Bonivant at Sandal. There is some archaeological evidence that the garrison of Sandal Castle was divided into four 'watches' in a similar fashion to the gentlemen and volunteers at Pontefract and it may have been Benson who instigated this system at Sandal. The garrison of 100 officers and men lived in cramped conditions. As has already been mentioned, some of the castle's buildings were in such poor order that lean-to buildings had been put up. The castle's kitchens seem to have been in good enough condition for the garrison to use as a hospital and the burials were found close to this area.

The garrison also seems to have been in regular communication with Pontefract Castle. Beacons on top of the keep of one castle could be seen from its counterpart at the other. At this stage of the second siege of Pontefract Castle the Royalists were still able to send mounted messengers between the two garrisons, as is evidenced by Captain Benson's ability to transfer between the two castles. Another incident that illustrates this took place on 27 May, when Lieutenant Wheatley, mentioned at Pontefract on several occasions, and a force of between forty and fifty horse drove a large herd of cattle from Sandal to Pontefract, where he handed them over to Captain Walker at Baghill, who then conveyed them into the castle.

Just after this incident Colonel Thomas Morgan and 300 dragoons arrived at Sandal to blockade the castle and prevent similar resupply attempts. On 18 June Morgan was appointed by Parliament to the command of the garrison of Gloucester. On 8 July he departed for his new command, taking his dragoons with him. The garrison must have been mightily relieved as they had been running short of fodder. The garrison sent out parties to gather food for the men and fodder for the horses. Two of these parties clashed with enemy patrols. In the first action the Royalists lost three men and sixteen horses and in the second twenty-six cattle were seized and the garrison suffered further losses.

On 20 July the garrison of Pontefract Castle surrendered and on the 21st the Parliamentary command summoned Sandal Castle to surrender. Colonel Bonivant refused in a letter signed by all his officers. In early September Sydenham Poyntz, Parliament's local commander, ordered Colonel Robert Overton to take the castle and supplied him with a siege train of four large guns from Hull. There is archaeological evidence for at least one culverin, firing a 16lb ball, and a cannon royal, firing a 60lb ball. Fragments of 11-inch mortar shells have also been found. One of these was found at the bottom of a Civil War grave and it has been suggested that the occupant may have been killed by the fragment found in the grave. It is possible that these artillery pieces may have been present at Scarborough as a 60lb ball was found in the castle ditch there. This could also be the reason why the final siege of Sandal Castle did not start until early September.

The defenders were well supplied by this time and had made preparations to stand a siege. Several earthworks had been raised to supplement the

Sandal Castle: the Barbican Tower was built directly onto the local bedrock, as can be seen in this photograph.

castle's medieval defences. One of these looks suspiciously like an artillery emplacement but there is little, if any, evidence that the garrison had any artillery. Among the Civil War remains archaeologists found fragments of medieval armour and arrow heads and it has been postulated that the defenders may have made use of some of these artefacts alongside their muskets.

Once his guns were emplaced Overton began his bombardment. The Well Tower, part of the keep, seems to have been one of the main targets of the bombardment and archaeologists found a large number of cannon balls in the ditch below the tower. They also found that the defenders had cut a trench across the top of the motte, which probably signified that the outer walls of the keep had collapsed. There is also artefact evidence for other parts of the curtain walls suffering during the bombardment. The gatehouse suffered severe damage and several breaches were made in the walls.

By 30 September Overton believed that one, or more, of the breaches were practicable and prepared his men for an assault. As Overton's men formed for the attack Bonivant sent a messenger out of the castle to seek a parley. Overton returned the messenger with a letter for the garrison commander:

In behalfe of our Countrey (which we serve) I summon you to render this Castle into our hands for the use of the Publique. And though our neglect of this place hitherto hath occasioned your Honour and some effusion of blood, be advised to close with the Almighties Overtures of mercy ere it is too late, otherwise the Justice of God and the civility of men will I doubt not most evidently appeare in the obstinate and wilfull destruction of yourselves. Sir, I wish this advice may prove effectual to you as it will be satisfactory to

Your humble servant
R. Overton

In a letter to the Committee in York, Colonel Overton admitted to allowing the parley because he was not confident that his assault would have succeeded. On the other side, Bonivant had asked for a parley because of the damage to his defences and his doubts at his troops' ability to stop an assault. He quickly replied to Overton:

To render ourselves prisoners we will not, but if you please that we may treat upon our march away, wee shall have done in two words and this is the resolution of

Your servant
Geo. Bonivant

Both of these letters were printed in *Mercurius Civicus*, a Parliamentary newssheet, for the period covering 1 to 8 October 1645.

The commanders agreed to a parley and discussions then took place. Representing Parliament were Majors Crook and Hooper, while the garrison was represented by Captain John Benson. It was agreed that the garrison would march out on the following day, 1 October, by ten o'clock in the morning. They would have four days to march to the nearest Royalist garrison outside of Yorkshire, which was at Welbeck House in Nottinghamshire. The

Sandal Castle: the entrance to the sally port. By the time of the Civil War its exits had been blocked. It may have been used as a toilet during the siege.

officers and gentlemen could carry one additional suit of clothes to those they were wearing, while the other ranks could only take what they stood in. Two officers would be allowed to take a horse, possibly Bonivant and Benson, but these were only on loan and should be returned when they reached Welbeck. No money was to be taken from the castle and if anyone was found carrying any they would remain as a prisoner. All arms and provisions would be left at the castle and two hostages would be provided by each side. A real change in attitude can be seen in these terms compared with those at the surrender of York fifteen months earlier, where the garrison was allowed to march away with the full honours of war.

On the morning of 1 October Bonivant and his men departed from the castle and headed south towards Nottinghamshire. The Parliamentary forces occupied the castle in the wake of the Royalist departure. Their tenure was to be of short duration. On 30 April 1646 Parliament gave orders for the castle to be slighted. Any modern visitor will agree that the workmen carried out their job efficiently.

Sandal Castle: the remains of a range of domestic buildings, including the Great Hall and kitchen. It is probable that the kitchen was used as a hospital during the siege.

Chapter 8

THE SIEGE OF BOLTON CASTLE

The Castle's Early History

Bolton Castle was completed in 1399 by Richard, first Lord Scrope of Bolton. He had been granted a licence to crenellate his manor house at Bolton by King Richard II in 1379. Little, if any, of the original manor house existed once the castle had been built.

The Scrope family seem to have supported both sides in the risings which followed Henry IV's usurpation of Richard II's throne in 1399. The Masham branch of the family supported Henry's opponents or tried to revolt against his son, Henry V. In 1405 Archbishop Richard Scrope, the son of Lord Scrope

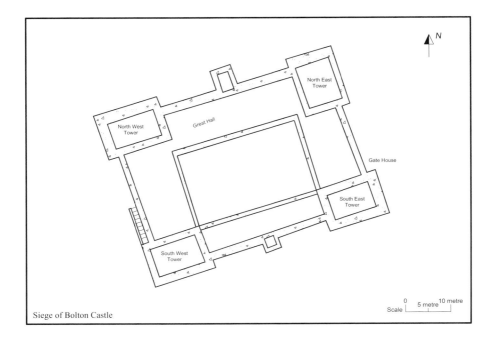

Siege of Bolton Castle

The entrances to Bolton Castle from its courtyard were defended by lowering doors.

Bolton Castle: a view looking through the entrance tunnel at the main gate.

of Masham, was executed for supporting Henry Percy, known as Harry Hotspur, in his revolt against Henry IV. In 1415, Henry, third Lord Scrope of Masham, was executed at Southampton for supporting the Earl of Cambridge's revolt against Henry V, while his Bolton relative, Richard, third Lord Scrope of Bolton, fought alongside Henry at Agincourt.

During the Wars of the Roses the Scropes of Bolton supported the Yorkists, which is hardly surprising as Richard, fourth Baron Scrope, was related to Richard, Duke of York, through marriage – his mother was York's sister-in-law. In 1459 John became the fifth Baron Scrope and trod a very dangerous line during the latter part of the Wars of the Roses. He was a staunch supporter of Richard III and later supported Lambert Simnel's revolt against Henry VII. Many others who followed a similar course felt the executioner's axe, but Scrope was pardoned for both offences. The only punishment he received was that he was required to live within 22 miles of London.

In 1536 another Scrope of Bolton crossed the King. This time John, eighth Baron, supported the Pilgrimage of Grace against Henry VIII. Henry's commissioner ordered the burning of Bolton Castle and John was ordered to

A view of Bolton Castle from the west.

Bolton Castle: the interior of the southeast tower, showing the number of floors and the thickness of the walls.

attend Parliament, where he was forced to remain until 1552. In 1568 Bolton Castle became a royal prison, with the arrival of Mary, Queen of Scots, on 15 July. She remained at Bolton Castle until 26 January in the following year.

In 1630, Emmanuel, the eleventh and last Baron Scrope of Bolton, died without a legitimate heir. His whole estate was bequeathed to his illegitimate son, John, who served as a colonel in the Royalist army and defended the castle against two sieges.

The Castle's Defences

Bolton castle is very different from the other castles covered in this book. It was built much later and incorporated the latest in fourteenth-century castle design. Older castles usually had a keep and one or more baileys surrounded by curtain walls, often reinforced with towers. Ranges of domestic buildings, such as kitchens, brewhouses and living quarters, were added inside the baileys. Bolton Castle had a rectangular shape, formed by ranges, several storeys high and with thick outer walls. At each corner of the castle stood a square tower and an open courtyard in its centre.

The castle was originally built with a single entrance; the doorways on the north and west sides were added in recent times. The main gate was on the eastern side of the castle, next to the southeast tower. It was protected by a thick wooden gate and two portcullises. An attacker would have to negotiate these obstacles in the gate passage and would then enter the courtyard, with the imposing bulk of the castle looming over him in every direction. The courtyard had five exits, each of which was defended by a thick wooden door which descended like a portcullis. If an attacker managed to break through one of these doors, he would then find himself in a maze of rooms, passageways and staircases. The interior of the castle was broken down into discrete sections so that if an attacker did manage to penetrate one section he would not be able to gain access to the other sections without returning to the courtyard and attempting to break through another one of the doorways.

The castle had been built with a siege in mind. All its domestic functions were contained within the ranges, making the castle self-sufficient. These included kitchens, a bakehouse, a brewhouse, a smithy and armourer's workshop, stables and even a horse-powered grinding floor. Very importantly, it had an internal well so its water supply could not be cut off.

The castle and Bolton village are built on a wide shelf on a slope descending from north to south and this introduced two weaknesses into its defences. First, the castle was overlooked from the high ground to the north. Fortunately, it would be very difficult for an attacker to mount guns on the high ground, although musketeers could bring fire to bear on any defenders on the ramparts. Second, the ground falls away to the south and this prevented the castle from having a moat, even a dry one.

The Sieges of Bolton Castle

Little contemporary evidence is available on the sieges at Bolton Castle and few, if any, modern writers have covered the sieges. Research continues.

The castle was standing its first siege by December 1644. A Parliamentarian force of 500 foot had been despatched by Lord Fairfax, commanded by

The eastern wall, southeast tower and main gate of Bolton Castle.

Colonels Lascelles and Wastell. This points to Bolton's garrison, commanded by John Scrope the castle's owner, not being very large. It is unlikely that the Parliamentarians had heavy guns with them as the Yorkshire Parliamentarians' heavy siege train was continually employed elsewhere: Helmsley, Knaresborough, Pontefract, Scarborough, Sandal and Skipton in succession. It is probable that Lascelles and Wastell planned to blockade the castle and starve its defenders into submission.

By March 1645, King Charles had a large army marching through the Midlands and Parliament feared that he would march it into Yorkshire, which had been a rich recruiting ground for the Royalists. The Parliamentarians were desperately short of men to gather in the south of the county to oppose the King should he move north. The Parliamentarian commanders at Bolton Castle were ordered to suspend the siege and march to Pontefract. The King's advance into Yorkshire did not happen and in June he was soundly defeated at Naseby by the New Model Army, commanded by Sir Thomas Fairfax.

Bolton Castle: a replica English Civil War cannon. The author visited on Halloween, hence the fake cobwebs!

A view of Bolton Castle from the northeast, showing the results of the slighting of the castle by Parliamentarian troops. Only one tower and one range of buildings were left habitable.

Colonel Lascelles was ordered to return to Bolton Castle and resume the siege. By early November 1645, the castle's defenders were in dire straits. Their provisions had run out and they had to resort to eating horses. By the 5th even this source of food had been exhausted and Scrope had no choice but to surrender. The garrison were allowed the honours of war but John Scrope had had enough of war.

By March 1646 Scrope was living in London and was fined £7,000 by Parliament, a huge sum at the time, which illustrates the value of the estate he had inherited. John Scrope died of the plague, at the young age of 23, before he had chance to pay the fine. The estate was inherited by his sister, Mary. In 1653 Mary married her second husband, Charles Powlett, sixth Marquess of Winchester, who became the first Duke of Bolton.

In 1647 Parliament ordered the castle to be slighted. Only the western range and the southwest tower were left inhabitable. In 1675 the family left the castle to move into the newly completed Bolton Hall.

Chapter 9

THE SIEGE OF SKIPTON CASTLE

The Early History of the Castle

The first castle at Skipton was begun by Roger de Romille in 1090 and was built as a typical Norman motte and bailey castle. In 1260 William de Forze, whose father had inherited the castle through marriage, began work on converting the timber castle into a stone one. This work would be continued by successive owners until Tudor times. In 1310 Robert, the first Lord Clifford moved north from Herefordshire to take possession of the Honour of Skipton.

Skipton Castle: the Conduit Court was built by Henry, 10th Lord Clifford (the Shepherd Lord). The yew tree was planted by Anne Clifford, Countess of Pembroke, in 1659. She retained possession of the castle after the Civil Wars.

The Cliffords seem to have been a warlike family, as their subsequent record shows. Robert was killed at the Battle of Bannockburn in 1314. The fourth Lord Clifford, another Robert, fought for Edward III at Crecy in 1346. Thomas, the sixth lord, died on campaign in Germany and his son, John, died on campaign in France with King Henry V. Thomas, eighth Lord Clifford, supported the house of Lancaster during the Wars of the Roses and was killed at the First Battle of St Albans in 1455. His son, John, inherited the lordship and continued to fight against Richard, Duke of York, and his supporters.

John Clifford was one of the Lancastrian commanders at the Battle of Wakefield in December 1460, where the Duke of York was killed, along with many of his supporters. In an act of revenge for the slaying of his father at St Albans, Clifford is reported to have murdered York's second son, the Earl of Rutland, in the pursuit after the Yorkist defeat. The chantry chapel outside which the murder is said to have taken place still exists. Shakespeare writes of Rutland as a young boy but, in fact, he was a 17-year-old man-at-arms, who had taken an active part in the battle. Clifford would survive only for another three months. During the night of 27/8 March 1461, he led a surprise attack on the advance guard of Edward IV's Yorkist army at Ferrybridge. It is not certain what the objective of this attack was, simply a raid on an enemy position or an attempt to destroy the bridge. The Yorkists counter-attacked but Clifford held his ground for some time, until he was outflanked by another Yorkist force which crossed the River Aire at Castleford. Clifford fell back towards the Lancastrian army, which was stationed close to Towton, south of Tadcaster, but was caught at Dintingdale. Clifford and most of his men were killed.

On the day after Clifford's demise, the Battle of Towton was fought (29 March 1461). The Lancastrian army was soundly beaten and the Yorkists came fully to power. Clifford's widow decided to send her son, Henry, into the Cumberland fells for safety and it was from this part of his life that he received the nickname 'the Shepherd Lord'. With the defeat of the last Yorkist king, Richard III, at Bosworth on 22 August 1485, Henry Tudor came to the throne as Henry VII and restored Clifford as the tenth Lord Clifford. At close to the age of 60, Clifford was one of the senior commanders of the English army at Flodden in 1513. He also made many changes to the interior of the main castle building, adding more comfortable apartments around the Conduit Court.

A view of the main part of Skipton Castle. To the left of the picture is the castle's entrance and to the right is the Tudor wing.

The Shepherd Lord's son, another Henry, was a close friend of Henry VIII. By this time castles were becoming more homes than fortresses and Henry Clifford, raised in the peerage to the first Earl of Cumberland, had a residential wing added to the castle, complete with a long gallery. The Clifford family continued to prosper and the castle remained one of their main residences. By the time of the English Civil Wars, Henry, fifth Earl of Cumberland, was in possession of the castle. He was appointed commander of King Charles's forces in Yorkshire but was the first to admit that he was no soldier, handing command to the Earl of Newcastle when his army arrived from the North East in December 1642.

The Castle's Defences

Skipton Castle was built in a very defensible position. The whole north side of the castle is protected by the cliffs of the gorge cut by the Eller Beck and was virtually impregnable. The castle and the Tudor wing were built along these cliffs. A strong Outer Gatehouse and curtain wall completed the castle's

Holy Trinity Church stands close to Skipton Castle and formed part of its outer defences during the Civil War sieges.

defences. During the early years of the First Civil War, the Royalists continued to reinforce the castle's outer walls with earth and raise platforms on which cannon could be mounted. Just outside the castle's curtain wall, to the west of the Outer Gatehouse, stands Holy Trinity Church. The church was occupied by Royalist soldiers and became an integral part of the castle's defences.

The First Siege

The garrison of Skipton Castle had been very active during the early years of the First Civil War. Colonel Sir John Mallory had been appointed as governor and tasked with retaining control of the Craven area and with keeping communications open across the Pennines with the Royalist forces in Cumberland and Westmorland. Troops from Skipton had been involved in relief attempts at several besieged Royalist garrisons, including Helmsley, where they had suffered a serious setback.

With the fall of Pontefract Castle on 21 July 1645, General Poyntz, the Parliamentarian commander in Yorkshire, was able to turn his attention to Skipton. Although his men were besieging the remaining Royalist garrisons, with the exception of Skipton, Poyntz's situation was worrying. First, he had a shortage of men and was actively trying to get reinforcements from Lancashire and County Durham. Second, and more worrying, was the state of his men's morale. His troops had not been paid for many months, some had not received their wages for over a year, and this was having a serious effect on their morale. Desertions had become rife, particularly among the newly conscripted foot soldiers. At Pontefract the Parliamentarians had to resort to cavalry patrols around the siege lines to try and prevent such desertions. On the march from Pontefract to Skipton Colonel Alured's regiment of horse protested to Poyntz about their lack of money and were only placated when the general promised to give them one month's wages.

By 1 August Ponytz's force had marched to within a mile of Skipton town. Here he paused for several days while he awaited the arrival of a number of reinforcements from Lancashire and Country Durham. It is not certain whether these reinforcements ever arrived. He did, however, receive the welcome addition of two companies of foot from Appleby, along with a small munitions convoy which accompanied them. Mallory despatched a

A view from Skipton Castle into the gorge of the Eller Beck. The beck formed an integral part of the castle's northern defences.

force of Royalist horse from the castle to try and intercept them and the Parliamentarians had a few casualties during the ensuing skirmish.

On Monday 3 August Poyntz ordered his troops to advance on Skipton in four columns. Mallory did not attempt to defend the town and withdrew his men to the castle and Holy Trinity Church. Poyntz's men quickly occupied the town and by nightfall were within pistol shot of the castle, probably no more than 100 yards. The townsmen's reaction to the Parliamentarian occupation was mixed. Some had picked up their weapons and joined the garrison, while others surrendered to the Parliamentarian soldiers.

Poyntz now offered Mallory terms, which the governor quickly refused. The Parliamentarian commander realized that he would need a siege train and wrote to the committee in York. The guns were despatched on the 6th. Poyntz began to raise battery positions to the south and west of the castle and managed to cut the castle's external water supply. This left only one small well within the castle to supply the needs of the garrison and the livestock enclosed within its walls. Poyntz was confident that the castle would fall.

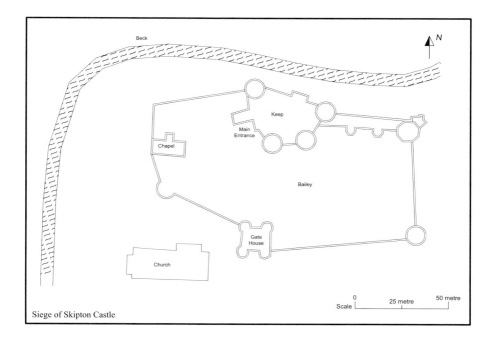

Siege of Skipton Castle

Skipton Castle: a view from the Eller Beck along the north side of the castle.

Skirmishing continued between the Royalist garrison and their Parliamentarian besiegers. Poyntz reported the capture of enemy troops and horses during these skirmishes but did not report his own losses. If the siege of Pontefract, where most of his men had been present, is anything to go by, the besiegers could have been taking casualties at a rate of four or five for every casualty the garrison suffered. The Parliamentarian soldiers must have had a real feeling of déjà vu – yet again they were besieging a castle which was defended by an active and aggressive enemy. Add to this the non-appearance of the month's pay promised by Poyntz during the march from Pontefract to Skipton and it is hardly surprising that some of his cavalry mutinied. Poyntz considered himself in more danger from his own men than from the enemy. Poyntz was in a very awkward situation. His foot, although more recently paid, also seemed in a rebellious mood. To try and alleviate the situation the Parliamentarian commander offered to send a message to the committee in York, detailing his troops' grievances.

Events outside the county now had an influence on the war in Yorkshire. King Charles had reached the large Royalist garrison at Newark and seemed intent on marching his army into Yorkshire, to recruit troops and, possibly, to relieve Skipton. The Parliamentarian committee in York took a decision to gather their troops in the south of the county. Most of these troops were engaged in besieging Skipton, Bolton and Sandal Castles and these sieges had to be abandoned. The Committee of Both Kingdoms in London wrote to General Poyntz on 13 August, ordering him to gather his forces and oppose the King's advance. On the 17th Poyntz withdrew his men from Skipton and marched southeastwards. The first siege had lasted only two weeks.

King Charles, and his army, entered Doncaster on 19 August. Two days later he turned southwards again and marched from Yorkshire. The King's advance and the mutinous state of Parliament's Yorkshire troops became a real cause of concern for both the committee in York and for Parliament itself. Parliament voted £20,000 to maintain the Yorkshire army, £5,000 of which would be used to pay Poyntz's troops.

October saw the arrival of the Northern Horse at Skipton Castle. The King had despatched Lord Digby and Sir Marmaduke Langdale, with about 1,500 of the Northern Horse, to reinforce the Marquess of Montrose, who was fighting a highly successful campaign in Scotland against the King's Covenanter opponents. Montrose was always short of cavalry, hence the despatch of the Northern Horse. On the morning of 15 October the Royalists had surprised the Parliamentarian garrison at Sherburn-in-Elmet, capturing most of them. While the Royalist troopers celebrated their victory and looted

Skipton Castle, Outer Gatehouse. The coat of arms is that of Henry Clifford, 5th Earl of Cumberland, owner of the castle at the start of the Civil Wars.

the town, a large force of Parliamentarian horse caught up with them. A cavalry action ensued on the ground between South Milford and Sherburn-in-Elmet, to the south of the latter. The Parliamentarian force was victorious and only 600 of the Royalist troopers, including Digby and Langdale, reached the safety of Skipton. After a short rest at Skipton the remnants of the Northern Horse set off across the Pennines for Cumberland, reinforced by 150 men from the garrison and 200 local volunteers. By the time they reached the Borders the Marquess of Montrose had been beaten. The Northern Horse were beaten and dispersed in an action close to Carlisle in late October.

The withdrawal of the Parliamentarian army in August had allowed the Royalists at Skipton to gather in the harvest and prepare for another siege, which was inevitable. With the surrender of Sandal Castle on 1 October only Skipton and Bolton Castles still held for the King. Parliament wanted the Yorkshire army to march into the Midlands to assist in the defeat of the King's remaining army but this could not be done until the two Royalist strongholds had fallen. The Parliamentary committee in York opened negotiations with Sir John Mallory for the surrender of Skipton Castle. On 8 November a meeting was held at Poppleton, near York, to discuss the surrender of the castle. Sir William List and Francis Pierrepoint represented the committee at York, while Colonels Leigh and Cobbe spoke for the Royalists. Mallory's terms were not accepted.

Although Skipton Castle was not slighted, Parliament would not allow the walls to be rebuilt to their original thickness. The thicker walls at the bottom of the photograph are the original medieval walls. The thinner upper walls are those built as part of the post-Civil Wars repairs.

The Second Siege

With the discussion unsuccessfully concluded, the Parliamentarians despatched Colonel Richard Thornton to Skipton, with a force of 2,000 horse and 2,000 foot, including 500 Lancashire foot. Thornton was close to the town by 18 November. By this time news had reached both sides of the surrender of Bolton Castle on the 6th.

Thornton's first move was to capture the town but this time Mallory's men did not withdraw to the castle and it took three days of hard fighting before the town fell to the Parliamentary forces on 23 November. With the town captured, Thornton sent for the siege train at York, although it took some time to reach Skipton due to the wet weather. The Royalists do not seem to have been as active as they had in the first siege, although they did carry out one sally in early December.

With the arrival of the siege train and the reoccupation of the batteries raised during the first siege, Thornton began a steady bombardment of the castle, which caused heavy damage both to the castle's material and to the defenders' morale. It must have become obvious that there would be no relief. Irrespective of what arms, ammunition and provisions were held in the castle it was obvious that it must fall. On 21 December 1645 the following terms were agreed between Colonel Thornton and Sir John Mallory:

1. That Sir John Mallory with all the rest of the Officers, Gentlemen, and Souldiers, shall march out betwixt this and Tuesday next before twelve of the clocke, surrendering the Castle, with all the Armes, Ordnance, and Ammunition, without any prejudice done to them, with all the goods and provisions whatsoever in the said Castle, not to be purloined or imbezzelled, and whosoever shall be found offending after the sealing of these Articles for the mis-disposing of goods, shall be given up to Justice, and treble satisfaction to be given for the goods so conveyed by the said party if he be worth it, if not, then to be made good by the Governour.
2. That all prisoners now in the Castle, of what quality or condition soever, shall be set at liberty upon the sealing of these Articles.
3. That after the signing of these Articles two such Officers as Col. Thornton shall appoint shall be admitted to go into the Castle, and see the Evidence-houses lockt up and sealed, and have an accompt of all spare Arms and Ammunition, and such a guard at such a time as Col. Thornton shall appoint to goe in.

4. That the Governour, Officers, and Souldiers of Horse & Foot with their horses and proper Arms as to horse & foot, shall march out accordingly to the Honour of a soldier with Colours flying, Trumpets sounding, Drums beating, Matches lighted on both ends, and Bullets in their mouthes, every Trooper and every Foot Souldier three charges of Powder, and the Officers of Commission to march with their wearing apparel that is properly their owne in their Portmantles, and not have any thing taken from them, and that the Common Souldiers shall not march away with any Bag and Baggage.

5. That all Gentlemen not in the condition of a Souldier, have their Horses and Swords, and be allowed to march to the King or his Garrisons, or their own homes, and be protected in either condition as they shall make choice of.

6. That all Officers and Souldiers of Horse and Foot, Gentlemen, Townesmen, or other persons what ever belonging to this Garrison, shall have liberty, conduct, & protection to go to his Majesty, or such of his Garrisons as shall be agreed of.

7. That all Officers, Souldiers, Gentlemen, Townesmen or others, desiring to goe and live at home, shall have free leave there to remain under the protection of the Parliament.

8. That all Souldiers or other persons that are sick or hurt, and not able to goe to their homes or other places where they desire, shall have leave to stay here at Skipton, and shall be allowed necessary accommodation untill it please God they shall recover, and then to have Passes upon their desires to goe to their home, or to such of his Majesties next Garrisons they shall make choice of.

9. That all women and Children within this Garrison be suffered to goe with, or to such as they shall desire to their own habitations.

10. That all the hangings & other goods given by Inventory to be the Countess of Pembroke, shall be there secured by themselves and not made sale of, untill the Lady Pembroke be made acquainted therewith, but to be prized with the rest.

11. That all the Evidences and Writings what ever, belonging to the Countesse of Pembroke, or to the Countesse of Corke, in any of the Evidence-Houses of this Castle, shall not be looked into by any, untill both the Countesses be acquainted therewith, and for that end, that two Moneths time for notice to be given them, and the Kayes to be delivered to Col. Thornton, who is interested with them in the mean time.

12. That all possible care be taken to preserve the Woods and Parks belonging to both these Ladies.

13. That those that intend to march to his Majesty, or any of his Garrisons, march but six miles a day, and free Quarter during all their march, and that a sufficient Convoy be allowed them, and may conduct them to Nottingham, and from thence to one of these foure Garrisons as shall there be named by them to the Commander in chiefe of the convoy, viz., Banbury, Worcester, Hereford or Litchfield.

14. That if any persons belonging to the Garrison shall misdemean themselves in the march, it shall not extend further then the parties offending, upon whom Justice shall be done according to the fault committed.

15. That if any Officers or Souldiers shall be necessitated to buy Horses, or any thing else in their march, shall have liberty for that purpose, and after payment enjoyment thereof, during the protection of the Convoy.

These seem to be very lenient terms. It should also be noted that Mallory's troops would not be allowed to join the garrison at Newark. When Mallory and his men marched through the gatehouse at Skipton Castle, no Royalist garrison existed north of the River Trent. Not only was Skipton the last Royalist stronghold in Yorkshire to surrender but also the last in the North.

Skipton Castle: the wall beyond the iron gate and fence follows the course of the original outer curtain wall.

Skipton Castle: a view of the imposing inner castle. During the siege the height of the wall was reduced by cannon fire to the level of the bottom of the second window.

As any visitor to Skipton Castle will notice today, although it was slighted at the order of Parliament, it was subsequently repaired. Lady Anne Clifford, the Countess of Pembroke, was married to the Earl of Pembroke, a staunch supporter of Parliament, who died in 1650. When Lady Anne came into possession of the castle she was given permission to repair it, as a plaque over the Tudor entrance commemorates:

This Skipton Castle was repayred by the Lady Anne Clifford, Countesse Dowager of Pembrookee, Dorsett, and Montgomery, Baronesse Clifford, West Merland, and Veseie, Lady of the Honour of Skipton in Craven, and High Sheriffesse by inheritance of the Countie of Westmorland, in the years 1657 and 1658, after this maine part of itt had layne ruinous ever since December 1648, and the January following, when itt was then pulld downe and demolish, almost to the foundacon, by the command of the Parliament, then sitting att Westminster, because it had bin a garrison in the then Civill Warres in England. Isa. Chap. 58, Ver. 12. Gods name be praised.

BIBLIOGRAPHY

Numerous contemporary accounts were used. By far the most detailed was Nathan Drake's Diary (see below). It gives a day-by-day account of the first and second sieges of Pontefract Castle. Guide books for Skipton and Bolton Castles were also consulted. Although they have no author, publisher or publication date, they are still available at the Castles.

Binns, J, 'A Place of Great Importance': Scarborough in the Civil Wars, Carnegie Publishing, 1996.

Binns, J, Yorkshire in the Civil Wars, Origin, Impact and Outcome, Blackthorn Press, 2004.

Butler, L, Sandal Castle, Wakefield: The History and Archaeology of a Medieval Castle, Wakefield Historical Publications, 1991.

Clark, J, Helmsley Castle, English Heritage, 2004.

Cooke, D, The Civil War in Yorkshire: Fairfax versus Newcastle, Pen & Sword, 2004.

Fox, G, The Three Sieges of Pontefract Castle, Old Hall Press, 1987.

Goodall, J A A, Scarborough Castle, English Heritage, 2008.

Holmes, R, The Sieges of Pontefract Castle, Old Hall Press, 1985.

Jackson, J, The Story of Bolton Castle, Dalesman Books, 1972.

Kershaw, M J, Knaresborough Castle, Harrogate Museums and Arts, 1998.

Leask, P, Valour is the Safest Helm: The Life of Sir Hugh Cholmley and Scarborough during the English Civil War, Jacobus Publications, 1995.

Quinn, J M V, 'These Unhappy Warres': The Civil War and Pontefract, Cluny Publications, 1992.

Reckitt, B N, Charles the First and Hull 1639–1645, Mr Pye Books, 1988.

Roberts, I, Pontefract Castle, West Yorkshire Archaeology Service, 1990.

Spence, R T, Skipton Castle in the Great Civil War 1642–1645, Smith Settle, 1991.

Spence, R T, Skipton Castle and its Builders, Smith Settle, 2002.

Stamp, A H, Cottingham in the Civil War, Cottingham Local History Society, 1991.

Walker, A (ed.), The First and Second Sieges of Pontefract Castle (Nathan Drake's Diary), Gosling Press, 1997.

Wenham, P, The Siege of York 1644, William Sessions Ltd, 1994.

INDEX

Acomb 32, 36, 39
Adwalton Moor, Battle of 4, 19, 20, 25, 26
Akin, William 68
Alford, Battle of 160
Almsley, William 69
Alured, Colonel 207
Anlaby 14, 15, 21
Appleby 207
Ashe, Simeon 33–5, 37, 38, 41–6, 55, 57, 60–2
Atkins, Richard 68
Auspice, Mr 159

Baillie, Lieutenant General 41, 160
Bamforth, Mr Thomas 113
Banbury 95, 213
Bannockburn, Battle of 204
Barnet, Henry 69
Barthrome, Captain
Barton, Sergeant 119, 126, 134, 135
Barwick-in-Elmet 107
Batley 19
Battley, Mr Robert 116
Baune, Nicholas 100
Beale, Captain 100, 101, 105, 119
Beaumont, Major Thomas 186
Beckett, Thomas 70
Belasyse, Colonel John 26–8, 171
Belvoir Castle 95
Benson, Captain John 117, 190, 193, 194

Bertie, Robert (Earl of Lindsey) 13–15
Berwick-upon-Tweed 26
Beverley 12–15, 21
Bishopthorpe 32
Bland, Major 105
Bland, Sir Thomas 159
Blockley, Cornet 120
Bolingbroke, Henry (later Henry IV) 72, 82, 195, 197
Bolling Hall 20
Bolton 4, 49
Bolton Castle 6, 55, 195, 197, 199–202, 209, 211, 212
Bolton Hall 202
Bolton (village) 200
Bonivant, Colonel George 105, 187, 190–4
Booth, Mr William 113, 134
Boroughbridge 52
Bosworth, Battle of 64, 164, 204
Boynton, Sir Matthew 177, 178
Bradford 16, 17, 19, 20, 27, 28, 53
Bradley, Lieutenant Edward 68
Brandling, Colonel 99
Bradley, Dr 116
Brereton, Sir William 55, 56
Bridlington 179, 181
Briggs, Brothers 90
Bright, Lieutenant Colonel 162
Browne, Captain 90, 91
Browne, Lieutenant 91
Boyle, Thomas 69

Bruce, Thomas 69
Buller, Mark 69
Burrough, Symon 69
Burt, Ensign Robert 68
Burton, William 68
Bury 49
Bushell, Captain Browne 167, 169
Bussey, Thomas 68
Byron, Sir John 27, 49, 50, 53–5
Byron, Sir Phillip 46

Callendar, Earl of 62
Canterbury 70
Carleton 134, 146, 148, 152
Carlisle 123, 211
Carre, William 69
Cartwright, Captain 138, 150
Castleford, 204
Catherine, Queen 72
Cattel, Elizabeth 93, 126
Cavendish, William (Earl of
    Newcastle, later Marquess of
    Newcastle) 3–5, 10, 16–21, 23–9, 32,
    34, 36–42, 44, 46, 48, 49, 52, 54, 55,
    60, 85, 168, 172, 205
Cawood 103
Cawood Castle 34, 117
Chappell, Thomas 69
Charles I, King 9–15, 18, 25, 27, 31, 39,
    42, 43, 49, 51, 54, 55, 75, 82, 83, 107,
    121, 123, 129, 138, 139, 178, 201, 205,
    209, 210
Chequerfield, Battle of 95
Chester 55, 107
Cholmley, Lady 179
Cholmley, Sir Henry 171
Cholmley, Sir Hugh 16–18, 20, 54,
    167–9, 171–6, 178, 179, 181
Clarke, Captain 150

Clavering, Sir Robert 55
Clifford, Anne (Countess of
    Pembroke) 213, 215
Clifford, Henry (5th Earl of
    Cumberland) 16, 75, 205
Clifford, Henry (10th Lord Clifford)
    204
Clifford, Henry (11th Lord Clifford,
    and 1st Earl of Cumberland) 205
Clifford, John (7th Lord Clifford) 204
Clifford, John (9th Lord Clifford) 204
Clifford, Robert (1st Lord Clifford)
    203, 204
Clifford, Robert (4th Lord Clifford)
    204
Clifford, Thomas (6th Lord Clifford)
    204
Clifford, Thomas (8th Lord Clifford)
    204
Clifton 34
Cobbe, Colonel 211
Constable, Sir William 57, 60
Copeland, Sergeant 119
Copley, Lieutenant Colonel 162
Cottingham 23
Coup, Bonny 128
Crawford, Major General Lawrence
    45–7
Crawford-Lindsey, Earl of 33, 41
Crecy, Battle of 204
Croft, Colonel 76
Crompton, Major 176, 177
Cromwell, Oliver 23, 24, 27, 52–4, 141,
    158
Crook, Major 193
Crossland, Sir Jordan 66, 68, 69, 169,
    173, 181
Cutler, Lady 146, 147
Cutler, Sir Jarvis 103, 131, 145, 146

Darrington 121, 134
Dawson, Quartermaster 102
De Lacey, Ilbert 72
De Lilburn, John 71, 76
De Mortain, Robert 63
De Moreville, Hugh 70
De Neville, Geoffrey 164
Dennis. Major 105
Dent, Captain 112
Derby 95, 128, 129, 132
Derringham 23
De Forze, William 203
De Romille, Roger 203
De Roos, Peter 63
De Roos, Robert 63
De Roos, Robert (Fursan) 63
De Roos, Thomas 63
De Warenne, John 183
De Warenne, William 182
Digby, Lord George 210, 211
Dixon, John 69
Doncaster 62, 95, 98, 117, 131, 132,
    134, 140, 147, 151, 157, 210
Drake, Nathan 85–8, 90–4, 96–105,
    107–14, 116–31, 133, 135, 137–43,
    145, 146, 148–51, 153–62, 190
Dudley, Sir Gamaliel 95–8
Durham 26, 28

Eadred, King 81
Eden, Colonel 104
Edmund, Earl of Rutland 185, 204
Edmund, Lord Roos 64
Edward I, King 8, 70, 164
Edward II, King 70, 76, 164
Edward III, King 71, 204
Edward IV, King 63, 82, 184, 185, 204
Elizabeth I, Queen 166
Elliot, James 92
Emson, Lieutenant 140

Escrick 33
Espec, Walter 63
Eure, Sir Ralph 166

Fairefax, William 69
Fairfax, Lord Ferdinando 3–6, 16,
    18–23, 25, 27, 28, 32–6, 38, 39, 41, 45,
    46, 48, 49, 53, 55, 57, 58, 60, 62, 65,
    67, 69, 74, 76, 77, 80, 85, 88, 89, 91,
    96, 98, 99, 136, 169, 171, 172, 186,
    187, 200
Fairfax, Sir Thomas 17–21, 23–5, 27,
    28, 33, 45, 52, 53, 65, 66, 69, 88, 138,
    154, 156, 158, 160, 186, 201
Fairfax, Sir William 41
Farrow, William 148
Featherstone 148
Ferrybridge 16, 28, 93, 97, 102, 109,
    110, 117, 119–21, 128, 138-140, 144,
    148, 150, 156, 204
Fevell, Lieutenant 104, 109, 119, 143
FitzEustace, Roger 82
Fletcher, Thomas 68
Flodden, Battle of 204
Flood, Captain 101, 106, 119, 126,
    134–6, 139
Forbes, Colonel William 66, 68, 85, 87,
    88, 91, 100
Foxcroft, 106
Freeman, John 69
Fulford 32

Gainsborough 21
Gaveston, Piers 70, 71, 164
George, Duke of Clarence 63
Gilbraith, Lieutenant Colonel 119,
    126, 134, 161
Glemham, Sir Thomas 10, 14, 41, 55,
    56, 58
Gloucester 190

Goring, Colonel George 18, 52, 53, 141, 154, 156, 158, 160
Graham, James (Marquess of Montrose) 160, 210, 211
Grames, William 69
Grantham 95
Greswick, James 69
Grey, Colonel 85
Grimstone, Captain 107

Hale Ford 49, 55
Halifax 16, 19
Hamburg 55, 168
Hammond, Colonel 41
Hanson, Thomas 117, 118, 122
Hardwick 134
Hare, Mr 159
Harper, James 69
Hart, Thomas 69
Helme, Edward 68
Helmsley 63–8, 78, 88, 173, 201, 205
Helmsley Castle 3, 6, 63, 65, 68, 76, 169
Hemsworth, Captain 104, 138, 159
Henrietta-Maria, Queen 11, 17–19
Henry II, King 163, 164
Henry III, King 164
Henry V, King 73, 195, 197, 204
Henry VII, 164, 197, 204
Henry VIII, King 8, 9, 22, 166, 197, 205
Hepborne, Sir Adam 60
Hereford, 213
Heslington 32
Hessay 48
Hexham, Battle of 63
Hill, Quartermaster 105
Hirst, Mr 132, 151, 159, 161
Hodgson, Mr 159
Hodgson, Leonard 69

Hodgson, William 69
Hooper, Major 193
Hopton, Sir Ralph 20, 25
Horsfold, Captain 115
Hotham, Captain John 10, 20
Hotham, Sir John 9–14, 20
Howard, Lord 33
Howley Hall 19
Huddersfield 17
Huet, Bernard 69
Hull 2–5, 8–16, 18, 20–5, 27, 53, 88, 128, 168, 169, 175, 179, 191
Humbey, Lord 41, 57, 60
Hunderly, Lieutenant William 68
Hutton, Sir Richard 41, 75, 85, 159–61

Ingram, Will 130, 131, 133, 136, 140, 161
Ipswich 173

Jackson, Mrs 108
James, Duke of York 11, 12
James I, King 166
Jarett, General 141
John, King 70, 164
John of Gaunt (Duke of Lancaster) 72
Johnson, Lieutenant George 68
Jubbe, William 124

Kellome, Mr 134, 137–9, 143
Key, Mr 132, 151, 159
Killingbeck, Ensign 119, 126, 134
King, James (Lord Eythin) 17, 55
King's Lyn 173
Kingston-upon-Hull 8
Kiplin, Edward 68
Kirby, Mr 121
Kirton, Sir Posthumous, 19
Kitchen, Captain 140

Knaresborough 48, 52, 66, 70–2, 74, 76, 77, 79, 80, 87, 103, 201
Knaresborough Castle 6, 68–70, 72, 73, 85
Knottingley 83, 84, 130, 132, 134, 148, 149, 157

Laiborne, Captain 90
Laipidge, Richard 132
Lambert, Colonel John 23, 24, 27, 28, 57, 66
Langdale, Sir Marmaduke 94–8, 121, 128, 156, 158, 160, 168, 210, 211
Lascelles, Colonel 201, 202
Lathom House 4, 49
Laud, Archbishop William 9
Leeds 16–18, 20, 53, 62, 103
Legard, Captain Richard 180
Legge, Captain William 9
Le Gros, William (Count of Aumâle) 163, 164
Leicester 15, 95, 129
Leigh, Colonel 211
Leslie, Alexander (Earl of Leven) 4, 26, 33, 34, 38, 39, 41, 45, 46, 49, 53, 55, 57
Leslie, Lieutenant General David 52, 54
Lichfield 213
Lilburn, Lieutenant Colonel John 77
Lilburn, Lieutenant Colonel Robert 77–9
Lincoln 21, 33
List, Sir William 211
Liverpool 4, 49, 50, 55
London 10, 53, 63, 168, 169, 202, 210
London, Tower of 11
Long Marston 48
Lowther, Captain 153

Lowther, Colonel Richard 86, 88–91, 100, 113, 118, 119, 121, 126-129, 134, 138, 144, 145, 147–51, 153, 154, 156, 158–62
Lowther, Thomas 117, 123
Lunn, Alderman 99, 102, 104, 114, 127, 128, 159
Lupton, Samuel 69

Mallory, Colonel Sir John 68, 206–8, 211–13
Malton 16
Manchester 34, 49, 52, 172
Manners, Francis, Earl of Rutland 64
Manners, Sir George 64
Manners, Katherine (Duchess of Buckingham) 64, 67
Market Harborough 95, 138, 141
Marston Moor, Battle of 3, 4, 51, 52, 54, 62, 65, 76, 168, 172, 186
Mary, Queen 166
Mary, Queen of Scots 166, 199
Massey, Mr 128, 129
Matterson, Captain Richard 68
Maullett, Captain 93
Maurice, Prince 123
Meldrum, Sir John 15, 23, 24, 34, 55, 56, 128, 171–7
Melton Mowbray 95, 138, 140
Metcalfe, Alexander 146
Metham, Sir Thomas 41
Middlethorpe, 32
Middleton, Lieutenant 134
Monks, Lieutenant 135, 136
Monks, Sergeant 105
Montagu, Edward (Earl of Manchester) 4, 23, 25, 32–4, 36–9, 41, 45, 47–9, 53–7, 60, 62, 77
Montague, Colonel 57

Montgomery, Colonel 105
Montgomery, Lord 118
Moore, Lieutenant 102, 134, 144
Morgan, Colonel Thomas 190
Morley 19
Munro, Captain 90, 101, 104, 119, 126, 134, 137, 159
Musgrave, Sir Philip 55

Nantwich 27
Naseby, Battle of 95, 138, 139, 143, 178, 201
Neville, Mr Gervase 160
Neville, Richard (Earl of Warwick) 82
Newark 19, 27, 28, 49, 95, 98, 110, 113, 115, 117, 118, 121, 129, 131, 132, 140–2, 147, 150, 154, 156, 160, 162, 179, 181, 209, 213
Newburn, Battle of 10
Newcastle, Duchess of 35
Newcastle-upon-Tyne 10, 25, 26, 35, 62, 168
Northallerton, Battle of 63
Northampton 141
Norwell House 95
Nottingham 6, 13, 15, 95, 213

Oates, Mrs 100, 109
Ogle, Mr 91
Ogleby, Captain 126
Ogleby, Lieutenant 126
Oldwark 98
Olley, Mr 116
Ormskirk 55
Otway, Ensign 119, 134, 144, 145
Overton, Colonel Robert 126, 128, 129, 131, 133, 136, 140, 142, 147, 149, 160–2, 191, 192

Oxford 18–20, 25, 95, 141
Oyston, Doctor 150

Parker, Sergeant 134
Pattison, Mr 87
Paull 14, 23
Pelham, Sir Peregrine 12
Percy, Henry (Harry Hotspur) 197
Perry, Lieutenant 103
Phillipa, Queen 71
Piercebridge 76
Pierrepoint, Francis 211
Pocklington 18
Pontefract 2, 3, 19, 77, 81, 83, 85, 94, 95, 103, 105, 107, 113, 120, 121, 128, 129, 131, 134, 138–42, 148, 150, 154, 155, 187, 190, 207, 209
Pontefract Castle 3, 6, 7, 16, 34, 38, 45, 72, 80-83, 85, 95, 99, 105, 122, 124, 125, 133, 162, 183, 190, 191, 206
Poppleton 52, 211
Porter, Colonel George 27, 28
Powlett, Charles (6th Marquess of Winchester and 1st Duke of Bolton) 202
Poyntz, Colonel Sydenham (later General) 91, 136, 138–40, 147, 149, 150, 153, 156, 158, 159, 161, 162, 191, 206–10
Preston 49, 52
Price, John 69

Rainsborough, Colonel Thomas 23, 24
Ramsden, Sir John 85, 159, 161
Ratcliffe, Captain 101
Redman, Captain 99
Redman, Peter 130
Richard II, King 72, 82, 195

Richard, Duke of Gloucester (later King Richard III) 63, 83, 164, 183, 197, 204
Richard, Duke of York 30, 82, 83, 185, 197, 204
Richard, Earl of Cambridge 197
Richardson. Lieutenant William 68
Richmond, 55
Rivers, Earl 83
Robson, William 69
Rockley, Master Robert 41
Rossington 95, 132
Rossiter, Colonel 95, 98
Rotherham 18, 98, 147
Rupert, Prince 4, 27, 34, 36, 38, 39, 42, 44, 45, 48–52, 54–6, 58, 61, 62, 68, 95, 98, 103, 151, 168, 172
Rusby, Alderman 100, 111, 124, 125, 127, 128, 137, 138, 147, 159
Russell, Colonel 41
Ruthven, Patrick (Earl of Forth) 74, 75
Rutland, Earl of 30

Sabden Brook, Battle of 4
Saint Albans, 1st Battle of 204
Salisbury, Earl of 30, 82
Samson, Lieutenant John 68
Sandal 117, 125–7, 133, 146, 151, 155, 157, 182, 190, 201
Sandal Castle 3, 6, 96, 102, 105, 110, 115–18, 120, 122, 124–6, 130, 133, 140–2, 147, 148, 150, 151, 154–7, 182, 183, 185–7, 190, 191, 209, 211
Saville, Sir John 19, 102, 105, 107–13, 120, 121, 187, 190
Scameden, Stephen 68
Scarborough 3, 6, 17, 18, 34, 55, 67, 69, 96, 103, 122, 128, 163, 164, 166–9, 171–3, 175, 179, 191, 201

Scarborough Castle 70, 122, 124, 128, 163, 164, 166
Scrope, Colonel John 199, 201, 202
Scrope, Emmanuel (11th Baron Scrope of Masham) 199
Scrope, Henry (3rd Lord Scrope of Masham) 197
Scrope, John (5th Baron Scrope of Bolton) 197
Scrope, John (8th Baron Scrope of Bolton) 197
Scrope, Mary 202
Scrope, Richard (Archbishop) 195
Scrope, Richard (1st Lord Scrope of Bolton) 195
Scrope, Richard (4th Baron Scrope of Bolton) 197
Sculcoates 21, 23
Seacroft Moor, Battle of 18
Selby 16, 18, 27, 28, 34, 103, 117, 181
Setle, Robert 69
Sheffield 18, 133, 186
Sheffield Castle 186
Sherburn-in-Elmet 4, 97, 210, 211
Sherwood, John 68
Short, George 69
Sigurdsson, King Harald 163
Simnel, Lambert 197
Skipton 52, 58, 76, 77, 201, 203, 205–13
Skipton Castle 3, 4, 6, 68, 76, 156, 203, 205, 206, 209, 211–15
Slingsby, Sir Henry 32, 33, 37, 38, 45, 56, 57, 74, 75
Smith, Captain 93, 100, 101, 109, 118, 119, 126, 134, 139
Smith, James 69
Smith, Lieutenant 109, 126, 142
Smith, William 69
Southampton 196

South Milford 211
Southome, Richard 69
Speight, Captain 105
Speight, Cornet 104
Spence, John 90, 91
Spright, Lieutenant 68
Squire, Cornet Thomas 68
Stables, Richard 130
Stables, Zachary 130, 131, 134, 148
Stafford, Thomas 166
Stamford Bridge 16, 27
Stephen, King 63, 163
Stevinson, Thomas 69
Stewart, Colonel William 173
Stockport 49
Strickland, Captain 23
Strickland, Sir Robert 41
Sunderland 26, 168
Sutton, Nathaniel 112

Tadcaster 16, 18, 28, 52, 97
Tadcaster, Battle of 85, 204
Tankert, Richard 69
Tanshelf 81, 121
Taunton 154
Taytom, Mr 107, 137
Thirsk 55
Thomas, Earl of Lancaster 71
Thompson, Lieutenant 117
Thorgils 163
Thornton, Colonel Richard 212, 213
Thurley, Cornet 117
Tickhill 132
Tickhill Castle 62
Tindal, Mr William 159
Towton, Battle of 3, 83, 185, 204
Turnbridge 99
Turner, William 68
Tuxford 131

Vane, Sir Henry 36, 39, 45
Van Tromp, Admiral 18
Villiers, George (Duke of
  Buckingham) 64

Wade, Captain 104
Wakefield 17–19, 62, 121, 140, 182,
  183, 185, 186
Wakefield, Battle of 30, 82, 185, 204
Wakefield, Mr 92
Walker, Captain Joshua 87, 125, 126,
  136, 137, 140, 190
Walton, John 69
Ward, Christopher 68
Ward Lieutenant 119, 126, 135, 137
Ward, Major 119, 186, 187
Ward, Mr 93, 94
Wardroy, John 68
Wark Castle 63
Warner, John 76
Warrington 49, 52
Washington, Captain 100–2, 104, 122,
  124, 125, 140
Washington, Colonel 138
Washington, Mr 154
Washington, Mrs 154, 155
Wasthill, Mr 162
Wastell, Colonel 201
Waterhouse, Captain 86
Welbeck 25, 133, 194
Wentbridge 94–7, 151–3
Wenthill 132, 150
Wentworth, Sir George 85, 159–61
Wentworth, Sir William 41
Wether, William (Belwether) 103, 104,
  107, 115, 117, 121
Wetherby 49, 52, 76
Wheatley, Lieutenant 101, 122, 124,
  126, 135, 140, 190

Wheatley, Lieutenant Colonel 159
Whitby 27, 171, 179
White, Colonel 41
Wickham, Captain 175, 176
Widdrington, Lord 41
Wike 8
Wilkinson, Alderman John 116, 138
Wilkinson, Robert 69
Wilkinson, Alderman Thomas 102
William I, King 63, 82
William, King of Scotland 63
Williams, Thomas 69
Willoughby, Lieutenant 119, 134, 137, 138, 142, 143
Willoughby, Lord 14, 23, 24

Wilson, Trooper 102
Winceby, Battle of 25, 27, 172
Wiose, Lieutenant John 68
Worcester, 213
Worcester, Battle of 181
Wray, Sir Christopher 76
Wright, Thomas 69

Yarm Bridge, Battle of 17
York 2–6, 10, 12, 15–18, 27–31, 33, 34, 36, 38, 40, 43–5, 48–50, 52, 54–8, 60, 62, 65, 66, 68, 76, 83, 91, 92, 103, 132, 136, 158, 161, 168–70, 175, 179, 185, 192, 208, 209, 211, 212
York Minster 38